ROUTLEDGE LIBRARY EDITIONS: THE VICTORIAN WORLD

Volume 10

THE LOWER MIDDLE CLASS IN BRITAIN 1870–1914

THE LOWER MIDDLE CLASS IN BRITAIN 1870–1914

Edited by
GEOFFREY CROSSICK

LONDON AND NEW YORK

First published in 1977 by Croom Helm Ltd

This edition first published in 2016
by Routledge
2 Park Square, Milton Park, Abingdon, Oxon OX14 4RN

and by Routledge
711 Third Avenue, New York, NY 10017

Routledge is an imprint of the Taylor & Francis Group, an informa business

© 1977 Geoffrey Crossick

All rights reserved. No part of this book may be reprinted or reproduced or utilised in any form or by any electronic, mechanical, or other means, now known or hereafter invented, including photocopying and recording, or in any information storage or retrieval system, without permission in writing from the publishers.

Trademark notice: Product or corporate names may be trademarks or registered trademarks, and are used only for identification and explanation without intent to infringe.

British Library Cataloguing in Publication Data
A catalogue record for this book is available from the British Library

ISBN: 978-1-138-66565-1 (Set)
ISBN: 978-1-315-61965-1 (Set) (ebk)
ISBN: 978-1-138-64559-2 (Volume 10) (hbk)
ISBN: 978-1-138-64560-8 (Volume 10) (pbk)
ISBN: 978-1-315-62806-6 (Volume 10) (ebk)

Publisher's Note
The publisher has gone to great lengths to ensure the quality of this reprint but points out that some imperfections in the original copies may be apparent.

Disclaimer
The publisher has made every effort to trace copyright holders and would welcome correspondence from those they have been unable to trace.

The Lower Middle Class in Britain 1870-1914

EDITED BY GEOFFREY CROSSICK

CROOM HELM   LONDON

© 1977 Geoffrey Crossick

Croom Helm Ltd
2-10 St John's Road, London, SW11

ISBN 0-85664-348-3

Printed in Great Britain by
Lowe & Brydone Printers Limited, Thetford, Norfolk

CONTENTS

Tables

Preface

The Emergence of the Lower Middle Class in Britain: A Discussion
Geoffrey Crossick   11

White Collar Values and the Role of Religion
Hugh McLeod   61

Society, Status and Jingoism: The Social Roots of Lower Middle Class Patriotism, 1870-1900
Richard N. Price   89

The Social Economy of Late-Victorian Clerks
G. L. Anderson   113

Religion, Culture and Social Class in Late Nineteenth and Early Twentieth Century Edinburgh
R. Q. Gray   134

Housing and the Lower Middle Class, 1870-1914
S. Martin Gaskell   159

The Small Shopkeeper in Industrial and Market Towns
Thea Vigne and Alun Howkins   184

Index   211

TABLES

1.1	White collar employees in Great Britain, 1851-1911	19
2.1	Social origins of men marrying in Anglican churches	84
2.2	Addresses of couples marrying in three Birmingham parishes, 1896-1905	85
2.3	Church attendances in London as a percentage of estimated population, 1886-7 and 1902-3	86
2.4	Church attendances in Liverpool as a percentage of population, 1851-1912	87
5.1	Places of worship in Edinburgh	154
5.2	Membership of churches	155
5.3	Boys' Brigade officers, 1891	156
5.4	Denominational breakdown of Boys' Brigade officers, 1891	156
5.5	Membership of St. David's Free Church Mutual Improvement Association, 1881	157
5.6	Residence and neighbours of professional, business and white collar members of organisations, 1891	158

PREFACE

This book has been assembled in the hope of beginning a discussion rather than ending one. It stemmed from a conviction that the neglect of the study of the lower middle class had seriously hindered our understanding of a range of issues in the development of modern British society, concerning central areas such as politics, ideology and social relationships. I knew that various people were working on subjects that, if not necessarily directly concerned with the lower middle class, required them to think seriously about the relationship between their more general research and that stratum. It therefore seemed a good idea to open up a more serious historical assessment of the problem by inviting essays that would sink shafts into the subject at specific points with a view to illuminating the issues. There are grounds for seeing a book of essays as not just a substitute for the massive monograph on the lower middle class that would answer all our questions, should such a thing be possible, but also a more productive way of beginning a debate. These essays do not necessarily agree with each other, and were not invited with that purpose. All that has been sought is an explicitness that would make differences clear. For the same reason, my contribution has not attempted to pull all the essays together but rather to discuss some of the broader issues and draw wider European comparisons in an attempt to set a context for the specific studies that follow it. The British lower middle class has received too little attention from historians, to the detriment of our understanding of British social history. If the book convinces of that point, illuminates some of the issues, and opens up the problem for wider discussion, then it will have served its purpose.

Hull, June 1976   Geoffrey Crossick

1 THE EMERGENCE OF THE LOWER MIDDLE CLASS IN BRITAIN: A DISCUSSION

Geoffrey Crossick

The neglect of the development of the British lower middle class by historians is unfortunate but not altogether unexpected. Indeed, there has been very little work on the history of the middle class as a whole.[1] The explanation for this skewing of emphasis towards working class history must lie in the way that social history has developed in this country; it was for a long time the banner under which the gross neglect of working class movements and popular experience was to be rectified. The motivation, guided by a political enthusiasm and concern for historical breadth that were inseparable, was laudable but may in the long run have proved inhibiting. In other countries, most notably France, a concern for theory and social analysis in history has driven social historians to examine the social process as a whole in order to explain its parts. The absence of these impulses, together with the empirical commitment of British historiography, have effectively narrowed the interests of too many social historians.

If this is the general explanation for the failure to attend to the development of the lower middle class,[2] there are also more specific reasons of which the most immediate is the sheer lack of heroism of this section of society. They fail to do anything very striking, it seems. They are not active on the historical stage. The contrast with the attention given to the *Mittelstand*, the generally equivalent group in Wilhelmine Germany, is instructive. This ambiguous and diverse group, more united in conception than in reality, is attracting serious attention from historians of Germany.[3] At one level this interest derives from a concern to trace back the dynamics of fascism, but it also grows out of the fact that the *Mittelstand*, whether as an entity or in its component parts, was an active and increasingly problematic group in political and social life, organising, pressurising and impinging on the political process. The British lower middle class was prominent neither in this ambiguous sense of corporate identity nor in organisation. This not only explains why it has escaped the historian's attention, but also the problems that it poses for historical analysis. There are few organisations, especially of a political nature, of the kind that provide so much evidence for the labour historian. The difficulty of penetrating lower middle class ideas and beliefs is therefore intimidating.

The lower middle class in Britain can be divided into two main groups. On the one hand was the classic petty bourgeoisie of shopkeepers and small businessmen, on the other the new white collar salaried occupations, most notably clerks but also managers, commercial travellers, schoolteachers and certain shop assistants. In addition there were probably the minor professional people, too frequently categorised as members of the established middle class, but probably containing amongst lesser solicitors and the like a range of small operators acting on the margins of their profession. The most immediate feature of the two main groups is their strikingly different market situations. The problems of establishing lower middle class stratification stem from that point. In effect, was there a single lower middle class? The question cannot be answered in this paper, though exploratory points might lead towards clearer definition and understanding. The formation of social strata always poses fundamental difficulties of analysis in social history, because it is not enough simply to show that people shared a common characteristic such as a certain level of income or a certain occupation. If stratification is to be shown then there is an axiomatic requirement to prove it through identifying actual social relationships and commitments.

One approach might be to seek contemporary opinions as to the composition of the lower middle class. These sometimes included labour aristocrats, and at other times excluded them. Charles Booth, in his *Religious Influences* series, firmly separated the lower middle class on the one hand from artisans on the other. Leone Levi did the same, including teachers, clerks, small shopkeepers, civil servants and, surprisingly, clergy in his higher stratum. Other observers were less sure. Contradictory evidence was offered to the enquiry on pupil-teachers, where witnesses revealed the inexactness of the label, and other instances can be accumulated of definitions of the lower middle class that included the better-paid skilled workers.[4] What does all this reveal, beyond an increasing use of the term 'lower middle class' during the period? It merely indicates that members of the established middle and upper class held a certain view of the social structure, and not even a consistent one. Given the undeniable respectability and stability of the non-manual lower middle class, the occasional inclusion of artisans with them presumably represents an important comment on how these observers from higher social strata saw the better skilled workers. A genuine definition of the lower middle class, however, must take far more account of both self-ascription and the effective stratification that is demonstrated through the evidence of social relationships. At that level there are grounds for believing that the distinction between marginal non-manual groups and labour aristocrats became an increasingly important one during this period. This will, indeed, be argued later. It is nevertheless difficult to tackle the realities of this stratification without studies of the place of these 'middling groups' in relationship to each other and to specific communities. It is upon the non-manual lower middle class that this essay will focus.

One contemporary view was offered in the *Spectator,* where a contributor felt that there was such a stratum but was confused about what to call it. He described George Gissing's *In the Year of Jubilee* as being about 'that vaguely outlined lower middle section of society which, in the matter of physical comfort, approximates to the caste above it, and in its lack of the delicate requirements of life has something in common with the caste below it, but which is, nevertheless, so recognizably differentiated from both, that confused classification is impossible even to the most superficial observer.' Gissing was the novelist of 'the families of the imperfectly educated but fairly well-paid manager or clerk, of the tradesman who has "got on" pecuniarily but hardly "gone up" socially, and, to speak generally, of the typical ratepayers in an unfashionable London suburb.'[5]

Yet are we correct in seeing these people as a class,[6] or as a single social group of whatever name? If the lower middle class was more than a residual category, then a major difficulty arises that is even more problematic outside Britain. Kocka observes that German writing in the decades before 1914 grouped together independent artisans, shopkeepers and salaried employees within the *Mittelstand,* with the peasantry placed in an ambivalent position.[7] He is correct to emphasise the need for firm analytical distinctions between the groups involved, yet the question remains as to why it was that in many parts of Europe at this time old petty bourgeois groups and new salaried occupations came to see each other as *in some ways* in a similar situation.[8] Some answers may emerge if we interpret these groups in terms of relationships rather than categories. Two key elements would then help explain the convergence. The first is that the groups in question were emphatically not working class, and felt stridently conscious of that fact. In other European countries popular culture emphasised and propagated this non-working class character, and the ensuing sense of honourable status gave a degree of unification to the lower middle class.[9] Rising labour movements and social democracy only exacerbated this. The second element drawing together these diverse groups was that they shared a similar position of marginality to the established bourgeoisie, although one resting on diverse market situations. They both supported the broad features of the property-owning capitalist economy and what they saw as its traditional ideology, while also suffering in distinctive ways from the main trends towards economic concentration during the period. In addition, both operated in areas of the economy under relatively free market conditions, with the petty bourgeoisie suffering the full force of the market over sales, competition and interest rates, while white collar workers were particularly poorly organised within the labour market.

There are thus *a priori* reasons why these groups should in some ways have identified with each other, but they do not remove the objection that the concept of a lower middle *class* is analytically a poor one, for their relations to the means of production were not those of a class, and their internal division was fundamental.[10] As a descriptive term for a contemporary observed reality it may, nevertheless, be usefully employed.

A final point of definition that is important is the local orientation of the lower middle class. Its members lived and operated within communities, and thus in the context of a complex stratification of both the middle class and the working class. They were in contact with a range of social groups, all of which intermeshed within a local society. The result was necessarily that different places would produce various forms of lower middle class social experience within the framework set by national economic and social developments. In small towns without a resident bourgeoisie or wealthy professional groups, or in working class districts of segregated towns, they were the social elite, running the churches and local government. It was shopkeepers and clerks who led the chapels in late-Victorian Bethnal Green, while the same was true of religious activity in the socially declining Kentish Town.[11] Booth's coloured street maps take us even further and show in the long red line cutting through poorer areas how it was shopkeepers clinging to their main road premises who survived as the superior class in totally working class areas.[12] Comparable social groups contributed to Gambetta's *couche sociale nouvelle*, but their more general importance in France stemmed from the fact that it was so much more emphatically a small-town society within which they might flourish.

In all these situations it is the local narrowness of the lower middle class that is so important. While the established middle class would be marked out by its external contacts, its links outside the locality with other towns and, for the most substantial, even national relationships, there was something irreducibly local about the lower middle class. This closed local dimension of its culture, in comparison with other groups, must have restricted severely its ability to cope with change, and must also have been responsible for much of the rigidity of values that only grew stronger as the period progressed.

After these preliminary points of explanation and definition, this essay will concentrate not upon examining the whole range of lower middle class experience, but on establishing the main dimensions that can assist an understanding of the wider social process. The former project is rendered impossible by the paucity of research on the subject, in addition to the necessary limitations imposed by the constraints of length. The most glaring deficiency lies in chronology. The precise dating of the processes discussed in this essay remains unclear, beyond generalised formulations, and this is a persistent problem of which I am conscious. Nevertheless, changes over time can be indicated, and areas for analysis presented. The essay will first examine the structural situation of the two sections of the lower middle class, the petty bourgeoisie and white collar workers. The differing levels of vulnerability of these groups will be raised as a preliminary to examining their aspirations, values and status consciousness. Finally, after a brief look at schoolteachers, a group whose relationship to this analysis is an ambiguous one, the historical significance of the lower middle class in the period will be examined. This will inevitably be partial but will focus specifically upon the rise of suburbia and commercial provision; the role of the lower middle class in the process of social mobility; the conservative force of the stratum within society and politics; and finally the impact upon the labour aristocracy of the expansion of this status-conscious lower middle class.

This essay will give more attention to white collar employees, but the classic petty bourgeoisie faced new pressures during this period through much of Europe. Yet there is a fundamental distinction within it between retailers, who might be expected to benefit from urbanisation and the widening of consumer markets, and independent artisans, especially those in small towns, many of whom were threatened by urban industrial development. There were, none the less, certain common challenges facing small businessmen towards the end of the nineteenth century. Small masters were squeezed by the concentration of capital, the advance of large-scale production, and the rise of cartels and monopolies. Although Hannah presents this process in Britain as narrowly based, it is only so in comparison with the greater-merger waves of the 1920s and 1960s. In the later decades of the century there appeared 'a systematic tendency to large-scale enterprises, created by sustained merger activity as opposed to occasional acquisition and extended partnerships' in manufacturing industry.[13] Awareness of this new kind of pressure must have been growing amongst the always unstable small businessmen.

The small retailer witnessed a similar process of concentration. New forms of retail operation were a striking feature of the period, and have been presented by Charles Wilson as evidence against the view that innovation was absent from British economic life.[14] Department stores grew from the 1870s, using advertising, display and amenities to attract mainly middle class customers, while multiple shops spread widely, mainly in the sale of food and footwear but diversifying from the 1890s.[15] The effects of the multiple invasion on the main streets of Camberwell have been clearly shown[16] and must have been mirrored in most towns. Finally there were the mainly working class co-operatives, ideologically the most explosive of all these innovations. They increased their membership thirtyfold between 1863 and 1914, and turnover by an even greater ratio.[17] By the beginning of the war, these three new types of retailing accounted for between 16 and 20 per cent of all retail sales.[18]

The impact of these changes was psychological as much as economic. Small businesses have always been crisis-prone, most notably over short-term credit problems. The sense of new and apparently unfair types of competition must have provided a ready scapegoat for what were often indigenous difficulties. The shop owned by H. G. Wells' parents was precarious at the best of times, but they felt especially threatened by the multiples and the Army and Navy vans which came 'to suck away the ebbing vitality of the local retailer.'[19] As suppliers grew larger, so their credit provision became more selective, and small retailers came to be increasingly dependent upon shark-like intermediaries.[20] The awareness of these difficulties was only compounded by the degrading of small shopkeeping skills that was implicit in the increasing branding and pre-packaging of goods, especially in the grocery trades.[21] At the same time they were faced with severe price competition, and the profit margins of the 'legitimate' retailer were consequently squeezed.[22]

Similar processes of concentration in other European countries often stimulated petty bourgeois organisation, sometimes specifically economic but at others with broader political ambitions. The problems of the petty bourgeoisie were consciously related to normative political decisions, and as such were believed to be capable of manipulation. Gellately, in a recent dense survey, has outlined the shopkeepers' organisations in Wilhelmine Germany and their political allegiances within the *Mittelstand*.[23] In Belgium intensive agitation by shopkeepers and independent artisans—there were 689 associations of the urban petty bourgeoisie by

1913—led to increasing government response. The establishment of a national commission on the petty bourgeoisie, and Ministries and departments for the protection of the small trader are significant even if they were mainly aimed at placatory measures. The flow of cheap capital was inevitably their principal concern.[24]

If in both Germany and Belgium the separate interests of artisans and shopkeepers provided an irregular source of tension within organisations, the contrast with Britain is none the less striking, for petty bourgeois groups there generally failed to organise at all, though experiencing similar difficulties to their European counterparts. The most that existed were ineffective retailers' associations of low ambition. Unimportant as a lobby, they could extract virtually no response from government. This lack of political weight was as much a reflection of the British political structure as of the weakness of petty bourgeois mobilisation. The retailers' associations concentrated on services to members and fostering the retail trade ethic. The one campaign of significance was the struggle for retail price maintenance, directed not at government but at the large manufacturers and distributors. Begun in the 1870s, it re-emerged in the 1890s to protest against 'unfair' competition. Local associations formed national ties amongst grocers, tobacconists and chemists, but with manufacturers reluctant and no political aspirations, they achieved little.[25] It was the co-operative store, posing an ideological as well as a business threat, that bore the brunt of their fury. The *Grocer* campaigned from the 1870s for a boycott of those who supplied them, and similar sentiments by J. Aubrey Rees just before the First World War, supporting 'the legitimate trader', indicate how little they had achieved.[26]

With these associations our survey of British petty bourgeois organisations exhausts its subject. This comparative failure to organise and to develop distinctive political perspectives clearly requires wide-ranging explanations. These would involve the somewhat lesser pace of business concentration in Britain,[27] but ideological factors would be paramount, especially the nature of the relationship between the intense individualism of the British petty bourgeoisie and their huge sense of vulnerability. Like the shop in Bromley owned by H. G. Wells' parents, all would be sunk in it and 'they had no means of getting out of it, and going anywhere else.'[28] It is this disbelief in the value of action that is striking. The subject would warrant more serious investigation.

The fast-growing white collar element in the lower middle class was more significant in Britain, certainly to contemporaries. It must be emphasised at the outset that the terms 'clerk' and 'white collar worker' mask a huge range of occupational status and income. B. G. Orchard, in his classic study of Liverpool clerks, noted their great heterogeneity.

> Their ranks embrace some who, though the servants of others, are enabled by their ample salaries to live in not the least ample houses at Claughton, or Aigburth, or New Brighton, or Birkdale; though others (equally 'clerks') must strive hard to exist on twelve shillings a week.[29]

The clerical income hierarchy in 1909 reveals the proportion of male clerks earning over £160 a year at its highest amongst those in insurance (46%) and banking (44%), then declining through central government (37%), local government (28%), and industry and commerce (23%), to the lowest group, railway clerks, of whom only 10 per cent earned above the income tax minimum.[30] White collar workers thus constitute a very diverse occupational group.

Precise enumeration of the expansion of these occupations is difficult, because of the familiar problems of consistency over time that accompany use of the census tables. Only one group causes problems here, the commercial clerks, who until 1881 were merely a residual group. Most commercial clerks were allocated by the census checkers to separate sectors before then. All other occupations remain roughly uniform in definition between 1851 and 1911, and comparative figures can therefore be relied upon. The data below will concern themselves with male workers, because the focus of this essay is upon the process of lower middle class stratification at a time when it was male occupations that defined status. The growth of female white collar workers[31] initially presented difficulties for male employees, yet we know little of the wider problems of social relationships involved. How do we locate female white collar workers—especially clerks and schoolteachers—within an analysis of stratification? Stratification theory, and especially studies of historical orientation, has great difficulty in coping with female occupations. The family is classically taken as the unit of analysis, and an uncertain extension of that uses the man's occupation as the main indicator of family status. More information about the marital status, social origins and family structure of female employees would help an understanding of the effect of female workers upon the perceived status structure.

Table 1.1 covers the bulk of white collar occupations and is self-explanatory, indicating that all these occupations were expanding numerically, to a total approaching one million by 1911, but that they grew at different speeds. Central government, male schoolteachers and law clerks all increased their numbers no faster than the male occupied population as a whole.

Table 1.1: White collar Employees in Great Britain 1851–1911

Male employees over 15 years as percentage of all occupied males over 15

	1851	1871	1891	1911
Civil Service	0.5	0.4	0.4	0.5
Local Government	0.1	0.2	0.2	0.4
Schoolteachers	0.5	0.5	0.6	0.6
Commercial Clerks[a]	0.7	1.3	2.6	3.0
Bank Clerks[c]	–	0.2	0.2	0.4
Insurance Clerks[b]	–	0.0	0.2	0.4
Law Clerks[c]	0.3	0.3	0.3	0.3
Railway Officials[c]	0.2	0.3	0.5	0.7
Commercial Travellers	0.2	0.3	0.5	0.8
TOTAL (%)	2.5	3.5	5.5	7.1
TOTAL (NUMBER)	144,035	262,084	534,622	918,186

– Not separately classified.
a Note the qualifications in the text concerning the figures for 1851 and 1871.
b The 1871 & 1891 tables aggregate agents and clerks. The 1911 division, with half in each category, was applied to produce a figure for insurance clerks in earlier censuses.
c The 1891 census for Scotland gave no separate figures for law, bank or railway clerks.
Source: Census Tables for 1851, 1871, 1891, 1911 (England & Wales; Scotland).

These figures must be qualified by examining their local distribution, for they were very unevenly spread round the country. While some jobs would exist everywhere, notably teachers and local government officers, most white collar employment was not only strikingly urban but concentrated in specific kinds of urban economies. In 1891 we can examine male white collar employees (those occupations in Table 1.1) as a percentage of all occupied males[32] in various communities that were separately listed in the census tables. The most concentrated places were the government and trading centres of Edinburgh (10.9%) and London (10.1%). At the other extreme were the overwhelmingly rural counties of Wiltshire (3.1%), Lincolnshire (3.1%) and Buckinghamshire (2.5%). More unexpected is how low are the figures for towns of a primarily industrial character such as Oldham (3.8%), Sheffield (4.9%), Northampton (4.9%), Nottingham (5.3%) and Birmingham (5.6%). It is the commercially important cities that had a substantially larger white collar workforce, whether the commerce rested on a base of local manufacture as in Manchester (7.5% with Salford) or more commonly on overseas and coastal trading links as with Aberdeen (8.6%), Bristol (8.3%), Liverpool (8.1% with Birkenhead), Newcastle (8.0%), Cardiff (7.9%), Glasgow (7.8%) and Hull (7.3%). The presence of the white collar lower middle class was thus strongest in the cities built upon trade, commerce and government.

The economic basis for these developments is clear in outline but hazy in detail. The origins lie at one level in the emergence of the imperialist and international economy of the late nineteenth century. The expansion of the financial and commercial significance of Britain, especially of the City of London, underpinned all else, and for these developments at least overshadowed any possible industrial retardation. In this period international trade probably attained the highest ratio that it has ever held to the value of world production,[33] and it is in the context of that international economy, with its increasing financial, commercial and administrative sophistication that Europe's salaried employees emerged. Although the internal service sector was no novelty, for the industrial revolution was as significantly a commercial transformation, its specific growth in the late-Victorian economy thrust to the fore just the non-manual employees with whom this essay is concerned. Retailing, marketing, distribution, banking and finance—all increased in scale and complexity. The main contribution of education to the expansion of white collar employment was increasingly dominated by female teachers. Finally, and perhaps far more importantly than over-generalised characterisations of the late-Victorian and Edwardian economy would allow, there was the commercialisation and bureaucratisation of the secondary sector. In 1911 42 per cent of all commercial clerks were employed in manufacturing industry—45,000 of them working for engineering and shipbuilding firms alone.[34]

The contemporaneous expansion of similar occupations in many European countries at this time, in spite of great differences in economic development, is striking, but detailed comparative statistics are hard to establish.[35] Paul Bairoch notes in his massive compilation of European population statistics that the occupational categories he uses for different countries are not strictly equivalent, and comparisons can not therefore be pressed very far.[36] Nevertheless, the group 'commerce, banks, insurance, real estate' is everywhere a prime lower middle class occupational sector, and it is therefore significant that according to Bairoch it undergoes a marked upward trend between 1860 and 1910 in all Western European countries. This is confirmed by other evidence. In the period 1882 to 1907 salary earners rose from 7.0 to 13.1 per cent of the German labour force, while the *employés* category in France rose from 772,000 and 5.0 per cent of the workforce in 1876 to 1,869,000 and 9.3 per cent in 1911.[37] This is not the place to explain that trend, but the growing unification and internationalisation of the world economy in this period, and the upward surge in population growth, are clearly important factors. One might also extend Gerschenkron's backwardness argument to say that other European economies at different levels of industrial development from Britain would enter not just at a higher technological level, but also at a higher commercial and bureaucratic level. Thus the expansion of white collar occupations would come far sooner after initial industrialisation in the rest of Europe than it had done in Britain.

The paradox of the expansion of the salaried workforce in Britain was that as it grew so its frustration increased, based most concretely on a sense of unfulfilled ambition. White collar workers were notorious for their aspirations for mobility, and this ambition had some real viability. There were three main dimensions to these aspirations. A man could rise to a partnership in his firm, a process particularly common in the wholesaling trades. He could set up in business on his own, especially if he was a broker's clerk for there it was who you knew and what you knew, rather than capital resources, that were the key. Orchard saw it as a characteristic of small offices based on dealing that 'men with genuine business faculty soon rise from the ranks.'[38] Finally, in areas such as banking, railways and insurance that were closed to the small man, there were the prospects of rising by merit in the clerical scale.

Individual ambition at work was built centrally into the employment atmosphere of the salaried lower middle class. The commercial traveller, for example, had a fiercely competitive understanding of his situation, and in his survey of those *Ambassadors of Commerce*[39] A. P. Allen made great play with those in the trade who had risen to high position. The United Kingdom Commercial Travellers' Association elected its presidents from top businessmen, preferably those who had risen from fairly lowly origins.[40] These origins might not have been as humble as first appearances would suggest, but the myth might yet persist, for it reflected what they wanted to believe. When George Grosch's father obtained a post in 1889 as manager of a Kentish Town corn and seed business, both he and his ambitious wife undertook it as a positive first rung on the ladder.[41] Charles Parsons recognised the importance of open mobility for clerks, for as early as 1876 he felt that the link between effort and reward was being too severely fractured for employees with such a self-help orientation. There was a great need, he felt, for a *fair* promotion system. The clerk needed to know that 'higher remuneration must follow his successful efforts.'[42] This persistent ideology of personal mobility was characteristic of the lower middle class and a dominant element in its values. It was an ambition quite distinct from that of the artisan for whom there was far less scope, and often far less desire, for a mobility structured into the job. This is not to deny, of course, selective artisan ambitions for inter-generational mobility. These will be discussed later.

It was these career aspirations that came to be challenged by late-Victorian experience for so many white collar workers, in a threat comparable to that experienced by the small businessman. The ambition of salaried employees was being undermined both by changes in the composition of their labour market and in the structure of firms.[43] Easier entry at the bottom end of the white collar world possibly followed the extension of elementary education, though it is unlikely that parents not obtaining an education for their children before 1870 would have been those seeking clerical and other salaried employment for them subsequently. The improvement in the quality of education with progressive urban school boards was probably more important. The closing of opportunities for advancement was more significant. Partnerships and setting up on one's own account became less accessible as the scale of enterprise and capitalisation grew, and increasing bureaucratisation fractured the promotion ladder by beginning the modern practice of multi-level recruitment[44] while the work for many clerks became increasingly menial. Work for an increasing proportion of white collar workers became routinised and impersonal, and processes similar to those discussed amongst clerks by G. L. Anderson in his essay below were experienced by commercial travellers. Their knowledge of the field and their contacts, together with their relationship with the employer, gave them pride and respect as well as prospects. The traveller had self-respect and great freedom of action. As business conditions hardened and management was made more bureaucratic, commercial travellers complained of increasing pressures, and of their work now being organised by disrespectful clerks who expected them to conform to rules, codes of behaviour and organised routes.[45]

Insecurity increased at the lower end of white collar occupations. Female labour was almost certainly less of a threat to clerks than oversupply in their own ranks.[46] Lower-grade commercial travellers, and even their longer established seniors, felt great competitive pressure in a similar way to clerks. There was far less security of employment, more commission work, and increasing pace and competition. More and more travellers chased sales that were growing at a slower rate. According to a correspondent in the travellers' newspaper, *On The Road*:

> we are constantly meeting in our commercial rooms with fresh faces; we see them once or twice, and in some instances a little oftener, but before we know them, they disappear.[47]

They also grew anxious about business combinations that restricted competition. Their assets were their goodwill and connections, and business combinations put these increasingly at risk.[48]

Commercial travellers and clerks shared in different ways the common problem of the aspirant and unorganised white collar worker in the late-Victorian economy. Their fears of falling, the obsession that vied in lower middle class minds with the prospect of success, were exacerbated. The terror of dismissal was growing, and jobs were far harder to find as men grew older. When George Grosch became bored with his job as a clerk, he went to sea. On his return he found it very difficult to obtain a clerical job again, for 'employers, it seemed, liked boys fresh from school.'[49] It was even worse for unemployed French office workers, charged a premium by a new employer under the guise of caution money.[50] The problem common to all forms of salaried white collar work was that because jobs were ostensibly careers with a single firm, the specificity of each job and the narrow limitations of a man's skill to the office routine he worked with, made re-employment difficult. The corollary of job security was thus fear of the sack. In Frederick Willis's street of lower middle class families this was the great fear. For the skilled mechanic it would only mean a short period of unemployment, but it often signified complete collapse for the residents of Burdock Road. 'No worker came down to destitution more rapidly than he.'[51]

It is the totality of what that fall might mean that was so important. It was not falling a rung on some notional occupational hierarchy that was involved, but collapse into the unskilled and casual. Outside office work, or whatever, the white collar employee had no skill, no ability, probably not even any strength. Thus casual job-hunting on the London docks was often the fate of those displaced elsewhere. David Crew has shown that although few non-manual employees in the German city of Bochum were mobile downwards in the late nineteenth century, those that were generally ended up amongst the unskilled at the next census.[52] There is no comparable evidence for Britain, but it would be surprising if the same were not true there.

The problems faced by lower middle class employees were thus partly a result of their market weakness and job specificity, but also a function of the nature of the aspirant ideology that exposed them to frustration and fear. All combined to put pressures upon them that they were organisationally and culturally ill-equipped to meet. Non-manual employees in Germany and France, under similar processes of closing opportunity, organised themselves during this period, but their counterparts in Britain were reluctant to do the same.[53] The petty bourgeoisie and white collar workers, groups sharing an inherent weakness in the market, were being exposed more seriously to the difficulties of a market economy at just the time when other groups in society—companies, employers, financiers, manual workers—were either organising or consolidating in order to reduce the impact of the market upon the individual. The failure of small businessmen to combine has already been indicated, and the same can largely be said of white collar employees. Although most sectors saw some form of association or trade union emerge during this period, they were on the whole very poorly supported. Only the Post Office unions, whose National Joint Committee could boast 61,000 members in 1914, and the Railway Clerks Association, which expanded in the years before the First World War and organised 61 per cent of their potential membership in 1918, made much headway.[54]

It is not enough to see the general failure of white collar unionism before 1914 as due to some generalised characteristics such as docility, deference, or lack of aggression. The absence of collective organisation could signify power rather than the reverse, indicating the strength of the individual bargain. This perhaps applied to the best clerks and local government officers on high salaries, and accounted for the weakness of their respective associations. The failure to unionise for the rest was due partly to the realities of their economic and social position, for only a rigidly narrow definition of proletarianisation would deny that the structural position of white collar workers militated against unionism. It was also a result of their ideological position and status consciousness. When George Bernard Shaw had been an estate agent's clerk in the 1870s he would on no account have contemplated joining a trade union, even if one had existed.

> Not only would it have been considered a most ungentlemanly thing to do—almost as outrageous as coming to the office in corduroy trousers, with a belcher handkerchief round my neck—but, snobbery apart, it would have been stupid, because I should not have intended to remain a clerk. I should have taken the employers' point of view from the first.[55]

Relations with the employer were thus thought to be explicitly different from those of a manual employee. Whatever the reality, there was a firm belief in some identity of interests between employer and non-manual staff, an identity often expressed in the emulation of the former's dress and manners. Career ambitions and a traditional security of income inhibited collective organisation amongst those who were essentially in competition with each other. In any case, trade unions were explicitly not respectable. There were other inhibiting factors, in addition to those mentioned by Shaw. The majority of firms were still small-scale, and white collar workers were widely scattered by work place and industry. Skills and even aspirations would be highly specific to a given firm, indicating a narrowness and a commitment that could only inhibit a wider consciousness. Finally, an individualistic and isolated life-style would make improbable the inclinations towards collective support that were so important to nineteenth-century manual trade unionism.

Trade union organisation was conversely most successful where the work unit was highly bureaucratised and impersonal, with standardised rules and procedures, and a widening gulf between employer and employee. The railways and the Post Office fit this generalisation very clearly, and white collar employees there would also be in close daily contact with a unionised working class. It is significant that similar factors explain the early unionisation of just the same white collar groups in the USA.[56] Sturmthal regards career blocks—these occurred in government employment and in the railways after amalgamations— as having the most strong inverse correlation with trade unionism amongst white collar workers throughout Europe.[57] In fact, the lower white collar grades could attract socially aspiring individuals for whom blockages were especially frustrating. The first organisation of Boy Clerks in the Civil Service—a grade classically used as a stepping stone for the sons of aspirant working class parents—was expressly aimed at persuading a Royal Commission that the dead-end Boy Clerk system should be abolished.[58] Schoolteachers, of course, provided the best and earliest example of strong association stimulated by frustrated and status-conscious men and women blocked from serious mobility in their profession.

Where associations and organisations were formed, the tentative, if ultimately unsuccessful, solution to the threat to respectability was to narrow their function to that of an individualistic and instrumental tool to achieve aspirations compatible with middle class status. Even clerks' associations that offered sick relief, unemployment benefit and job information had difficulties in recruiting because they might appear to be acting like trade unions in spheres that lower middle class ideology restricted to self-help.[59] Trade unionism was vigorously rejected. The United Kingdom Commercial Travellers' Association explicitly denied any trade union approach, of which the most basic element was seen as interference between employer and employee. The Association, founded to support the commercial travellers' demand for weekend railway concessions, concentrated on that together with a legal service and pressure for uniform hotel charges.[60]

These pressures for only safe associations can be seen in most aspects of white collar organisation. The Association of Teachers in Technical Institutions stressed its professional role. The President claimed in 1907 that

> since the inception of this Association we have all, I think, agreed that it should become in no sense a Trade Union of Teachers, but that our labour of love should be for the benefit of technical education... Teaching is one of the greatest professions.[61]

The income bargain was resolutely left to the individual, as it was in the National Association of Local Government Officers. NALGO grew out of the local guilds such as that in Liverpool, which aimed at 'social intercourse', 'improvement and advancement', and 'knowledge of the principles of local government.' The authorities gave their support, and the concentration was upon leisure activities—literary societies, pierrot troup, drama and choral activities, football, and so on.[62] This atmosphere continued even after the 1905 amalgamation and the Bolton guild was not alone when it asserted that 'there is no trade unionism about [our movement] .We are not to battle councils, but to assist them.'[63] Even the call for grading and an examination-based promotion system was rejected on the grounds that a scale would dull ambition and kill incentive, and that grading would make NALGO akin to a trade union.[64]

In such ways would the ideological damage of organisation be minimised for members of the lower middle class. The distinctions were fragile, however, and most resisted even the weak organisation that did exist. According to Strumthal, a lasting feature of white collar unionism throughout Europe has been to keep open a free opportunity-based employment situation, maintaining the channels of occupational mobility and making them dependent upon merit.[65] Few such associations in Britain went even that far before 1914, but outside the two main areas of clerical unionisation the orientation of the small white collar associations that did exist was precisely to set the framework for individual self-help.

Associations of any kind were the exception. The lower middle class in this period was expanding yet, at the same time, frustrated and lonely. In autobiographies in particular there is an atmosphere of a self-imposed isolation and loneliness. 'There is a real home life,' wrote Masterman, 'strong family affection, little gardens and ornamented villas, ambition for the children.'[66] The availability of space in the lower middle class home allowed a family centredness, a degree of privacy and isolation that was impossible for most working class families who consequently spilled into the street, the public house, the external entertainment. It was also the individualistic ideology of the lower middle class that drove them inwards into the security of a family life that was often incapable of bearing the strains imposed upon it. If the bread-winner felt under pressure, if the status of the family seemed vulnerable, a further turning in could result. For Richard Church the tightly closed family that he experienced as a child was typical of the stratum. 'I see it, in retrospect, as a place, a pocket of civilisation utterly quiet and self-sufficient.'[67] The world outside her home was alien to Helen Corke, daughter of a small shopkeeper in Sussex and Kent towns, who was eight years old before allowed to enter the house of a neighbour.[68] Domestic entertainment was in this context paramount. Hence the symbolic importance of the purchase of a piano.[69] For wife and children the repressive force must have been enormous. Without wider contacts of any real intimacy, with an isolated existence in a shapeless suburb where appearances had to be maintained, and entrance into the street had to be regulated for display, the tedium and frustration must have been intense. The novels of Keble Howard paint an affectionate picture of just that atmosphere.[70] This internalisation and individualism precluded organisation for defensive purposes or for collective support and company. Even the lower middle class use of friendly societies would often reject those of the mutual and socially active kind supported by most artisans, in favour of 'ordinary societies' like the Hearts of Oak with collectors and no meetings.[71]

These inhibitions to organise were less powerful amongst the more homogeneous rural petty bourgeoisie of many European countries. In Belgium, for example, it was the rural rather than the urban petty bourgeoisie that organised most extensively in the face of economic pressures.[72] Yet there was more to it than that. Christopher Caudwell captured it in an extreme form. 'It is the peculiar suffering of the petit bourgeoisie that they are called upon to hate each other.'[73] Competitive instincts he saw as fundamental, and there does certainly appear to have been a normative resistance to any collective social life. The commercial travellers enjoyed the traditional conviviality of the hotel commercial rooms, with their elaborate dining rituals,[74] but this was an abstracted social life of ever recomposing groups of isolated individuals rather than one of continuing social support. It was in any case denied to the women and children trapped in suburbia.

Those lower middle class associations that did exist were formal ones based not on community but on interest. Helen Corke's adolescent social life illustrates this well.[75] Even the artificial constructs of such associations were slow to develop in suburbia.[76] In religious activity, most of all, they could perhaps seek to overcome the isolation to which they were condemned by their life-style and aspirations, and enable them to make contact with others of similar status.[77] Booth was certainly convinced that the churches' role in London as a social centre for clerks was vital in explaining the success of specific institutions.[78] When the lower middle class, neither gregarious nor collective by nature, joined voluntary associations, they did so in a one-dimensional and almost instrumental way.

All this led necessarily to highly individualistic analyses of their own difficulties. The social imagery of the marginal middle class is one that locates movement and success as due to individual initiative and talent. Helen Corke's shopkeeper father was convinced that his own repeated business failures were due to his personal incapacity and lack of judgement.[79] As clerical opportunities for advance closed, and as the labour market was flooded at the lower end, the response was to seek external scapegoats of the kind discussed by G. L. Anderson below, rather than to trace the problem back to their own vulnerability as individuals. The solutions were equally individualistic, as in the upsurge of interest in commercial education and the blind faith in the power of shorthand. Adult education became the individual's chance for salvation. Commercial classes at Nottingham University College in the 1880s had been overwhelmed by white collar workers, and twenty years later classes at Toynbee Hall were flooded with clerks and shop assistants.[80]

This individual self-help response was what was expected of them. It was ideologically unacceptable to make calls for government aid of the kind demanded by the German *Mittelstand*. Nor could they organise vigorously for mutual strength, only tentatively to construct a context for individual endeavour. Ideology and situation would interlock, and problem-solving became a lonely quest. The result, given the increasing vulnerability of their status and economic position, was a sense of threat and frustration. Opportunities were closing, yet that was hard to believe. Business was concentrating and apparently threatening small men of ambition, whether rival small businessmen or white collar employees. Most serious of all was a growing sense of being threatened by both the organised and unorganised working class. H. G. Wells' mother knew that there had to be a lower stratum, but was disgusted to find that anyone belonged to it.[81] For many others, lack of contact would only aggravate fears, while the terror of themselves falling socially made the abyss seem even blacker. The absence of a party with the revolutionary tone of the German SPD made little difference, though it might provide one reason why the British lower middle class failed to develop an extremist politics. The sense of embattlement was one that Masterman characterised well.

> The Rich despise the Working People; the Middle Classes fear them ... In feverish hordes the suburbs swarm to the polling booth to vote against a turbulent proletariat ... He has difficulty with the plumber in jerry-built houses needing continuous patching and mending. His wife is harassed by the indifference or insolence of the domestic servant ... He would never be surprised to find the crowd behind the red flag, surging up his little pleasant pathways, tearing down the railings, trampling the little garden; the 'letting in of the jungle' upon the path of fertile ground which has been redeemed from the wilderness.[82]

An ever more insistent status consciousness was one consequence of these trends. The assertion of status can often be a defensive response to a sense of threat. We lack detailed studies to document this in Britain, but an interesting example of such responses to the rise of labour can be seen in Henning's study of Westphalia and the Rhineland between 1860 and 1914. In the early years of that period lower civil servants (whom he took as representative of educated white collar workers) had a degree of open contact with manual workers, especially as indicated by marriage links. Industrialisation advanced from the 1890s, and the response of white collar workers, feeling increasingly threatened by the rise of labour, was a more status conscious exclusiveness. They sought titles and offices to mark themselves off, and marriage contacts markedly declined.[83]

It is this kind of response that helps understand the insistent status consciousness of the British lower middle class. The archetypal lower middle class obsession with what was proper and respectable was lampooned endlessly in the novels of the time, most notably *The Diary of a Nobody*.[84] There is always a danger that we overstate this aping of the values and life-style of others and the extent of the passionate respectability. H. G. Wells certainly did not find it in his Westbourne Park lodging house.[85] Nor do we know how often what appears to us as dull and artificial imitation was in reality a quest for a more substantial achievement. E. M. Forster recognised this in his characterisation of the tragic Leonard Bast.[86]

With these qualifications in mind, it still remains necessary to insist that for a stratum for whom belief in mobility and achievement was high, status aspirations were always essential to allow the satisfaction of ambitions that genuine social mobility could not afford to many. The problem became especially serious for trapped salaried employees whose consequent counter-attack involved for some a turn to socialism but, for the great majority, increasing status anxieties and more strident assertion of their non-manual character. This was not altogether new. The clerk was always seen as comically self-important, and in the 1860s Fitzjames Stephens gave a clear conception of an identifiable stratum of mercantile clerks, small shopkeepers, newspaper reporters and commercial travellers, united by their pretensions.[87] Yet these pretensions and the concern for display became increasingly strident and forceful. Dress was always important, marking off the non-manual employee in Britain in the same way as the long fingernail in Italy. We glimpse in letters to the *Evening News* in 1912 from lower middle class suburbanites how fragile they felt their status was. They complained endlessly of the aggression or simple contamination of the lower classes. Children played at the end of the High Street in naked feet. Twickenham dustmen and roadsweepers importuned excessively for summer outings and Christmas dinners.[88] Display and status security became of increasing importance; so did the sense of threat implicit in these letters.

Respectability and other components of the status consciousness of members of the late-Victorian lower middle class were fundamentally a means of living with inequality. The process appears in a fascinating way in the changing content of YMCA propaganda, which had in earlier decades encouraged ambition for advance amongst this stratum, but was adjusted in the late nineteenth century as speakers emphasised the benefits of respectability, self-education and a sense of pride.[89] This assertiveness was most unfortunately necessary for just that expanding lower end of the stratum whose economic position was both more insecure and more insufficient than previously. Proper standards became all-important. Masterman was surprised. 'There are often set up quite astonishing standards of "respectability" in politics and religion.'[90] The need to maintain an elevated status on what was often little more than a working class-sized income was a constant problem. Status had to be visible, because on a salaried hierarchy salary indicated level, and only display could reflect salary. It was this need for visible respectable expenditure, on clothing, housing and assistance in the home, that put such pressures on income. Parsons was not alone in believing that many artisans were better off without the need to impress neighbours that their circumstances were much better than they in reality were.[91] The obsessive questioning about the amount on which a man may marry reflected these problems.[92]

The most revealing evidence of these status anxieties is a controversy in the letter columns of the *Daily Chronicle*[93] over the minor clerk depicted in Gissing's novel *The Town Traveller*. The whole dispute demonstrated a fascinating sensitivity to status, with self-styled 'minor clerks' condemning the unrefined and undignified Christopher Parish, others condemning the first writers for exposing their own pretensions, and the painting of a total picture of acute sensitivity to the public image of their stratum. Only lengthy extracts from the letters, for which there is no space here, could convey the flavour of anxiety and determination to do what is correct by middle class standards that pervades the whole correspondence. In a neat editorial, the *Spectator* observed just how odd was the sensitivity of these clerks.[94]

One group who suffered these status problems in a more acute and earlier form requires some separate mention. Schoolteachers were by the 1850s exposing the rigid complexities of the English (though not necessarily the Scottish) status system, earlier than any other salaried white collar group. Many pupil-teachers were the children of artisans seeking upward mobility,[95] and this was both a cause of their frustration and, given the sensitivity of their work, of the criticisms levelled at them. The 'social condition' of schoolteachers was repeatedly an issue, either through criticism of their conceit, over-education and over-ambition, or their own anxieties about their social position. In the mid-Victorian period they provide an early example of a status-conscious white collar group with unfulfillable ambitions. They were soon complaining about their inability to obtain promotion, while the school managers would not accept them as social equals. One witness to the Departmental Committee on the Pupil Teacher System noted that in France and Germany 'the position of the elementary teacher is so much more highly esteemed than in this country. His social status is quite different from what it is in this country.'[96] They were elevated in France both by the increased importance attached to education, and by their symbolic role in the struggle for the Republic against the Church.

Similar anxieties persisted to the turn of the century, but by then the schoolteacher was taking the brunt of a diffuse attack directed by the old middle class against popular education and against the new white collar stratum.[97] The social isolation remained, for the schoolteacher was indeed over-educated for the lower middle class to which he or she was assigned.[98] Admired for having risen, they were despised for their airs. In the context of these problems, career blocks, and a new local government employer emerging after 1870, it is not surprising that the National Union of Teachers was the strongest of the non-manual trade unions. They were assisted by their sense of identity as a professional group, and by the absence of a competitive career situation. Although the union stressed professional interests rather than trade union ones, the pressures of their situation drew them into more trade union-style activities, and from the 1890s into an uneasy relationship with the labour movement.[99] The complexities of the schoolteachers' problems marked them out from other salaried occupations, but it is striking that in many respects they pre-dated developments amongst other white collar groups.

In the present state of our understanding of the British lower middle class, any discussion of their historical significance must of necessity be partial. The points that follow are also consciously speculative, growing both out of the earlier sections of this essay and the developments examined in the book as a whole. The rise of suburbia and lesser commercial operations aimed at the lower middle class market will be examined first. Subsequent discussion will raise three central points of intersection between the lower middle class and the social structure as a whole: its place in the process of social mobility; the lower middle class as a conservative force in politics and society; and its impact upon the aristocracy of labour and thus upon the working class as a whole.

According to the snobbish T. H. Crosland, 'Man was born a little lower than the angels, and has been descending into suburbanism ever since.'[100] From the image of romantic anti-urbanism and the rejection of uniformity, the suburb had come to represent all that was mediocre and dull. The flooding of the lower middle class into cheap and regular imitations of the middle class villa residence must play a large part in explaining that transformation. The arrival of the shopkeeper heralded the decline, in Crosland's eyes. Though they might have moved on, 'the spirit of them remains and abides, and is reflected in everything suburban.' Then came the clerks, the warehousemen and the bagmen.[101] Dislike of the self-righteous superiority that pervades Crosland's book can not prevent agreement that mass suburbia was a creation of the lower middle class. Booth's *Religious Influences* series offers excellent examples of this in London, and examples abound elsewhere, usually linked to transport extensions from the 1870s. Railway access, together with proximity to the status of Hampstead, meant that there was a 'practically complete colonisation of West Hampstead and Kilburn by the petit bourgeoisie.'[102] If the railway was the main influence in London, it had the same impact in Liverpool where bulk commuting began in the last decades of the nineteenth century, with the building of modest houses for the lower middle class northwards up to and beyond Waterloo and Crosby. In Manchester and Birmingham it was the tramway and omnibus that were more important.[103]

The difficulty in preserving residential exclusiveness meant that there was a lack of homogeneity in lower middle class suburban housing that makes generalisation dangerous. It was often located on the fringes of areas changing in social composition. In Dalston and West Hackney the better-to-do were leaving, and 'in the homes and in the churches their places are taken by a lower middle grade.'[104] Similar pressure could drive them from areas being invaded by artisans to those such as Lewisham and Lee where 'the incomers are clerks and managers, many coming from Peckham and Brixton.'[105] The older inner London suburbs were being progressively invaded by the better-paid working class, especially from the 1890s, but, in terms of the process as a whole it is the lower middle class role in the suburban housing market that was dominant. The mass of working men and women were reluctant to seek suburban life, whether for reasons of transport or amenities, or for others with more normative content.[106] Status was the key to lower middle class movement. G. S. Layard, advising a solicitor's cashier on £200 a year on where to live, told him to choose 'the clerks' suburbs' of Clapham, Forest Gate, Walthamstow, Kilburn or Peckham. 'His neighbours will be of his own class' and this would be important to the wife and children who were to spend most of their time there.[107] The growth of such carefully defined suburbs, or at least suburban zones, was not just a feature of London. Manchester boasted commuter suburbs clearly defined as based on clerks, warehousemen and book-keepers.[108] Similarly, the southern suburbs of Edinburgh that grew from the late nineteenth century were dominated by shopkeepers, small businessmen, accountants and clerks, together with some engineers. On the edge of the same town the red sandstone terraced speculation at Saughtonhall was mostly inhabited by clerks, travellers and shopkeepers.[109] If the process was less distinct than these generalisations would allow, and some further qualifications will be offered towards the end of this essay, John Kellett firmly concludes that suburban zoning had clear tendencies towards social homogeneity.[110] As one would expect from the nature of housing zoning, they were rarely large uniform suburbs, but contained sub-areas and areas in change. Yet it is clear that the role of the lower middle class in the creation of a new status-conscious suburbia was paramount.

Commercial provision for the lower middle class extended beyond the bricks, mortar and bays of suburbia. Specific innovations catered for them. Selfridges, most notably amongst department stores, was directed at the lower middle class consumer demand.[111] Similarly in publishing, where the *Daily Mail*, carefully tailored for an aspiring readership, was the most notable example. Masterman felt that the 'yellow press' was directed precisely at them, and they certainly were eager readers of *Tit-Bits* and *Answers*.[112] In fact, Crosland saw them as the key to the new commercial and cultural innovations. He advised his readers to go to Clapham, and there understand the market for half-penny journalism, gramophones, pleasant Sunday afternoons, golf, tennis, high-school education, miraculous hair restorers, and prize competitions.[113]

The basis for the broad commercial provision for a lower middle class market was initially simple growth of numbers, but equally significant were earnings—their size, regularity and security. We are talking about F. G. D'Aeth's groups of small shopkeepers and clerks on £150 a year, and his smaller business class on £300 a year.[114] Here was the central lower middle class. Below it lay the poorer clerks for whom the struggle was often desperate, while above it were groups whose life-style and occupations became more and more akin to the substantial middle class. Far more important than the simple level of earnings were the relative security and the promise of some kind of salary scale. This was the vital difference between the labour aristocracy and the lower middle class, even at those points at the margin where notional rates of pay appeared the same. Artisan earnings related far more to the vagaries of the trade cycle, local employment fluctuations, sickness, the possibilities of overtime, and other uncertainties. Amongst clerks living in four working class districts of London in 1887—we are therefore examining mainly lesser clerks—a survey revealed in them a great sense of the regularity of their work. Their pay was level with the best artisans, but they were paying above average rent, indicating both a normative attachment to better housing and a sense of security that allowed longer-term rent commitments. Their unemployment in the previous six months was far lower than for skilled workers. Most interesting of all, when asked whether their employment was regular or irregular—in other words, when asked to reveal their own sense of security—90 per cent of clerks judged it regular. Skilled workers were all far lower, and the only higher groups were policemen, postmen, railway workers and, for some reason, sugar bakers.[115] It should be noted that this sense of security existed amongst clerks in fairly ordinary working class districts. The effects must have been even greater on those with larger salaries and higher positions. It was this, together with the aspirations that encouraged status-conscious expenditure, that was the basis for the commercial market that was constructed amongst the lower middle class.

The lower middle class plays a very specific role in the process of social mobility, whether of a career or an inter-generational type. It is available for those seeking to rise out of the working class, whether into white collar occupations by means of a fairly rudimentary education, or by small capital accumulation into the petty bourgeoisie. Whereas the former generally implied some conscious separation from the manual working class, the latter did not always do so. Some shifting from worker to shopkeeper, or even more so to small master, might see it as an occupational change implying no social mobility, and would still identify with working class social values. Others saw it positively as a social advance, and aspired to middle class norms of behaviour.[116] The changing structure of the lower middle class clearly signifies changing mobility prospects for the working class. Small businesses, while still the ambition of many, were less feasible, especially as a means of advance to anything but the most precarious of existences. The real mobility prospects were offered through salaried non-manual employment.

Where did this growing stratum come from? It had to be recruited from either members or offspring of other classes, either the working class moving upwards or the more established middle class down. From what we know of lower middle class attitudes, their aspirant but not desperate tone, upward mobility seems more likely. Yet, in reality, we know virtually nothing about occupational recruitment during this period.[117] In Kentish London during the mid-Victorian years male clerical workers were recruited more specifically from amongst non-manual strata in the 1870s than they had been in the 1850s, with a lower proportion the sons of skilled workers, and a very small number with unskilled fathers in either period.[118] The main change was increased recruitment from amongst shopkeepers' sons, indicating perhaps a use of white collar occupations to solve a fundamental petty bourgeois problem, the placing of non-inheriting sons in positions of adequate status. The early expansion of white collar employment was thus used more successfully by the small business class in Kentish London than by the skilled manual workers who seem to have benefited most from the more substantial expansion towards the end of the century, though the absence of studies of late-Victorian occupational recruitment means that we can only speculate. Vital to these issues is the growing differentiation amongst salaried occupations. As the lower end of the scale grew, and differentiated prospects for advancement became more evident, working class children seem to have obtained the lower jobs. It is not surprising that most railway clerks in Liverpool in the 1870s were already the sons of artisans,[119] for railway work offered least of all prospects, whether of moving up the clerical scale or into independent business. The importance of contacts and nepotism in skewing the advantages in the favour of clerks from non-manual backgrounds can only have increased. Banking and parts of insurance were the prestigious areas for ambitious clerks, and D'Aeth thought that it was the smaller business class earning £300 a year who put their sons into such positions.[120] Hugh McLeod, in Table 2.1 of his essay below, presents evidence to confirm this differential recruitment pattern.

Career mobility did exist. In the Royal Arsenal at Woolwich, for example, skilled workers and even secure labourers could become 'writers' (minor clerical workers) and thus enter the clerical hierarchy and perhaps advance.[121] Other examples would involve stepping into management by supervisory grades on the edge of the manual workforce. Overall, however, mobility for children of manual workers was more important. What would the consequences be of this kind of social mobility? The expansion of white collar occupations gave a new dimension to parental aspirations. Did the working class origins of many white collar workers have a marked effect on lower middle class culture and life-style? Neither contemporary observers nor historians have noticed this, except to the extent that the marginality of the new stratum seems to have produced a vigorous rejection of the main features of working class culture—its street life, its collective mutuality, its pub-centred leisure, its assertion of the value of manual work and of working class organisations and traditions. A more careful probing of lower middle class values might find some more subtle continuities, of which the search for both dignity and self-respect by the self-educated artisan might be one of the most fruitful. That search was after all itself undergoing in the mid-Victorian years a change of emphasis that drew out its instrumentality.

The escape from manual employed work offered by these lower middle class occupations could have acted as a stabilising social force by compensating parents for their own poor position, even defusing a degree of working class frustration. In some cultures, especially that of Italian and Jewish immigrants into the United States of America, mobility for children might be an acceptable compensation for the failure of the parents, but the strength of such values in Britain seems far more dubious. The possibility still remains that a particular type of working class parents saw white collar work as a desirable aim for their children. It is the apparent weakness of mobility from the unskilled which confirms this, for whereas the lower ranks of manual workers might have had good reason to seek any form of escape for their children, this was less true of skilled workers whose pride in their own craft produced some degree of contempt for the puny and parasitic clerks.[122] How does one distinguish the majority of Rowntree's skilled men in York who found apprenticeships for their sons in the same or some other skilled trade, from those others whose sons frequently became clerks and who saw it as a social advance?[123] Was there something exceptional within the working class that made certain parents or children desire white collar work? Robert Roberts noted that only a few in his Salford slum had specific aspirations. 'Shopkeepers, publicans and skilled tradesmen occupied the premier positions, each family having its own sphere of influence. A few of these aristocrats, while sharing working class culture, had aspirations. From their ranks the lower middle class, then clearly defined, drew most of its recruits—clerks, and, in particular, school-teachers.' This minority tried to get on by imitating 'what they believed were real middle class manners and customs.'[124]

Roberts offers no clue as to what distinguished this minority. The constant dissatisfaction experienced by W. J. Brown's plumber father was not simply caused by his frequent unemployment. 'He was conscious of a great disparity between his innate powers and the place he held in life . . . He brooded and became melancholic.' Under his father's pressure Brown prepared for the Civil Service examinations. As his father told him, and here we glimpse a distinguishing characteristic, 'if you get into the Service you're made for life—a permanent job all your life and a pension at the end of it.'[125] It is thus dangerous to assume that society's status ladders join on, one to the other. A selection by aspiration as well as by opportunity and ability must have existed.

A basic problem of lower middle class status was that of maintaining it and even progressing beyond it. It was significant for white collar workers, anxious not to have to resort to manual work for their children, but was even more difficult for the petty bourgeoisie. Demographic necessity will preclude most families with continuing businesses from the ideal situation of a single surviving heir. Maintaining status for non-inheriting children was thus a persistent problem. Marriage was one solution, though a far more fragile one than with the great landowners, the other group faced with the same problem but on a larger scale. The other way out was sideways mobility into other occupations of comparable status, with the hope of advance beyond. It was a continuing dilemma throughout Europe, though more serious where there was a small peasant class rather than England's mainly urban petty bourgeoisie. English elementary education might provide a means of reaching the white collar lower middle class, but the structure of secondary schooling and of the higher reaches of occupational and professional recruitment offered no such benefits of mobility through education for the lower middle class itself. The weakness of lower middle class education, noted by the Taunton Commission,[126] advanced little in terms of the mobility it might provide, for it offered no access to the educational system of the ruling class.

Personal contact was of a unique importance for obtaining even lower middle class positions in Britain compared with other European countries where educational qualifications could provide an excellent route for advance. The British position is notorious. As G. L. Anderson shows in his essay below, personal recommendation, and some degree of even indirect contact with employers and managers, was vital to clerical employment. When Sidney Ford's father lost his clerical job, he obtained a new position only 'through the good offices of a friend of the church.'[127] It is H. G. Wells' early life which provides the clearest picture of this process. As his shopkeeping mother sought a position of adequate status and opportunity for her son, personal contacts led him through a series of jobs as cash clerk with a draper in Windsor, a pupil-teacher in Somerset, a chemist's assistant in Midhurst, and a draper's assistant in Southsea.[128]

France, on the other hand, offers an example of a system of highly structured and, at least until the reforms of the later Third Republic, theoretically egalitarian educational system linked to occupational mobility. The rise of the individual from low to high social position by means of education was a great popular belief of the Third Republic, compared by Dupeux to the American rags to riches myth.[129] At the level of sideways mobility, Patrick Harrigan has indicated the role of secondary education, and especially the *Ecoles d'Arts et Metiers*, in providing access to the lower and middle civil service and the lesser professions such as secondary teachers, pharmacists and veterinary surgeons.[130] The real barrier in French education was the financial one between primary and secondary schooling. From the latter to higher education there was no institutional chasm of the British kind. The large urban *lycées* contained a substantial lower middle class of the sons of *employés* and shopkeepers in the 1860s, while the smaller provincial *lycées* were used predominantly by the farmers and rural lower middle class.[131] From there to the *grandes écoles* providing access to elite positions in the professions and government there was no inevitable block, and Harrigan finds some 40 per cent of the students at these *grandes écoles* during the Second Empire to have come from lower middle class and artisan backgrounds.[132] It is thus clear that French secondary education allowed some to proceed beyond narrowly lower middle class occupations, while also allowing members of that stratum to obtain sideways mobility for their children. For a variety of reasons analysed above, British society, having created this aspirant lower middle class, was rigidly incapable of guaranteeing it stability of status or offering the real chance of continued mobility. To this must now be added the consequence of a highly stratified educational system.

The conservatism of the lower middle class must not be oversimplified. There was no homogeneous social ideology, nor was its conservatism simply of political dimensions. There was a more fundamental defensiveness manifested in the concern for status, in the shift to the political right, in the clinging to an ideological individualism which reassured while it undermined. Masterman saw the suburbanite 'with custom dominant, accepted and inherited students of judgment, contempt for the classes below it, envy of the classes above it, and no desire for adventure or devotion to a cause or an ideal.'[133] This social fear and self-protectiveness are remembered by many. Richard Church's parents' fear of his brother Jack's musical talent is an unusually revealing demonstration of this anxiety about anything not comfortingly normal.[134]

The political dimensions of this social conservatism most concern this essay, but they weave endlessly into one another, most emphatically in the once radical commitment to both an economic and an emotional individualism. The drift of the lower middle class toward Toryism was one facet of the declining viability of mid-Victorian liberalism. This had been constructed as community politics, as the binding together of the forces of independence and vitality in British urban life as they fought outdated ideas about the political nation, economic affairs and social values.[135] It was the product of a particular social climate, before the economic anxieties, the social segregation, and the tensions between middle class and working class liberals had demonstrated the fragility of the Gladstonian myth. The lower middle class of shopkeepers and small businessmen had played a vital role in binding together that liberal expression of a small town social life, at times injecting it with a radicalising attack on privilege and protection. This fragile unity began to fragment during the closing decades of the century. From the working class position it was the reality of Gladstonian Liberal government, now that it could be contrasted with the myth, that created the tensions, but even more important was their treatment at the hands of the local caucuses. When one inserts into the equation the changing economic viability of that optimism upon which the mid-Victorian movement had rested, the Great Depression, the speeding up and craft dilution of the 1890s and the anti-trade union offensive; then liberalism as an ideal and as a movement was a declining force, whatever its vote-winning successes. The community politics of the 1860s fragmented under the force of the increasing social segregation within most towns and was exacerbated from 1884 by the establishment of single-member parliamentary constituencies.

These were not the only forces pushing the lower middle class into a more conservative posture. The rise of a hesitantly independent labour politics, aggressive trade unionism, especially of the unskilled, and the growing insecurity and frustration of the lower middle class itself all contributed. So did the historically important shift of the business elite into the Tory party, making it emphatically the party of property and stability. This drift towards 'Villa Toryism' seems to have carried much of the lower middle class with it. James Cornford sees the rise of white collar workers, schoolteachers, professionals, small shopkeepers and the rest to a new numerical prominence from the 1850s as central to the Tory party's late-Victorian success. 'They provided at least a potential rank and file for a non-working-class party.' Lord George Hamilton ascribed his conservative success in Middlesex as early as 1868 to the growth of these voters in his constituency.[136] Yet the real impact came from the last quarter of the century. Henry Pelling has noted the conservative trend in specific lower middle class suburbs, such as Fulham (London), Ormskirk (Liverpool) and Newington and Morningside (Edinburgh).[137] A writer in the *Club and Institute Journal* had no doubt as to the lessons to be learned. 'Until (the clerk) . . . can be laid hold of, villadom will prevent headway being made in Radicalism.'[138] Masterman agreed and saw the suburban lower middle class, terrified of the advance of labour, as responsible for giving the Moderates control of the London County Council. 'In feverish hordes,' he wrote, 'the suburbs swarm to the polling booths to vote against a truculent proletariat.'[139]

If conservatism grew as the dominant force amongst this stratum, extremist right-wing movements were absent. The continuing commitment of the lower middle class to mainstream party politics warrants investigation, particularly when compared with the German experience. There were organisations of a militantly right-wing complexion, such as the Liberty and Property Defence League and the Anti-Socialist Union,[140] yet both were backed by large-scale business interests to counter socialism and state intervention, and neither were the kind of extra-parliamentary organisation to mobilise the small man or appeal to his interests and fears. After 1918 the Middle Classes Union appeared, with a perspective similar to that of movements in Belgium and Germany. The Chairman told his members,

> If you are properly organised ... you can possibly hold up all the workers, you could hold up the capitalists, or you could even hold up the Government. You must see to it that you are not crushed or squeezed.

This rare statement of a clear *Mittelstand* tone continued, 'the unorganized middle, the section which is the butt, the buffer, and the burden-bearer when capital and labour are contending, has no standing and representation.'[141] This was a rare organisation in both tone and membership, directed against the growth of socialism, and proposing strike breaking and the organisation of essential supplies in emergencies.[142] Its distinctiveness and lack of impact only emphasise the absence of wider lower middle class political or economic organisation.

Arno Mayer refers to the 'erratic and intermittently frenzied politicisation' of the lower middle class in Europe, based essentially on insecure panic.[143] While there is much truth in this, it undervalues the uneven mobilisation of that stratum in Europe that preceded the involvement in fascism. Fears of proletarianisation and a squeeze induced by the concentration of capital stimulated different levels of response. The variables involved are clearly diverse, but the rate and type of economic development on the one hand, and the nature of the existing political structure on the other, are obviously central.

France, for these reasons, experienced far less explicit lower middle class mobilisation than Germany. The formation of self-conscious middle strata was retarded by the slow development of French industrial capitalism, but it is important that most politics in France at that time were precisely for these small men. A conservative drift can be detected in the later stages of the Third Republic, but the mainstream radicalism of the era as a whole was 'une radicalisme de refus'. It was an increasingly conservative doctrine based on classically petty bourgeois principles: the Republic as the descendant of the Revolution, the importance of education for social mobility, the rights of private property and especially of the small peasant proprietor, and the importance of the independent artisan class as the means of escape for workers.[144] Little challenged that faith in the early years of the Third Republic, and the result was a great variety within this small town and small man politics. Yet the radicalism was narrowly political, resting on an increasing social conservatism. These were compatible because of the peculiarity of French radicalism, its commitment to ideals of specifically political consequence such as formal democracy, the Republic, anti-clericalism, and low taxes. To André Siegfried the egalitarian republic, resting on the support of peasants, *employés*, and small businessmen, applied only in politics.[145]

This small town constituency was undergoing a conservative electoral drift from the 1890s, and Eugen Weber has shown how pressures from the labour movement and socialism increasingly frightened the small shopkeepers, shop assistants and office workers of Paris. Their radicalism became ever more conservative in its social content and their fears of oppression from above and of losing their identity in the proletariat below offered excellent opportunities to a demagogic nationalism such as that of the revival after 1905.[146] Such a movement was not the norm, though, and it is not until after the Second World War that we find a major and distinctive lower middle class entry into politics that rejected existing formations. Only when this stratum felt no longer protected by the political system as it stood could movements like Poujadism emerge, rejecting the existing economic and political establishment, albeit from a petty bourgeois Jacobin tradition.

The contrast with Germany is marked. There, both the old *Mittelstand* of independent artisans and retailers, and the new *Mittelstand* of white collar employees were important elements in pre-1914 nationalist and socially conservative movements.[147] These occupational groups faced diverse markets that posed insuperable obstacles to united economic organisation. There were indeed various levels of occupational and economic association, but whatever the difficulties posed by market position and the experience of urban industrialisation, political organisation was always possible. Although this becomes most insistent from the inflationary decade that began in 1914, it was advancing before the war.

It is increasingly clear that the term *Mittelstand* conceals a complicated and fragmented group whose major division mirrors the divide within the British lower middle class. Yet the very pervasiveness of the *Mittelstand* concept blurred the differences, and partially hid those distinct economic interests, encouraged by the landowning aristocracy and others who sought their support for the anti-socialist and anti-democratic cause. If the tensions were clear and at times persistent during the Wilhelmine period, it was the differential experiences of the First World War that tore the two sides apart. As Winkler has observed, 'the War demonstrated that not common economic interests but a common self-image created a fictitious unity for the *Mittelstand*.'[148] The tensions could be emphatic before the War, as in 1909 when the *Mittelstandsvereiningung* wanted to include white collar workers in its organisation, only to lose its angry Dusseldorf section as a consequence.[149] The insistent claims came from the white collar workers. In 1907 of 53 associations of them, 32 were also open to the self-employed.[150] They were in a peculiar position, dependent for their expansion upon the results of capitalist industrialisation, yet defining their status largely in terms of pre-industrial notions more relevant to sections of the old *Mittelstand*. The hesitant but real unity was provided not by economic and social reality, but the forces of aspiration and fear.[151] The political identification developed outside the formal structure, with substantial *Mittelstand* mobilisation in reactionary organisations such as the Army and Navy Leagues. If it appears that the old *Mittelstand* was more likely to be reactionary than the new, it remains true that the largest white collar unions, such as the German Federation of Salaried Commercial Employees, subscribed to an ideology that was racist, imperialist and radically anti-socialist.[152] Faced with a socialist labour movement most white collar workers stressed their non-proletarian allegiances more emphatically as the pay and working conditions of the two groups converged. They fought to mark out their distinctiveness, maintain traditional privileges, and stress ideological differences.[153]

The failure of the lower middle class in Britain to organise in the way that their counterparts in Germany did, and the failure to develop a distinctive political response to their situation, derives from the different social and ideological development of the two countries. Whatever the division of experience and consequently often of organisation within the German *Mittelstand*, there was still a real consciousness of structural and ideological positions and a specific function in society.[154] They were encouraged in this by the traditional ruling class, who claimed the *Mittelstand* as a bulwark against social unrest and moral decay. The conception of a middle stratum that was a stabilising force in society was rare in Britain. The chairman of the Middle Classes Union claimed it, and to G. S. Layard in 1910 'the lower middle class of which we write is the backbone of the commonwealth.'[155] In Germany the conception of an unincorporated *Mittelstand* being ground between organised labour and organised capital developed without a political framework that could contain the disruptions and subsequent struggles of industrialisation. This was the specific German situation that permitted a *Mittelstand*-based right radicalism. In Britain these developments never took place, and a full account would have to examine the more gradual evolution of industrial capitalism, the less stark polarisation of large and small capital, the absence of a peasantry, the early establishment of a liberal democratic tradition, and the persistent hegemony of competitive capitalist free trade ideas.

There can be distinguished in Britain no traditional ideology of a pre-industrial petty bourgeois kind around which discontented groups could focus. As a result there was no distinctive consciousness in relation to industrial and commercial capital. The lower middle class was offered no foothold on to wider political and social tradition, and the absence of a vigorous class of small property owners,[156] in particular a peasantry, marks the British experience off most clearly from that in a number of other European countries. The demoralised Scottish and Irish peasantry could never play that role, and while there was a Jacobin-style political radicalism it carried few social implications. This was the small shopkeeper radicalism that had identified with many early working class movements.[157] The nature of that early working class radicalism, with its defence of property and concentration of attacks on monopoly, privilege and landed control made this identification easier. This Jacobin ideal of the small-scale society of free property owners had no real purchase in late-nineteenth-century economic and social life. Nor did it have a place in the new context of either socialist or consciously labour politics. It was always too close to a small-town liberalism as well as too ideologically fragile to provide the basis for a strong urban lower middle class ideology.

Against the absence of a distinctive petty bourgeois ideology for the expanding lower middle class to make contact with, there was the deeper hold in Britain of competitive free trade ideas. Traditional *Mittelstand* ideology in Germany, however, transmuted by the differential economic experiences of the groups involved, espoused a set of values that were non-industrial capitalist, centring on the fact that the stability and survival of the small man as a middle group within German society was vital to the nation. This organic conception proposed a natural and hierarchical social order, with the *Mittelstand* as the stablising stratum between the classes.[158] Those arguing for aid to the Belgian petty bourgeoisie made similar claims, arguing that only they stood between the country and violent class struggle.[159] However different the experiences of industrialisation for peasants, urban petty bourgeois and salaried employees, the response to pressures was often to reassert a traditional ideology that might provide identification and security, and in terms of which they could formulate demands. The problem was caricatured by 'Simplicissimus' in a cartoon at the end of the war showing a slender member of the *Mittelstand* crushed between a fat capitalist and a fat worker.[160] The distinctiveness of *Mittelstand* ideas and of German social thought is significant, for the solution was to call for state protection and assistance for the small man against large-scale business, specific benefits for white collar employees, anti-labour legislation, and so on. Whatever the differences between one occupational and economic group and another, state intervention to protect the *Mittelstand* was the most general demand. The German left-liberal *Fortschrittliche Volkspartei*, during the period when it argued that self-help alone would help the petty bourgeoisie in their competitive economic struggle, could attract little *Mittelstand* support.[161] In the years leading up to the First World War it softened its economic policy in an attempt to improve its appeal, and always attracted some white collar support.

Winkler suggests that the protectionist impulse of the German *Mittelstand* might have been the exception, rather than the failure of the British small businessman to make such demands. Yet in France, Belgium and Switzerland he finds a far greater protectionist call from the 1880s than in Britain. The depth of dependence on state assistance in Germany was notable, but must not override the outstanding feature that he finds in Britain, that of small businessmen and white collar employees 'it is questionable whether one can speak at all of a political profile.'[162] In Britain comparable groups to the *Mittelstand* were tied into an existing laissez-faire ideology and neither small producers, retailers, nor white collar workers turned to the state in the way that they did elsewhere. In any case, the state was committed to a form of laissez-faire ideology that defended concentration as unavoidable and rational, and political leaders, not seeking allies against other movements, did not encourage such demands. No distinctive position developed in terms of which an expanding salaried stratum could orientate itself. The difference between orientation and total identification must be stressed, because in Germany the old and new *Mittel-*

stand did not basically mix, rather they shared a varying identification with a certain sector of society, and with its organic populist interests against large-scale capital and organised labour. The whole conception reassuringly denied the necessity of class conflict.[163]

The main intention of this argument has been to contrast what is, admittedly, an excessively clear-cut picture of a complex German situation, with the lack of organisational and political identity of the British lower middle class. The most striking explanation amongst all those offered is the ideological dominance in Britain of those middle class free trade ideas which had struggled for supremacy since the early nineteenth century. The lower middle class clung longer and more persistently than others to these values, at just the time at the turn of the century when the established middle class and political leaders were relaxing their grip on the ideology's most rigid premises. The result was that the lower middle class voice had none of the bite and penetration of the *Mittelstand* critique, and was characterised by an ideological weakness and diffuseness.

The social marginality of this lower middle class that was noted above led to an exaggerated anxiety to achieve a middle class life-style. Their aping of superior standards became a subject of contemporary scorn, yet it mirrored a wider desire for emulation that espoused culture and values as much as mere style. As Christopher Caudwell perceptively noted of the stratum:

> it has no traditions of its own and it does not adopt those of the workers, which it hates, but those of the bourgeoisie, which are without virtue for it did not help to create them.[164]

The culture could thus seem superficial, but any scorning of their snobbishness would provoke a reinforced assertion of their respectable middle class character. The combined effect of their economic position and work situation, status anxieties, and aspirations for success led to a formulation of their interests that was akin to classic laissez-faire, emphasising individualism, self-help, and the defence of private property.[165] Especially important was the faith in a rational competitive individualism and, for small businessmen, a view of the economic order that invested symbolic moral importance to the free enterprise system.[166] But it was more widespread than that for, as discussed above, the white collar work situation encouraged the conception of a social order in which achievement and failure depended upon individual initiative and energy. As Giddens has noted, struggle in this imagery is at the level of the individual not of the class.[167] The attempt by the small National Union of Clerks to wean clerks from economic individualism and self-help, and therefore from existing clerical associations, made little headway.[168] A. P. Allen emphasises this competitive individualism and the faith in its potential.

> The truth is that the commercial traveller, and especially the town representative, is more absolutely the pioneer of his own fortune than any other class of men employed in commerce.

He ascribes to this their predominant political conservatism.[169] This explains why the main travellers' attacks on the concentration of retailing that they saw as unfair interference with a free market economy were directed at co-operative societies. They represented both unfair concentration and proletarian organising. 'Co-operation', according to an article in their journal *On The Road* in 1906, 'was a very aggravated form of class selfishness, and consists of the miner, the bricklayer, the engineer, the rivetter, the caulker, the plater combining together to rob the grocer, the draper, the butcher, and the baker of their right to make a living.'[170]

The deep commitment to traditional values is important in any assessment of the significance of the lower middle class. In economic values, in social ideas, in aspirations and aggressive respectability, there prevailed an increasing conservatism in political and social life. As a marginal group between the established middle class and the manual working class it might thus serve to legitimise existing structured inequality. Yet all this needs severe qualification. Lower middle class radicalism ought to be cited, whether ILP socialists[171] or others more vaguely left, like Richard Church's father who switched from the *Daily Mail* to the *Daily Chronicle* and started to air egalitarian views, but these were 'neither coherent nor clear and they had little political stamina', constituting only a muttered resentment.[172] One might also point to a religious diversity, with sometimes a radical and evangelical nonconformity dictating a different life-style, as shown by the Ford family's work built around their chapel and slum-mission, and spilling over into an enthusiastic liberalism.[173] There was also the substantial representation of clerks, salesmen and teachers amongst the office-holders of the Salvation Army in the 1880s. If the values of work, morality and discipline were fairly orthodox, the methods were most definitely not.[174] One could even point to individuals, to the great optimism and lack of caution of V. S. Pritchett's father, 'walking in and out of jobs with the bumptiousness of a god.'[175]

It is therefore important to take care not to caricature, and much of this assessment of lower middle class conservatism has been highly generalised. The overall proposition none the less remains for consideration, that there developed within the lower middle class an increasingly widespread conservatism, but one that merely followed the values and convictions of other social groups. Its own ideological position was weak and diffuse, and thus could remain genuinely conservative, as distinct from the more specific right-radical movements of the mobilised German *Mittelstand*.

The final area of lower middle class significance singled out for discussion in this essay is its impact on the working class, and especially the aristocracy of labour. A key explanation of the relative social calm of the mid-Victorian period focuses on the existence of a labour aristocracy that saw itself as an elite of working men, and built its politics on viable if sometimes tense urban community relations,[176] but towards the end of the century there was a turn from exclusiveness back into the manual working class. The labour movement that emerged from the 1880s onwards represents a growing identification by the politically active working class of their political interests with those of the working class as a whole. If broad structural explanations are now being used to explain the position of the mid-Victorian labour aristocracy, then an explanation of the way that the stratum turned back into a wider labour movement at the end of the century must rest partially upon their changing position both within the economy and in relation to other social groups. A range of factors are involved, amongst them the situation at work, especially the challenge to skilled men involved in speeding up, the threat to trade unions, and the emergence of new semi-skilled grades operating self-acting machinery; a continuing process of residential segregation that destroyed the mid-Victorian liberal community; and increasing tactical conflicts with organised liberalism. To these must be added the paradoxical success of labour aristocracy elitism in breaking down that craft sectionalism of the early decades of the century that could only have inhibited a wider labour consciousness. There was also the effect of the emergence of a larger and more self-conscious lower middle class.

Labour aristocrats of the mid-Victorian period could feel that their secure position was above that of the mass of the working class and below the established urban middle class in a way rare for continental Europe, where other groups competed for that intermediate position.[177] This more typical European pattern developed in late-nineteenth-century Britain with the emergence of a growing intermediate social stratum that sought to distinguish itself socially from manual workers. This all needs qualification, of course. A sense of superiority was not unknown before, nor did the social separation of this period occur with any precision or homogeneity. The trend however was discernible both in the number and importance of the people involved and in their degree of self-conscious separation.

An intense white collar status-consciousness was the main component of that separatism, as salaried workers under pressure sought to mark themselves off from prosperous artisans as the only way to demonstrate their superiority. As lower middle class educational advantage declined as a force, so the area of distinction seemed to narrow both in scope and in range. The consequently vigorous and at times over-sensitive assertions of status have already been noted, but one specific aspect was an aggressive rejection of manual work, symbolising as it did a whole range of working class characteristics that were unacceptable to this superior stratum—insecurity of employment, lowly origins, dependence on authority, trade unionism, and working class social life. In response was the assertion of a lower middle class superiority that was not just coincidental with non-manual work but actually dependent upon it for status.[178] As resources were mobilised for speculative suburban housebuilding, the final aspect of this changing relationship appears as a process of residential segregation that progressively demolished the mid-Victorian liberal community and isolated the manual working class.

These points of tension are not mutually exclusive. Thus the status-consciousness and the anti-manual stance of much of the lower middle class manifested itself in, as well as being reinforced by, increasing residential segregation. Furthermore, the development of each of these pressures was a relative not an absolute change. Residentially the strata never became entirely distinct. In many towns, where the lower middle class was only small, a distinct housing market for them did not emerge. It has already been noted that even in larger towns homogeneous lower middle class suburbs were rare. Many developments, as indicated by Martin Gaskell in his essay below, were pitched ambiguously at a lower middle class and artisan market. Sometimes this could be deliberate policy.[179] In other places it was the forces of the temperamental market in status-oriented developments that broke the intended exclusiveness of a lower middle class housing area, and reluctantly accepted artisan incursions, and therefore a tapping of only the lower reaches of the lower middle class. T. E. Gibbs' Kentish Town development is a good example.[180]

Even within apparently mixed developments, however, there would have been considerable differentiation by housing type, street, or neighbourhood. Gordon identifies in Edinburgh a great complication of status areas between 1855 and 1914, with smaller zones but clear differentiation. In the mid-Victorian years he can point only to combined lower middle class and artisan districts, but by 1914 certain areas were more specifically white collar and petty bourgeois, such as Saughtonhall, Lauriston Bridge and good quality tenement areas in Marchmont. Housing for clerks and shopkeepers grew up in Springvalley, while in the closing decades of the century the white collar groups came to dominate the small terraced housing at Craighouse and tenement flats in Marchmont and Comely Bank.[181]

This process in Edinburgh, confused rather than simplified by the vertical status complexities that tenement housing could create, took place in most large towns. Frederick Willis' inner suburb of South-East London had once been balanced between working class residents and the fairly comfortable middle class. He was born, however, in Burdock Road, a new street

> designed to fill a long-felt want; it was intended to house the class in between, which was then increasing and not very well provided for... the managing clerk and similar type of employee.

The division had clear status implications, for

> the working class of the neighbourhood had a great prejudice against the City swells of Burdock Road and, accordingly, the Burdock Road residents kept the rest of the district at arm's length.[182]

Even in the socially mixed district of Battersea, with artisans, labourers and lower middle class families in different but proximate streets, Richard Church observed a firm segregation. On the whole, 'birds of a feather flocked together street by street.'[183] Booth found the same in areas of mixed artisan and lower middle class housing in parts of North London. 'We are told that contingents from different streets would never mix.' There would be quite distinct gymnasia, summer treats and so on.[184]

The Board of Trade cost of living enquiry of 1908 in some towns refers to a specific lower middle class housing type but not in others. The smaller industrial towns, such as Bolton, Crewe and Derby identify only a single clerk/artisan housing type.[185] In Preston this was specifically ascribed to the role of female earnings in narrowing differentials,[186] but it would seem that small town mixing was a result both of the local social structure and of its implications for the housing market. There were specific lower middle class housing types in the suburban areas of larger towns. The best five-roomed houses in Birmingham were occupied by 'clerks, foremen, insurance agents, shop assistants, &c.' In Liverpool the six-roomed house was occupied by clerks and shop assistants rather than 'by people of the kind usually included in the term "working class"'. The artisan areas of Wolverhampton spread to the east, while tradesmen and clerks followed the substantial middle classes to the western outskirts. This upward blurring of residential areas was widely acknowledged in London. In Ealing, for example, six-roomed houses were 'usually occupied by clerks, shop assistants, &c. They are usually built with back additions and vary greatly in convenience and character, merging gradually into the middle-class villa.' In Leytonstone housing was similar to that inhabited by artisans in nearby Leyton, but 'nearly all the houses, though small, are occupied by clerks and professional workers.' The main differences were location and 'superior appointments and character.'[187] The trend does seem to be one of specifically lower middle class areas emerging in the suburbs of larger towns; but also of a more subtle segregation by street or group of streets, often distinguished by housing type. A finer mesh than that provided by literary sources is needed to capture these developments more precisely.

If housing patterns are one area where we can distinguish an emerging gulf between labour aristocrats and the lower middle class, there were other areas of social contact where either mixing (church or chapel could have served such a purpose for a minority of artisans[188]), or tensions could have arisen. Such tensions were not new. A wheelwright in Woolwich explained the artisan's reluctance to use mechanics' institutions. He identified

> a class of fast young fellows who rejoice in the nomenclature of shopmen and clerks, who keep up a strict line of demarcation, and not only monopolise the daily journals, but likewise the conversation. And if a labouring man ventures a sentiment, he is met with either a universal grin or a personal taunt, and therefore he soon becomes disgusted with that society that fails to reward him for the trouble and expense of attending.[189]

If the tensions were not new, they became far more significant in a period when these white collar workers were no longer a thin layer above the labour aristocracy, but a substantial stratum whose very anxieties exacerbated their rejection of those below them. The hostilities were not simply one way. The artisan resented lower middle class incursions into his social club, for 'here it is that the working class club man feels himself the patron rather than the patronised, that he really unbends and feels himself socially free.'[190] The *Club and Institute Journal* noted the massive social distance between the clerk and the skilled working man, revealing itself in the former's refusal to participate in the latter's clubs. 'Possibly his tastes bear no comparison with his pocket, and he scorns the idea of mixing with "working men".'[191] Yet the tension was inevitably mutual. If clerks did move into facilities aimed at the working class, there would be a fast fall in attendance by those for whom it was initially provided. Booth noted this for various educational facilities in Kentish Town, and a similar process took place in classes at Woolwich Polytechnic and Toynbee Hall.[192]

In all these tensions what is of importance is neither their novelty nor their uniformity,[193] but their increasing size and frequency within a changed context in which the labour aristocracy no longer faced the economic securities and the community reassurances of the mid-Victorian years. It was in these changing circumstances that a social separation emerging between the core of the lower middle class and the core of labour aristocrats served as one factor among a number that turned that elite of skilled men back towards a broader political identification with the working class as a whole.

This essay, consciously offered as a discussion, has concentrated on propositions concerning the development of the lower middle class and its significance within British society in the late-Victorian and Edwardian periods. That stratum has been neglected by British historians, and part of the explanation may be found in C. Wright Mills' comments on American white collar workers. 'Whatever history they have had is a history without events; whatever common interests they have do not lead to unity; whatever future they have will not be of their own making.'[194] Only the Anglo-American experience could produce a judgement so sure and so belittling. Yet the absence of dynamic activity, the lack of cohesion and the quest for individual status that is so easy to parody can not themselves justify that neglect, for it is partly through these weaknesses that the lower middle class has exerted its specific influence upon British social development. The changing social structure during the period of the international and imperialist economy is a fundamental problem of British social history. It is in those areas that this essay has posed questions, concerning the growth and identity of that stratum, its place within the social structure, and its values and ideology. The lower middle class was important. The precise implications of its development need far more discussion, for which the essays that follow must be seen as the first contribution. The problem is that new approaches are needed to understand such a stratum. As Theodore Zeldin recently observed of French clerks, shop assistants and bureaucrats, 'they need to be dealt with through a different approach, which involves studying not institutions or catastrophes, but largely silent ambitions, which take one out of the realm of economics or politics, beyond quantity and conflict in its simple forms, to the search for satisfactions which were seldom clearly formulated.'[195] The silence of those ambitions must not lead to neglect of their historical importance.

Notes

I am grateful to Geoff Eley, Robbie Gray and Rita Vaudrey for their helpful comments on this essay.

1. The most significant study is J. A. Banks, *Prosperity and Parenthood*, Routledge and Kegan Paul, London, 1954.
2. Arno Mayer has recently observed the same neglect in his article 'The Lower Middle Class as a Historical Problem', *Journal of Modern History*, vol. 47, 1975, pp. 409-11. The most important works referred to below are principally studies of specific occupations.
3. Amongst the growing body of work in English, the most important include Robert Gellately, *The Politics of Economic Despair: Shopkeepers and German Politics 1890-1914*, Sage, London, 1974; Jurgen Kocka, 'The First World War and the "Mittelstand": German Artisans and White-Collar Workers', *Journal of Contemporary History*, vol. 8, 1973, pp. 101-23; Herman Lebovics, *Social Conservatism and the Middle Classes in Germany, 1914-1933*, Princeton University Press, Princeton, 1969.
4. Charles Booth, *Life and Labour of the People in London*, London, 1902 ed., 3rd Series; Leone Levi, *Wages and Earnings of the Working Classes*, London, 1885, pp. 51-2; Departmental Committee on the Pupil-Teacher System, PP 1898 xxvi, see for example Q8-10, 161, 3521; the same inconsistency between witnesses can be seen in the report of the Board of Trade Inquiry into the cost of living, PP 1908 cvii; G. S. Layard, however, included 'certain skilled mechanics' in his lower middle class, 'A Lower-Middle-Class Budget', *Cornhill Magazine*, New Series vol. 10, 1901, p. 657; so did Walter Warren in R. Mudie-Smith (ed),*The Religious Life of London*, Hodder & Stoughton, London, 1904, p. 141.
5. P. Coustillas & C. Partridge (eds), *Gissing, The Critical Heritage*, Routledge & Kegan Paul, London, 1972, p. 238.
6. S. Ossowski attempted to resolve this problem in *Class Structure and the Social Consciousness*, Routledge & Kegan Paul, London, 1963, pp. 75-9.
7. Kocka, op. cit., p. 101.
8. For a generalised discussion of the European lower middle class in this period, see Peter Stearns, *European Society in Upheaval: Social History since*

1800, Collier-Macmillan, London, 1967, pp. 236-48.
9. Mayer, op.cit., p. 418.
10. See the opening remarks of Gray's essay below, with which I am in broad agreement.
11. Hugh McLeod, *Class and Religion in the Late Victorian City*, Croom Helm, London, 1974, pp. 106-7; Booth, op. cit., 3rd Series, vol. 1, p. 175.
12. Ibid., p. 72.
13. L. Hannah, 'Mergers in British Manufacturing Industry, 1880-1918', *Oxford Economic Papers*, vol. 18, 1965, p. 190.
14. C. Wilson, 'Economy and Society in Late-Victorian Britain', *Economic History Review*, vol. 18, 1965, p. 190.
15. J. B. Jefferys, *Retail Trading in Britain 1850-1950*, Cambridge University Press, Cambridge, 1954, pp. 20-24.
16. H. J. Dyos, *Victorian Suburb. A Study of the Growth of Camberwell*, Leicester University Press, Leicester, 1966, pp. 150-2.
17. Jefferys, op.cit., p. 16.
18. Ibid., p. 29. The proportion must therefore have been immeasurably higher in key areas of urban retailing.
19. H. G. Wells, *Experiment in Autobiography*, Gollancz, London, 1934, p. 65.
20. Ibid., p. 366.
21. W. B. Robertson observed in 1911 that 'knowledge of a shopkeeping trade is not nowadays considered nearly as necessary as purely commercial ability,' Jefferys, op cit., p. 26.
22. Ibid., pp. 37-38; B. S. Yamey, 'The Origins of Resale Price Maintenance: A Study of Three Branches of Retail Trade', *Economic Journal*, vol.lxii, 1952, pp. 523-4.
23. Gellately, op.cit., *passim*.
24. B.-S. Chlepner, *Cent ans d'histoire sociale en Belgique*, Editions de l'Université de Bruxelles, Bruxelles, 1972, pp. 141-5.
25. Hermann Levy, *Retail Trade Associations*, Kegan Paul, London, 1942, p. 18; Yamey, op.cit., pp. 529-43.
26. Jefferys, op.cit., p. 18; Levy, op.cit., p. 17.
27. P. L. Payne, 'The Emergence of the Large-Scale Company in Great Britain, 1870-1914', *Economic History Review*, vol. 20, 1967, pp. 519-42.
28. Wells, op.cit., p. 60.
29. B.G. Orchard, *The Clerks of Liverpool*, Liverpool, 1871, p. 4.
30. F. Klingender, *The Condition of Clerical Labour in Britain*, Martin Lawrence, London, 1935, p. 20.
31. For an investigation see Lee Holcombe, *Victorian Ladies at Work*, David and Charles, Newton Abbot, 1973. The census tables show their expansion to be almost entirely limited to commercial clerks (144,000 in 1911), schoolteachers (202,000), and civil service (32,000), these last being mainly post-office and telegraph clerks.
32. Both figures are for those over the age of 10 years, except for the Scottish cities where it is for those over 15 years of age.
33. A. J. Brown, 'Britain and the World Economy, 1870-1914', *Yorkshire Bulletin of Economic and Social Research*, vol. 17, 1965, *passim*.
34. 1911 Census Tables, vol. x (i), Table 28, pp. 560-589.
35. On Germany see G. Hartfiel in Adolf Sturmthal (ed), *White-Collar Trade Unions*, University of Illinois Press, Urbana, 1966, pp. 162-3; also Kocka, op. cit., p. 102; T. B. Caldwell, 'The *Syndicat des Employés du Commerce et de l'Industrie* (1887-1919). A Pioneer French Catholic Trade Union of White Collar Workers', *International Review of Social History*, vol. 11, 1966, pp. 228-30 offers similar explanations for the rise of French white collar employment.

36. P. Bairoch, *La Population Active et sa Structure*, Université Libre, Bruxelles, 1968, p. 127.
37. G. Bry, *Wages in Germany 1871-1945*, Princeton University Press, Princeton, 1960, p. 28; G. Dupeux, *La Société Française 1789-1960*, Armand Colin, Paris, 1964, p. 169.
38. Orchard, op.cit., pp. 21-36.
39. A. P. Allen, *The Ambassadors of Commerce*, London, 1885, p. 112.
40. B. J. Avari, 'British Commercial Travellers and their Organisations 1850-1914' (University of Manchester M.A. thesis 1970) pp. 396-401.
41. Alfred Grosch, *St. Pancras Pavements. An Autobiography*, John Gifford, London, 1947, pp. 9-15.
42. Charles Edward Parsons, *Clerks; their Position and Advancement*, Provost, London, 1876, p. 11.
43. G. L. Anderson discusses these problems at length in his essay below.
44. David Lockwood, *The Blackcoated Worker. A Study in Class Consciousness*, Allen & Unwin, London, 1958, pp. 62-3.
45. Allen, op.cit., pp. 101-4; Avari, op.cit., pp. 61-6.
46. See G. L. Anderson, below. The mass of female clerks earned less than £80 per annum, Klingender, op.cit., p. 20. Nevertheless, the early spread of female clerks shows great local variations. According to the 1891 census tables, although Bristol, Manchester and Leeds had only 6% of their commercial clerks female, and London 9%, 20% of all Birmingham commercial clerks were women and 25% of those in Edinburgh. These early variations might warrant closer examination.
47. *On The Road*, February 1886, cited by Avari, op.cit., p. 75.
48. W. Davidson, *Fifty Years on the Road. Recollections of a Commercial Traveller*, Edinburgh, 1928, pp. 31-2; Avari, op.cit., pp. 77-91.
49. Grosch, op.cit., p. 42.
50. Caldwell, op.cit., p. 230.
51. Frederick Willis, *Peace and Dripping Toast*, Phoenix House, London, 1950, p.16.
52. David Crew, 'Definitions of Modernity: Social Mobility in a German Town, 1880-1901', *Journal of Social History*, vol. 7, 1973, p. 53.
53. James Bonar, 'German Clerks and Shop Assistants', *Economic Journal*, vol. 3, 1893, p. 321; Caldwell, op.cit., p. 246.
54. On Post Office unions see the essay by Guy Routh on the United Kingdom in Sturmthal, op.cit., p. 181; on railway clerks, Lockwood, op.cit., pp.148-9.
55. Cited in Holcombe, op.cit., pp. 152-3.
56. E. M. Kassallow in Sturmthal, op.cit., pp. 329-30; on the importance of standardisation in this context see R. K. Kelsall *et al.* 'The New Middle Class in the Power Structure of Great Britain', *Transactions of the Third World Congress of Sociology*, vol. 3, 1956, p. 322.
57. Sturmthal, op.cit., p. 390.
58. W. J. Brown, *So Far . . .* , Allen & Unwin, London, 1943, p. 51.
59. For a discussion of such clerks' associations and their problems in Manchester and Liverpool see G. L. Anderson, 'A Study of Clerical Labour in Liverpool and Manchester 1850-1914' (University of Lancaster Ph.D. thesis 1974), pp. 189-211. Rare exceptions were the Railway Clerks' Association and the small National Union of Clerks, see Lockwood, op.cit., pp. 156-64.
60. On the UKCTA see Avari, op.cit., pp. 360-428; Allen, op.cit., pp. 126-30.
61. David Farnham, 'The Association of Teachers in Technical Institutions (1904-14). A Case-Study of the Origins, Formation and Growth of a White-Collar Organisation', *International Review of Social History*, vol. 19, 1974, pp.394-5.
62. Alec Spoor, *White-Collar Union. Sixty Years of NALGO*, Heinemann, London, 1967, pp. 14-15.

63. Ibid., p. 47.
64. Ibid., pp. 27-8.
65. Sturmthal, op.cit., p. 390.
66. Mudie-Smith, op.cit., p. 192.
67. Richard Church, *Over The Bridge. An Essay in Autobiography*, Reprint Society edition, London, 1956, pp. 22-3.
68. Helen Corke, *In Our Infancy. An Autobiography Part I: 1882-1912*, Cambridge University Press, London, 1975, p. 38. Sidney Ford talks the same way about his family life in Paul Thompson, *The Edwardians*, Weidenfeld & Nicolson, London, 1975, pp. 99-106.
69. The best example of this ubiquitous event is in Corke, op.cit., pp. 56-7.
70. An example is *The Smiths of Surbiton*, Chapman & Hall, London, 1906. See p. 28, 'It is just as easy to make acquaintances in Surbiton as it is difficult to make friends.'
71. Ordinary societies appealed to the lower middle class and only a distinctive minority of artisans. P. H. J. H. Gosden, *Self-Help. Voluntary Associations in Nineteenth-Century Britain*, Barnes & Noble, New York, 1974, pp.62-3.
72. Chlepner, op.cit., p. 140.
73. Christopher Caudwell, *Studies in a Dying Culture*, Bodley Head, London, 1938, p. 79.
74. Allen, op.cit., pp. 50-67; Davidson, op.cit., *passim*.
75. Corke, op.cit., pp. 88-136.
76. H. J. Dyos, *Victorian Suburb*, op. cit., pp. 136-137 argues that the Waverley Park Estate at Nunhead was fairly typical in this respect.
77. McLeod, op.cit., p. 145.
78. See as an example his discussion of the West Hackney Church. Booth, op. cit., 3rd Series, vol. 1, pp. 93-4.
79. Corke, op.cit., p. 88.
80. McLeod, op.cit., p. 84; Helen Meller (ed), *Nottingham in the 1880s*, University of Nottingham, Nottingham, 1971, p. 42.
81. Wells, op.cit., p. 94.
82. C. F. G. Masterman, *The Condition of England*, Methuen, London, 1911 edition, pp. 66-7. On 'the violence of the street, the crass mob, the ever-rising waters of the indifferent masses' see Church, op.cit., p. 61.
83. Hansjoachim Henning, *Das Westdeutsche Bürgertum in der Epoche der Hochindustrialisierung 1860-1914*, Franz Steiner, Wiesbaden, 1972, as reviewed by Andrew Lees in *Journal of Social History*, vol. 7, 1974, pp.96-104.
84. George and Weedon Grossmith, *The Diary of a Nobody*, Penguin Books edition, Harmondsworth, 1965.
85. Wells, op.cit., pp. 268-9.
86. E. M. Forster, *Howards End*, Penguin Books edition, Harmondsworth, 1973.
87. Anon (Fitzjames Stephens), 'Gentlemen', *Cornhill Magazine*, vol. 5, 1862, pp. 327-42.
88. A. A. Jackson, *Semi-Detached London. Suburban Development, Life and Transport. 1900-39*. Allen & Unwin, London, 1973, p. 43.
89. For an excellent discussion of the way in which this model of success was redefined see G. L. Anderson, op.cit., pp. 173-80.
90. Mudie-Smith, op.cit., p. 193.
91. Parsons, op.cit., p. 13; G. S. Layard makes the same point, op.cit., pp. 660-1.
92. Examples are Layard, op.cit., p. 656 and Orchard, op.cit., p.64. On the increasing Victorian middle class obsession with the proper time to marry see Banks, op.cit., pp. 32-47.

93. The correspondence appeared in the *Daily Chronicle* for the issues of 29 and 30 September, 1, 4, 5, 6 and 8 October 1898.
94. *Speaker*, 8 October 1898.
95. See the Departmental Committee on the Pupil-Teacher System, PP 1898 xxvi, *passim*, though by then white collar and shopkeeper backgrounds were increasingly significant.
96. Ibid., Q.6272.
97. Asher Tropp, *The School Teachers. The Growth of the Teaching Profession in England and Wales from 1800 to the present day*, Heinemann, London, 1957, p. 147.
98. According to Harold Hodge, 'The Teacher Problem', *The Fortnightly Review*, vol. 66, 1899, however, 'they are half-educated persons belonging to the most narrow-minded element in our population, the lower-middle class.' p.858.
99. Tropp, op.cit., pp. 113, 149-50.
100. T. W. H. Crosland, *The Suburbans*, John Long, London, 1905, p. 80.
101. Ibid., pp. 11-12.
102. F. M. L. Thompson, *Hampstead. Building a Borough, 1650-1964*, Routledge & Kegan Paul, London, 1974, p. 375.
103. John R. Kellett, *The Impact of the Railways on Victorian Cities*, Routledge & Kegan Paul, London, 1969, pp. 356-361.
104. Booth, op.cit., 3rd Series, vol. 1, pp. 78-9, 110.
105. Ibid., vol. 5, p. 77.
106. See the scattered evidence to the Select Committee on Artisans and Labourers Dwellings Improvements, PP 1881 vii, 1882 vii; Sidney J. Low hoped that greater leisure would enable artisans to follow the clerks into the suburbs and benefit in a similar way, 'The Rise of the Suburbs', *Contemporary Review*, vol. 60, 1891, p. 557.
107. Layard, op.cit., p. 659.
108. Board of Trade Enquiry into the cost of living, op.cit., p. 301.
109. George Gordon, 'The Status Areas of Edinburgh. A Historical Analysis' (University of Edinburgh Ph.D. thesis 1970), pp. 133-6.
110. Kellett, op.cit., p. 411.
111. R. Pound, *Selfridge. A Biography*, Heinemann, London, 1960, p. 102.
112. Masterman, op.cit., pp. 82-4; Corke, op.cit., p. 59; Church, op.cit., p. 90; Robert Roberts, *The Classic Slum. Salford Life in the First Quarter of the Century*, Penguin Books, Harmondsworth, 1973, p. 163.
113. Crosland, op.cit., pp. 80-3.
114. F. G. D'Aeth, 'Present Tendencies of Class Differentiation', *Sociological Review*, vol. 3, 1910, pp. 270-1.
115. Condition of the Working Classes, PP 1887 lxxi, pp. 309-315. It was noted in the 1930s that the main impetus behind working-class children becoming clerks was that same quest for security, *Men Without Work: A Report made to the Pilgrim Trust*, Cambridge University Press, Cambridge, 1938, p. 144.
116. F. Bechofer and B. Elliott, 'A Progress Report on "Small Shopkeepers and the Class Structure"', SSRC Research Report, 1975, Part 3, p. 19. Vigne and Howkins provide some interesting oral evidence relating to this issue in their essay below.
117. The contrast with the USA is striking, where studies of social mobility appear with astonishing regularity. One of the most important recent studies is Stephan Thernstrom, *The Other Bostonians: Poverty and Progress in the American Metropolis, 1880-1970*, Harvard University Press, Cambridge, Mass., 1973.
118. Geoffrey Crossick, 'Social Structure and Working-Class Behaviour: Kentish London 1840-1880' (University of London Ph.D. thesis 1976), pp. 196-7.

58 *The Lower Middle Class in Britain 1870-1914*

119. Orchard, op.cit., p. 32.
120. D'Aeth, op.cit., p. 271.
121. Crossick, op.cit., p. 135.
122. For an example of working class contempt for those seeking to escape their background by some spurious mobility into white collar work see the music-hall audience cited by G. Stedman Jones, 'Working-class culture and working-class politics in London, 1870-1900: Notes on the Remaking of a Working Class', *Journal of Social History*, vol. 7, 1973-74, p. 493.
123. B.S. Rowntree, *Poverty. A Study of Town Life*, Macmillan, London, 1902, p. 720.
124. Roberts, op.cit., pp. 17-18.
125. Brown, op.cit., pp. 19, 37.
126. H. J. Perkin, 'Middle-Class Education and Employment in the Nineteenth Century: A Critical Note', *Economic History Review*, vol. 14, 1961-62, p. 124.
127. P. Thompson, op.cit., p. 100.
128. Wells, op.cit., pp. 116-175.
129. Dupeux, op.cit., p. 184.
130. Patrick J. Harrigan, 'Secondary Education and the Professions in France during the Second Empire', *Comparative Studies in Society and History*, vol. 17, 1975, pp. 356-62; This has been confirmed by Robert Anderson, 'Secondary Education in Mid-Nineteenth Century France: Some Social Aspects', *Past and Present*, 53, 1971, p. 136.
131. R. Anderson, op.cit., pp. 129-33.
132. Harrigan, op.cit., p. 370.
133. Masterman, op.cit., p. 75.
134. Church, op.cit., p. 162.
135. J. R. Vincent, *The Formation of the Liberal Party*, Constable, London, 1966. The viability of a broadly based liberalism, emphasising the ideological factors that bound in the labour aristocracy, is discussed in Crossick, op.cit., pp. 362-443.
136. James Cornford, 'The Transformation of Conservatism in the Late Nineteenth Century', *Victorian Studies*, vol. 7, 1963, pp. 59 & 65.
137. Henry Pelling, *Social Geography of British Elections 1885-1910*, Macmillan, London, 1967, pp. 41, 278, 388. On suburban migration hardening London's political divisions, Dyos, op.cit., p. 24.
138. John Taylor, *From Self-Help to Glamour: the Working Man's Club, 1860-1972*, History Workshop, Oxford, 1972, p. 25.
139. Masterman, op.cit., p. 66.
140. Edward Bristow, 'The Liberty and Property Defence League and Individualism', *Historical Journal*, vol. 18, 1975, pp. 761-789; N. Soldon, 'Laissez-Faire as Dogma: The Liberty and Property Defence League, 1882-1914', in K. D. Brown (ed), *Essays in Anti-Labour History*, Macmillan, London, 1974, pp. 208-233; K. D. Brown, 'The Anti-Socialist Union', ibid., pp. 234-261. See also the UK Property Owners' Federation set up in 1913, with a more explicitly *Mittelstand* language used by its President, R. Lewis and A. Maude, *The English Middle Classes*, Phoenix House, London, 1949, p. 75.
141. Lothrop Stoddard, *Social Classes in Post-War Europe*, C. Scribner's Sons, New York, 1925, pp. 95-100.
142. Chris Cook, *Sources in British Political History 1900-1951: Volume 1*, Macmillan, London, 1975, p. 220.
143. Mayer, op.cit., p. 434.
144. Dupeux, op. cit., pp. 185-6.
145. Ibid., p. 204.
146. Eugen Weber, *The Nationalist Revival in France, 1905-1914*, University of California Press, Berkeley & Los Angeles, 1959, pp. 149-51.

147. Lebovics, op.cit., pp. vii, 14; Charles S. Maier, *Recasting Bourgeois Europe, Stabilization in France, Germany and Italy in the Decade after World War I*, Princeton University Press, Princeton, 1975, p. 40.
148. Heinrich A. Winkler, 'From Social Protectionism to National Socialism: The German Small-Business Movement in Comparative Perspective', *Journal of Modern History*, vol. 48, 1976, p. 6; Kocka, op.cit., pp. 106-119.
149. Gellately, op.cit., pp. 25-6.
150. Kocka, op.cit., p. 103.
151. Lebovics, op.cit., pp. 5-7.
152. Stearns, op.cit., pp. 242-4. On the political stance of German white collar unions: see Bonar, op.cit., *passim*, and Hartfel in Sturmthal, op. cit., p. 137.
153. Kocka, op.cit., p. 103; Winkler, op.cit., p. 6.
154. Winkler, op.cit., p. 4.
155. Layard, op.cit., p. 656.
156. For a study of this small propertied and independent producer class in an *apparently* more radical situation, see Edward Shorter, 'Middle-Class Anxiety in the German Revolution of 1848', *Journal of Social History*, vol. 2, 1968-69, pp. 189-215. In reality these ideas reflected the conservative anxieties of petty bourgeois producers around 1848.
157. On shopkeeper radicalism see T. J. Nossiter, 'Shopkeeper Radicalism in the 19th Century', in T. J. Nossiter (ed),*Imagination and Precision in the Social Sciences*, Humanities Press, New York, 1972, pp. 407-438.
158. Kocka, op.cit., pp. 105-6.
159. Chlepner, op.cit., p. 147.
160. Reproduced in Gerald D. Feldman, *Army, Industry and Labour in Germany 1914-1918*, Princeton University Press, Princeton, 1966, p. 2.
161. Gellately, op.cit., pp. 182-3.
162. Winkler, op.cit., pp. 13-16. See also the material on Austria in Stearns, op. cit., pp. 244-5.
163. Lebovics, op.cit., p. 9.
164. Caudwell, op.cit., p. 77.
165. For a discussion of this see G. D. H. Cole, *Studies in Class Structure*, Routledge & Kegan Paul, London, 1955, pp. 95-6.
166. Frank Bechofer and Brian Elliot find this amongst small shopkeepers today, and see it as the persistence of the traditional bourgeois world picture amongst this group, op.cit., Part 3, p. 7.
167. Anthony Giddens, *The Class Structure of the Advanced Societies*, Hutchinson, London, 1973, p. 185.
168. G. L. Anderson, op.cit., pp. 304-313.
169. Allen, op.cit., pp. 157, 24-25. The railway companies were monopolies representing spurious competition, so the commercial travellers' support for the railway nationalisation campaign just before the First World War did not really contradict their faith in competitive laissez-faire.
170. Avari, op.cit., pp. 44-6.
171. Deian Hopkin, 'The Membership of the Independent Labour Party 1904-10: a Spatial and Occupational Analysis', *International Review of Social History*, vol. 20, 1975, pp. 175-97; Paul Thompson, *Socialists, Liberals and Labour. The Struggle for London 1885-1914*, Routledge & Kegan Paul, London, 1967, p. 231.
172. Church, op.cit., pp. 96-7.
173. P. Thompson, *The Edwardians*, op.cit., pp. 105-6.
174. C. Ward, 'The Social Sources of the Salvation Army 1865-1890' (University of London M.Phil. thesis 1970), pp. 149-54.
175. V. S. Pritchett, *A Cab at the Door*, Penguin Books, Harmondsworth, 1970,

p. 21.
176. There is a growing literature on this. See especially E. J. Hobsbawm, 'The Labour Aristocracy in Nineteenth Century Britain' in *Labouring Men: Studies in the History of Labour,* Weidenfeld & Nicolson, London, 1964, pp. 272-315; Royden Harrison, *Before the Socialists,* Routledge & Kegan Paul, London, 1965, *passim*; Geoffrey Crossick, op.cit., *passim*; R. Q. Gray, *The Labour Aristocracy in Victorian Edinburgh,* Clarendon Press, Oxford, 1976, *passim.*
177. Hobsbawm, op.cit., pp. 296-7. On the continuing degree of contact between the labour aristocracy and a fluid non-manual stratum in the mid-Victorian period see Crossick, op.cit., pp. 223-5.
178. Hobsbawm, op.cit., pp. 295-6.
179. Dyos, op.cit., pp. 180ff.
180. F. M. L. Thompson, op.cit., pp. 356-363.
181. Gordon, op.cit., pp. 116-174.
182. Willis, op.cit., pp. 14-15.
183. Church, op. cit., p. 16.
184. Booth, op.cit., 3rd Series, vol. 1, pp. 150-1.
185. Board of Trade Enquiry into the cost of living, op.cit., pp. 100, 166-7, 182.
186. Ibid., p. 382.
187. Ibid., p. 85 (Birmingham); p. 279 (Liverpool); p. 488 (Wolverhampton); p. 50 (Ealing); p. 52 (Leytonstone).
188. For an example in Deptford see Booth, op.cit., 3rd Series, vol. 5, p. 16.
189. Henry Knell, *Chips from the Block,* London, 1860, p. 84.
190. Workingman, *Working Men and Women,* London, 1879, p. 36.
191. Taylor, op.cit., pp. 24-5.
192. Booth, op.cit., 3rd Series, vol. 1, pp. 177-9 & vol. 5, pp. 124-5; McLeod, op.cit., p. 84.
193. Booth, for example, who gives so much evidence to support the view of a growing divide, also finds contradictory cases, such as the lack of 'any marked social distinctiveness' between the upper artisan and lower salaried classes on the Flower Estates in Clapham. Booth, op.cit., 3rd Series, vol. 5, pp. 158-9. The emphasis in this essay on the trend must not be allowed to hide its diversity.
194. C. Wright Mills, *White-Collar. The American Middle Classes,* Oxford University Press, New York, 1956 edition, p. ix.
195. In *Times Higher Education Supplement,* 14 May 1976, p. 14.

2 WHITE COLLAR VALUES AND THE ROLE OF RELIGION

Hugh McLeod

The lower middle class of later Victorian England had two parts: small property owners and non-manual employees occupying subordinate positions. My concern here will be entirely with the latter, the 'black coated' or 'white collar' workers, and my purpose will be to distinguish the way of life and system of values characteristic of this group in the later nineteenth and early twentieth centuries, and the part played within these by religious beliefs and institutions.

The middle class proletariat included certain peripheral groups, such as journalists and entertainers, but its core was made up of that part of the wage-earning population which came into direct contact with the established middle class by working beside them in their offices, by handling their money in the banks, by representing them as commercial travellers, or by serving them in the 'quality' shops, together with those who moulded the children of the masses in the elementary schools. For these tasks the requirements (besides literacy) were respectability in manner and appearance (so that the credit of their employers would be maintained, and offence not caused to those whom they served or assisted), together with a respectability of background which, it was hoped, would make them worthy of trust (especially where the handling of large sums of money was involved) and, if they were teachers, would make it more probable that their influence would be 'healthy' and 'elevating'.[1]

The nineteenth-century middle class attempted to amalgamate the social and moral meanings of respectability. Like the dominant classes of most earlier periods they contrasted their own civilisation with the brutalisation of the mass of the people. They also claimed to be morally superior—to have achieved 'respectability' in terms of property and social position by the exercise of qualities of industry, honesty and self-control that the economically unsuccessful generally did not possess. They protected themselves from contact with the dangerous masses by means of this intermediate stratum of those who, though not 'gentlemen', were 'gentlemanly'.[2] For acting this role, white collar workers received a measure of social status and certain privileges summed up in the word 'salary', though in both instances far less than they tended to consider their due.

Each generation of clerks and commercial travellers looked back to a golden age, just before their own day, when their predecessors had been regarded as gentlemen. Yet, as early as 1852, the contradictions in their position were exposed in a pamphlet by J. S. Harrison, one of the first of many spokesmen for the white collar stratum, who put forward their claims to middle class status and income and complained of the fact that their full merits were so seldom recognised. He started from the assumption that clerks and book-keepers belonged by nature to the middle class:

> The qualifications usually required of clerks and book-keepers are, that they should be men of respectability, education and address: these are more or less indispensable according to the nature of the engagement. It will no doubt be allowed as a general fact, that their occupation or position are necessarily of a more improving or elevating tendency, involving a greater degree of respectability of habit and appearance, and too often more anxiety and mental effort than most regular mechanical occupations. And this being the case, a constant and unavoidable influence is thereby exerted in respect to their position and connection in society.[3]

But every detail of their actual circumstances led towards his conclusion that their 'deterioration and absorption into the lower class is imminent'. The various norms of middle class life were listed, and in each case lack of means largely precluded white collar workers from complying: saving, giving their children a good education, contributing to charities, above all, keeping servants, in order to preserve middle class women from the degradation of manual labour. Yet he continually harped upon the intrinsic respectability of white collar work and the greater affinity between clerk and employer than between clerk and workman. For 'a clerk's duties bear greater similarity to those of the principal, and are of a more enlightening and improving nature than manual work', and 'their tendency is not only to keep up but decidedly to induce a more susceptible and sensitive state of mind than rougher and less mental pursuits'.[4]

This tendency, in fact, lay not in the work itself, but in what employers required of those performing it; and it was not clerical skills that were in relatively short supply, but this 'susceptible and sensitive state' that was a part of respectability. It was not, however, in such short supply that the majority of clerks could claim a middle class income: their reward lay in the various privileges that enabled them to claim middle class status in spite of their income.[5]

A minority of white collar workers—including, most notably, those employed in banks—was securely middle class. The best index of middle class status in Victorian England was the keeping of a servant, since any middle class man 'shrank', to use the terminology in which such subjects were usually discussed, from reducing his wife to the level of a 'drudge'.[6] About a quarter of the white collar households in Metropolitan London passed this test in 1891.[7] By most objective criteria the affinities of the remainder of the stratum were with the working class. A considerable proportion of them came from working class families;[8] they were generally educated at the same schools; they spoke with the same regional accents and used the same grammatical peculiarities (while tending to fall short of the 'broader' or 'rougher' local forms); middle class observers often counted both together in a single mass. Most white collar workers had an income typical of the better-paid manual worker,[9] and they shared with the wage-earning population generally, and in greater degree than some skilled craftsmen, the experience of subordination: the denial of initiative, responsibility, perhaps even knowledge of the larger process of which their activities were a part—and dependence on the whim of those in authority over them.

This dependence was the more acute because, as the General Secretary of the National Union of Clerks told Charles Booth in 1895: 'The general run of clerks consider themselves above the kind of machinery used generally by workmen to improve their position.'[10] For, as this complaint suggests, their aspirations and characteristic values separated them as decisively from the working class as their incomes excluded them from the established middle class. These values were reflected most clearly in their choice of homes. In spite of the cost in time and money of travel to city-centre offices, clerks preferred the healthier and more genteel surroundings of the suburbs.[11] The distinctive organisation of their lives was also reflected in a difference between working class and white collar marriage patterns, even within predominantly working class areas: where working class men generally married a woman living in the same neighbourhood, often in the same street, the community within which lower middle class partners met (though still fairly limited) tended to embrace a suburb or a group of adjoining suburbs.[12] Neighbourly controls were probably weaker, and certainly less direct than those imposed in working class districts; at the same time, social mobility, and perhaps geographical mobility, made them less subject to family controls.[13]

While, therefore, some white collar workers were well integrated into the middle class, and thus experienced the various pressures that middle class status imposed, and others, probably, were well integrated into the working class, with its intense localism, most were in a more uncertain and socially isolated position.

Because of this lack of clear reference points generalisation about lower middle class behaviour was hazardous. The lack of agreement is particularly evident in comments on the church-going habits of each class. From Engels in 1845 and Mann in 1851 to Charles Booth in 1902 it was a commonplace that the middle and upper classes were in general church-goers, while the working class was not—though Booth (and subsequent research) showed that these generalisations had to be modified to allow for differences between the sexes, between age, occupational and ethnic groups, and between the regions.[14] About the lower middle class, in so far as it was mentioned at all, there was no such consensus. Some observers saw them as a sub-branch either of the working class or of the middle class, sharing the same basic characteristics. Thus George Haw, writing about the outer suburbs of London in the light of the *Daily News* religious census of 1902-3, claimed that:

> That very large section of the working classes represented roughly by clerks, shop assistants and warehousemen, who feel a sense of pride at being able to afford to live out of London, diligently spend their Sundays by visiting and entertaining friends. Games and concerts in their little parlours beguile many a Sunday night. Thoughts of taking part in public worship are as remote from their minds as thoughts of taking part in public life. Sunday morning is a time for tending their tiny gardens. The treat of the afternoon is the cigar after dinner. Sunday evening, as we have seen, is given up to friends.[15]

Charles Masterman, however, writing on South London in the same volume, apparently counted the clerk as an example of the 'suburban dweller', with whom:

> Vigour may be more conspicuous than breadth of attitude or intellectual agility, and there are often set up quite astonishing standards of 'respectability' in politics and religion. But there are compensating elements in the widespread material comfort, enjoyment of simple pleasures, and (as we shall see) a very real and active religious life. It is here that the churches and chapels are crowded, that their activities

blossom out on week-days into mutual improvement associations, debating clubs and innocuous amusement.[16]

Those who distinguished white collar workers as a separate group also differed in their estimate of their habits. For instance, incumbents' replies to the Bishop of London's visitation questionnaire in 1883 drew the usual distinction between the middle class (if any) who came to their churches and the working class, who did not. But the few who made special mention of the lower middle class made varying comments. At All Saints', Stoke Newington, the parishioners were 'chiefly the poorer middle class, consisting of mercantile clerks and assistants in shops'; congregations were fair and 'one is most kindly received everywhere almost', but there was 'a considerable amount of apathy or religious indifference to be deplored'. At St Mary's, Stoke Newington, and St Thomas's, Camden Town, however, the lower middle class was singled out as a prominent element in the congregation.[17] This uncertainty is particularly evident in Charles Booth's parish by parish tour of the metropolis—though in the many hundreds of pages of his 'Religious Influences' series this group could remain almost invisible to anyone who was not specifically looking for it. One point seemed to be agreed: that south-west London was less of a church-going area than the north, and that Putney was particularly resistant to organised religion. This was partly attributed to the large element of 'theatrical and music-hall people', and to the fact that Putney was 'a great place for sporting men and swarming with bookmakers', but the 'small clerks and city people' of Wandsworth, and indeed the middle class population generally in this part of London, were said to be 'almost more stubborn and difficult to reach than the working classes'.[18]

Elsewhere the picture seemed to vary from one district to the next. Booth indicated the essential fluidity of the religious pattern in this section of society when he suggested that 'the most hopeful chances for the religious fishers of men' lay in:

> a distinct grade of small salaried people, minor officials and the upper ten of the working class world. These people, who are more often on the upward than the downward track are sometimes religious and sometimes not. In De Beauvoir Town they do not seem to respond, and we had a similar account of them in Dalston; but it is probably otherwise in Stoke Newington and Highbury. Much depends on their antecedents and on the character of their employment, and much, too, on the habits of those whose way of life they seek to imitate.[19]

There was thus no dominant pattern of white collar behaviour either in church-going habits or in many of the related areas. This was partly because of the social range that the stratum covered, extending as it did from the 'pound-a-week clerk' to those like the Pooters who were able to afford regular supplies of port to celebrate their son's frequent engagements.[20] But it also reflected the distinctive character of the social controls operating in the lower middle class.

The tightly-knit working class neighbourhood disciplined its inhabitants in extreme cases by rough musickings, and more typically by sendings to Coventry, refusals of help or simple rudeness. In many such communities there was a collective position of antagonism to most aspects of organised religion, though this attitude was more ambivalent than it appeared at first sight, and there was generally a significant minority rejecting in some degree the prevailing point of view. In the established middle class, and even more strongly in the upper class, there was also a kind of collective viewpoint. People in these classes were imbued with a sense of their own position in society and the standards of propriety required of them; they were also willing to sacrifice some of their wealth and leisure in what they conceived of as being society's interests.[21]

In the lower middle class there was no such collective viewpoint. White collar workers and small shopkeepers seldom felt much hostility to the churches: thus the 'general friendliness' noted by the Stoke Newington vicar. Though sometimes mildly radical they were not bitterly resentful of the social order. On the other hand, by middle and upper class standards their sense of social duty was weak; and though sensitive to the issue of their own respectability, they had far less to lose by any act of nonconformity, and most did not have servants to keep them up to the mark. Social disciplines were thus a little looser than in other sections of society, and more dependent on the strength of individual motivation; in church-going habits, there being no well-established norms, individual temperament or experience, family background, the influence of fellow-workers, or the efforts of particular churches might each exercise a decisive role.

This situation was reflected in intermediate rates of church attendance, in the multiplicity of denominations, and in the relative strength of Nonconformity. In London, for instance, comparison between the wealthiest suburbs and those populated by middle income groups shows in the latter far fewer Anglicans and more non-church-goers, but about the same number of Nonconformists.[22] In Liverpool, counts in 1902 and 1912 showed the white collar suburbs rather below wealthy Garston (as well as the Catholic districts), rather above Protestant working class areas.

But while Anglicans were much more numerous in Garston, Nonconformist strength varied considerably, being sometimes at the same level as in Garston, sometimes (Walton and Toxteth East) much greater.[23]

The distinctive character of formal religion in the lower middle class suburb can be illustrated by a comparison between church attendance in wealthy Knightsbridge and suburban Catford, as recorded in the *Daily News* religious census of 1902-3. The adult rate for Knightsbridge (31.5 per cent) was well above the average for London, and the 6,000 worshippers were divided into only five congregations, four of them Anglican and one Roman Catholic. In Catford the rate of 18.2 per cent was much closer to the average, but adult worshippers were divided between thirteen congregations, varying in size from 38 to 689, and including besides Anglicans and Wesleyans (the two largest groups) Baptists, Congregationalists, Free Methodists, Bible Christians and Disciples of Christ.[24] The churches of Catford, though more sparsely attended than those of Knightsbridge, must have provided a wider range of types of Christianity, their atmosphere must have been more intimate, and a higher proportion of attenders must have been involved in their day to day life.

While personal choice played an important part in the religious alignments of white collar families, there were certain aspects of the collective situation of the group that limited or enhanced the role of organised religion, and it is these that will be considered in the remainder of this paper. On the one side, the scope of religious ideas and organisations (or those of any other kind) was limited by the distinctively 'proletarian' mentality and way of life that many white collar workers shared with members of the working class. On the other side, their importance was enhanced by the characteristic lower middle class organisation of social life, by the Victorian association between 'religion' and 'respectability', and by the fact that Christianity was still by far the most important channel for idealism and the impulse to service, and that the churches were for many people the most attractive available sources of 'culture' and intellectual stimulus.

The formal church-going of most members of the middle and upper classes, together with many of the smaller property owners, was associated in many individual cases with strong personal convictions. More generally, it was part of a pattern of obligations that went with their position in society. Shopkeepers and small employers probably conceived of this society in relatively local terms, and their obligations were fulfilled by participation in local government or by acting as churchwardens.

Members of the elite groups tended to think in wider terms: they saw questions of government policy as being to some extent their personal concern, and they felt equally bound to take some interest in more abstract political, social and religious issues. Proletarians, black coated or otherwise, felt no such automatic concern, and their sense of identification with the nation, county, borough or parish was generally much weaker. A hierarchical society largely denied them responsibility and respect; it expected little of them and offered them very little. They in turn tended to respond with a system of proletarian parochialism, which was at once a means of justifying their lack of involvement in the affairs of society at large, and of demarcating a more limited community within which they enjoyed a measure of status and their actions were of some significance.[25]

White collar workers, almost as much as the working class, concentrated knowledge, interest, personal contacts within a small local world, regarding with indifference, sometimes with fear and distrust, questions relating to, and ideas and customs intruding from a wider world beyond. 'Philosophers have interpreted the world; the point, however, is to change it': it was a basic assumption of this parochialism, which more ideologically committed observers termed 'apathy', that both enterprises were a waste of time. This disposed, among much else, of most questions of national politics, as well as all those of political or religious theory. Instead proletarians concentrated their attention on the immediate, the relevant, the practical, the local. White collar workers also tended to believe that such a concentration could help to bring about at least some improvement in their individual circumstances. Meanwhile, within this local world small boundaries assumed huge proportions, and petty feuds took on an importance incomprehensible to the outsider.[26]

This parochialism, as it existed in the lower middle class, has been well described by Richard Church in his account of his parents, a GPO sorter and a board school teacher, in Battersea at the beginning of the twentieth century. If Church's reconstruction fifty years after the event is accurate, the focal point of their lives seems to have been the quest for security. For Richard Church himself, his father's craving for security and his fear of the risky or the unconventional was epitomised in the moment when he forced his son to give up a scholarship to an art college and to become a civil service clerk instead—an action which poisoned their relationship for some time.

> No doubt the poverty and hardship which he had known in childhood had fixed in his character an obstinacy born of hunger and

degradation. He was too innocent and too lacking in intellectual self-confidence to contemplate going out to fight for himself in the open market. He had a curious belief that money-making was a dirty game, something not even talked about, and all he asked was that he be assured of a regular income, no matter how small. He saw the Civil Service as the only way for himself and therefore his sons must follow him . . . Like most people at that time and in that walk of life [he and his wife] were grateful for small assurances: a safe job, a respectable anonymity, a local esteem. Outside that limit lay a dangerous unknown which included crime, genius, fame, notoriety and exalted rank. All the people who came to our house (few and infrequent) were of this persuasion, unanimous in their social and moral quietism. Behind my own parents' acquiescence in this lay an element of mystery, revealed only occasionally by oblique remarks and references, and by father's perverse attitude towards the aristocracy and to all manifestations of ambition, or of pursuits larger than he could comprehend.[27]

These fears and exclusions extended, Church implies, even into the field of music, where the father, puzzled by his son's enthusiasm for Schubert, demanded, 'one of our old favourites. There's nothing like the old friends.' And the mother, though a good pianist, played the same pieces every Sunday evening, and showed no interest in experiment.[28]

The tone of many lower middle class families, domestic, without either the brashness of the 'rougher' working class or the fastidious sense of decorum of the established middle class, was caught by a Hammersmith vicar, whose formerly well to do parish was being invaded by clerks and those of similar status:

The newcomers are quite quiet, respectable and inoffensive, but on warm evenings they will sit at their open windows in their shirtsleeves, drinking beer out of a pot, and though they do it quite quietly it is not what I am accustomed to.[29]

'Quiet, respectable and inoffensive': this particular combination of virtues or limitations was equally characteristic of a large section of the more prosperous working class. Yet there was one important difference. It is suggested in Richard Church's reference to his childhood home as 'cosy, passionate, instinctive, and almost completely isolated'.[30] If the working class found security in the community of the neighbourhood, the white collar proletarians tended to flee both the great world in which they counted for so little, and the neighbourhood, with its vulgarity and roughness, in which their black coats branded them as snobs. Powerless as individuals, and without the strength of numbers or a capacity for violence; distrusted by the 'masses' yet despised by the 'classes', they could find safety and self-respect within their own homes, in the family circle or in the company of those who shared their social position and way of life, and who would not tar them or their children with the brush of 'roughness'. Such friends were most commonly met at work or through formal associations. The intimate (though not necessarily friendly) relations between neighbours that characterised many working class districts were much rarer in the lower middle class. Indeed, the Thompson and Vigne interviews, in which some 450 men and women born between 1872 and 1906 have been questioned about their early life, suggest that the sharpest single difference between white collar and skilled working class families at this time may lie in the degree of intimacy of their relations with neighbours.[31]

The reason for this pattern of relationships lay in the respectability that was the basis not only of the white collar worker's pride in himself but of his livelihood. Employers of white collar labour were as much concerned with the dress, manner and style of life of their present and future employees as with their formal skills. Similarly, it was those who set store by the 'respectability' of their work (or whose parents did) who were most likely to seek white collar jobs.

An essential principle of the working class 'neighbourhood' was that status and recognition were accorded to all those who accepted the local mores and did not make themselves conspicuously unpleasant to those around them. White collar respectability required that they be fussier. Neighbours posed a double threat: on the one hand, they might infect the household with inferior standards in cleanliness, language and so on; on the other hand, they might come to spy on the often rather pinched reality behind the more prosperous facade. One of those interviewed by Thompson and Vigne describes as follows the philosophy of her mother, who had been born about 1865 and was the wife of a Manchester clerk:

> No use being poor and seeming poor, always put on a good face outside. And when you'd be saying about windows she would say, I must have the windows right because more pass by than come in. We had to dress to the public, you know what I mean when I say that. Always give people a good impression.[32]

The maintenance of standards, often against considerable odds, is a recurrent theme in interviews with those brought up in a white collar milieu. The wife of a Hackney clerk would 'come into that class to-day I think that although she'd qualify for a rates rebate you'd have a dickens of a job to get her to apply for it', while the wife of a Manchester railway goods checker 'had a horror of getting anything on credit or tick'. Clothes were another symbol: the son of an insurance agent from the Potteries defined the social stratum in which he grew up as those who 'would never go out without they was dressed up'.[33] Negatively these standards were defended by 'keeping yourself to yourself' and by a tendency to keep out of public houses (not necessarily because of 'temperance' principles, as they might well take back bottles of beer from the off-licence).[34] More positively, a strong home life was built up and leisure outside the home was concentrated on certain protected environments of assured respectability.

It was in the lower middle class that the family unit, unencumbered by servants, undivided by the sharp separation of 'male' from 'female' worlds, had a sacred character. The early years of the lower middle class child were dominated by his two parents; and while mothers in all but the servant-keeping classes were bound to the home and seldom escaped, here their husbands often bound themselves voluntarily. Sometimes the father had his one private hobby; but many lower middle class fathers seem to have had very little leisure apart from the rest of the family.[35] Saturday afternoon was the time for cycling, rambling or visits to the park;[36] Saturday evening for theatres and music-halls;[37] Sunday evening for music at home, sometimes with friends or relatives, sometimes just the family, the more devout concentrating on hymns, while other families mixed sacred and secular.[38] In Richard Church's family, his father's ideal of shared leisure was symbolised by the two tandems, one to be ridden by his wife and himself, the other by his two sons. This ideal was frustrated by his wife, who was even more devoted to her family, but less interested in cycling. But the unity, intensity and isolation of family life is continually stressed by Church, who claims that the 'closer and fiercer' 'intimacies' and the 'close, hugger-mugger home atmosphere' of the lower middle class made him and those like him 'over-emotional, unadventurous and matriarch-ridden'.[39]

At the same time, the independence of the white collar household was jealously guarded. Not only were neighbours kept at arm's length: they emphatically did not accept charity from philanthropists or the 'parish'.[40] For one old woman born in the 1880s in lower middle class Manchester, the most vivid memory from childhood seems to be a smacking for accepting a jam buttie from a mission soup-kitchen, delivered with the words, 'I'll teach you to ask for charity'.[41] In some respects this zeal for independence contrasted oddly with the attitude required of them in working hours. Clerks and shop assistants had to behave in ways that many manual workers would have regarded as demeaning: they not only had to work for their employers, but they had to dress and speak in ways acceptable to them, and often to make some show of deference towards employers or customers. They were thus open to charges of 'flunkeyism',[42] and shop assistants in particular could find this role oppressive. But, for the most part, white collar workers were unaware of the inconsistency, since they adopted 'respectable' standards as a matter of course or with conscious pride, rather than in a spirit of calculated subservience.

Some lower middle class families seem to have compulsively maintained standards for an audience consisting of no one but themselves. For many others, respectable values were a matter of accepted convention rather than deep conviction. But in one area nearly everone felt the pressure of these values: the bringing up of their children. The protection of the children from corrupting or vulgarising influences, or simply from physical danger, provided the strongest motive for maintaining the unity and isolation of the household, and it was the success of the children in growing up 'straight' and, preferably, in rising in the social scale, that could most clearly vindicate their parents. The parents accordingly would make sacrifices to give them an education, though often one that was conceived of in narrowly instrumental terms. And in the process the children sometimes developed intellectual and cultural interests that led them to question the values of their parents: so that education, instead of vindicating the lower middle class parent, became the chief means of alienating his children from him.[43]

Of those protected environments outside the home in which members of white collar families met old friends or made new ones, the most important was the church or chapel. In spite of the great variety of individual religious commitment and (by middle and upper class standards) the relatively low level of church attendance, the churches performed a number of characteristic functions in lower middle class life.

One of these derived from the ambition that many white collar families entertained, but few unmistakably achieved: in nineteenth century England a certain amount of church-going was among the 'recognised proprieties of life',[44] and those who aspired to middle class status would feel that their claims were enhanced by renting a pew and attending services fairly regularly. The pluralist English Sunday brought together the 'respectable' sections of the population in a moral unity that in some degree overrode differences of sect and party, providing a means of identifying those who, though poor, were honest,[45] and separating the wild men from those whose loyalties were basically sound.[46] In the eighties and nineties this association between religion and respectability was beginning to be eroded;[47] but apart from their personal convictions, white collar workers were still likely to feel that connection with a church or chapel was a normal part of middle class life. It also offered other advantages especially relevant to those in their social position.

It was around the middle of the social hierarchy, in the lower middle class and among some of the upper working class, that churches and chapels acted as centres of amusement and education, and as places where adolescents could meet those of the opposite sex in approved surroundings. White collar workers and those of similar status were isolated by their desire to escape the demeaning intimacies of the working class neighbourhood and their ineligibility for the society and institutions of the established middle class. This isolation may have been particularly acute in a small town such as Guildford: around 1910, according to the son of a small trader, professional men stood at the top of local society, monopolising, of instance, membership of the town's leading golf club. High Street traders were one stage lower, occupying leading positions in the big central chapels (and presumably the borough council) and meeting in the Tradesmen's Club which, in turn, excluded 'small business people' with shops in the back streets or on the roads leading away from the town centre. The working men, meanwhile, would have their pubs and clubs. Those, however, whose standards were emphatically respectable, but who had little money or social status, were obliged to fall back either on family life and private hobbies, or on membership of organisations that applied no social test. Thus, the small-trader parents of the Guildford man just quoted found one of their chief sources of amusement in cycling and the other in activities at their parish church. And a contemporary brought up in the same town, where his father was a railway clerk, remembers an early life focused on the Salvation Army, with Saturday afternoons devoted to rambles in the country, and weekday evenings to practising the cornet that his father played on Sundays.[48] In a larger city a wider range of commercial or privately organised amusements might meet some of these needs. But for those who were respectable yet with little social status there was nowhere that could offer so much at once.[49] This was especially so for the adolescent seeking a base in a city where he had newly arrived, or one that was independent of his parents and the neighbourhood in which he had grown up.[50] And for those who lacked 'connections' membership of a church could act as an alternative means of personal contacts and evidence of respectability and integrity. In the 1890s, 'A steady young man commencing life in Liverpool without capital or good friends' could not do better for his own future than by joining and becoming active, useful and respected in a large dissenting congregation.'[51]

The intensity of family life was probably greatest and parochialism most complete where attachment to church or chapel was relatively superficial. As this commitment deepened, the individual, while no doubt believing ever more strongly in the sacredness of 'the family', tended to be drawn into a wider world, and one in which a significant part of his free time was spent outside the home. A limited involvement could help to justify and to reinforce a passive respectability; deeper involvement tended to undermine the prevailing parochialism by making a person read more widely, and often by leading him into social and political work.

The point can be illustrated by a comparison between the Ford and Arthey families, members of which were interviewed by Thompson and Vigne.[52] Both lived in London and were headed by clerks; neither had a servant, though the Artheys seem to have been more comfortably off; both seem to have had a strong family life and relatively little contact with neighbours. But the life of the Artheys seems to have been very largely privatised: they were High Anglicans, though not, as far as it appears, very actively committed; they voted at elections and went to concerts and music-halls, but there is no mention of any other social, political or intellectual interests. The Methodist Fords inhabited a wider world in at least two senses: they were readers (Dickens, the Brontes and Tennyson are mentioned), and the parents devoted two or three nights a week to social work in connection with a mission in Haggerston (in particular, work with crippled children). Moreover, the Haggerston people whom they met through the mission, rather than being kept in a separate compartment of their lives, were freely invited to their flat in Hackney. They were also said to be keen Liberals (though it is not clear how actively this allegiance was expressed): in Victorian England political and religious commitment tended to be associated, the one often deriving much of its distinctive character from the other[53] — though sometimes the relationship took a negative form, as with those who had passed through a period of intense religiosity, ending with disillusionment and the transfer of all their energies and idealism into the political sphere.

In this period most lower middle class church-goers were, like the Fords, Nonconformists.[54] At chapel they mixed with upper working class families,[55] sharing a common moralism: the belief that a large part of the world's ills are caused by individual and collective moral failure, and could be cured by greater moral effort in private and in public life. This seems to have been reflected in a distinctive view of social stratification: the dividing line most emphasised by strongly church-oriented white collar families was that between 'rough' and 'respectable'. As the daughter born in 1905 of a Tyneside post office sorter put it:

> we didn't drink and we didn't gamble and we didn't buy on the never-never and we didn't swear. So I suppose that's a kind of class strata in its way too.[56]

A similar set of prohibitions was observed by most of the Nonconformist families represented among Thompson and Vigne's respondents. The reasons for these are seldom stated, and by the end of the nineteenth century they had become so much shibboleths setting off the devout, especially those who were Nonconformist, from the rest, that the individual scarcely needed any rational justification for adopting them. Yet there was a certain underlying logic. One theme was the ideal of independence, and there was a clear connection between this and the bar on any unearned benefit. But the great symbol of the unregenerate life was drink. At a conscious level, the chief reason for this was a revulsion from the violence and the neglect of wife and children to which it often led, and the taboo on this predominantly male activity was a part of the exaltation of family life;[57] less consciously, this humane concern could be stimulated by an obsession with work, or by a preference for everything that was clean, orderly, restrained, controlled.[58] The cult of work was probably more characteristic of small businessmen, haunted by the fear of bankruptcy or allured by the hope of riches; but a cult of cleanliness arose more naturally from the situation of the white collar worker, its particular advantages, and the qualities required of him.

Nonconformist moralism and the ideal of 'character' could have a mainly conservative function:[59] it tended to set its adherents apart from their neighbours, and could produce a preoccupation with moral differences between individuals, and a readiness to identify 'success' with 'character', and 'failure' with the lack of it. On the other hand, this moralism was generally directed against institutions as well as individuals, and it did not necessarily include any belief that the social system was essentially just, or that rising within it was a sign of virtue. In this period, especially, it characteristically did not lead to an exclusive concern either with the personal or with the social causes of society's ills, but to an insistence on their inter-relationship. According to the prominent Baptist minister, John Clifford, institutions were embodiments of ideals of human life 'true' or 'false'. They, in turn, fostered qualities that were socially useful or socially harmful. In particular the system of economic individualism was both a product of human greed and of the false 'competitive' ideal, and a cause of bad morality—providing some with excessive leisure, imposing on others extremes of poverty (each potentially debilitating), and denying to the many the exercise of responsibility that was essential to 'character'. It was because of considerations such as these that many Nonconformists were to be found on the radical wing of the Liberal Party, and later in the Labour Party.[60]

If the white collar family's freedom of action was limited by their ideas of respectability this was much less true of the fairly large white collar sub-cultures of unmarried shop assistants living-in, of young clerks in lodgings, and commercial travellers between week-ends. Here, unconstrained by family or neighbourly controls, the room was widest for the individual to devote himself to improving the world or his own self, or to having a good time.

In Victorian England the authority of religion was greatest in the home. It was there that mothers taught their children to say their prayers, and that fathers imposed on their children (and even to some extent conformed to themselves) standards that they would never think of observing elsewhere. But when men met, free from the restraining influence of wives and children, indecency and blasphemy began to come into their own, and the devout were in danger of being branded as killjoys, provocatively unamused by their companions' tales, adhering to a language quaintly swept clean of oaths, embarrassing those about them by the weakness of their thirst. And in all-male communities the religious could find themselves in a beleaguered minority. If commercial travellers and drapers' assistants scarcely compared for virile barbarism with sailors or navvies, the commercial room and the living-in quarters were still said to bear the stamp of an all-male environment. As a member of the Commercial Travellers' Christian Association put it:

> The atmosphere of the commercial room seemed to bleach the Christianity out of a man. There many a coarse man trotted out unwholesome jests and lewd stories for the edification of the more in-

experienced novices, and when a religious man protested he was generally marked—'He is a humbug without doubt, a whining Methodist or a Salvation Armyist' . . . Commercial men are too polite to say it to his face, but he is made to feel it.[61]

At the week-ends the 'coarse men' were back with their families, and their 'unwholesome jests' were no doubt forgotten for the time being. But for many young shop assistants the living-in quarters were for several years home. Early supporters of the YMCA, the chief mission of which was to the living-in draper's assistant, gave lurid accounts of the kind of homes that they were;[62] and some of the same features occur in a novel published in 1907 describing the adventures, if that is not too strong a word, of a clerk beginning his working life in lodgings in Kennington, far from his parents.[63]

But within this world of the relatively rootless and the relatively free the hedonism of some was fully matched by the earnestness of others. These latter could devote all of such free time as they had to the search for the key to life or, having found it, to the task of converting others, and they often carried this activity over into working hours. W. J. Fish gave this account of the assistants at the large Whitechapel drapers where he worked in the 1880s:

> There were two distinct sections among us 'Livers In'. There were those who preferred the more joyous side, or, to be more correct, what *they considered* to be the more joyous. I have my doubts. Some would have called their view of joyousness 'racketiness', but I take exception to this, and prefer the word I have used, 'joyousness'. The other section were religiously inclined. Somehow or other I seemed to fluctuate between the two.[64]

(Partly, it seems, because of his passion for a girl cashier who worked for the Spitalfields Lodging House Mission.) Naturally those who later came to recall their late teens and early twenties in memoirs had generally belonged to the more earnest party. W. J. Brown, for instance, was to look back to the years around 1910, when he was a boy clerk at the Post Office Savings Bank and lodging in Battersea, as the happiest of his life: he would study for an hour before breakfast, then take a row in Battersea Park, walk to work, and spend a good deal of the day exchanging ideas with his workmates, talk being permitted; after work there remained 'five glorious hours of freedom', many of which were spent at the library reading on politics, religion and science, though he also became increasingly active in open-air preaching for the Methodists and the ILP.[65]

Up to about 1890 the more serious had probably been mainly evangelical. But a less conventional form of earnestness was now beginning to develop among young white collar workers—that which found its chief expression in the Clarion Clubs, though it also had its representatives in the more 'advanced' chapels, and among High Anglicans repelled by what they saw as the excessive respectability of Anglican and Nonconformist evangelicalism. In Liverpool, for instance, one such church seems to have been Pembroke Baptist, which had its Clarion Fellowship, and where the Social Reform League was a centre of the women's suffrage movement in the city.[66] But around 1900 there was still a degree of tension between the lower middle class rebels and respectability of any kind. It was probably from lapsed chapel-goers that this culture drew many of its recruits —young men and women with all the sense of commitment together with the capacity for reading that the chapel demanded, but freed from the compromises with the established and the secure that all but a few fringe chapels tended to involve their members in.

This new culture of socialism, cycling, general free-thinking and the flouting of respectable norms seems to have been particularly strong among some of the clerks, teachers, shop assistants, telegraphists, and the floating population of white collar youth generally in and around Manchester during the first decade of this century. Norman Swindin, who came in 1901 to work as a draughtsman in a Manchester firm, has described the process by which he exchanged the 'middle class morality and piety' of his Yorkshire home for a life in which Blatchford was the leading influence and Jackson Street Social Democratic Federation Club the focal point (sometimes varied by visits to the Hallé or walking in Derbyshire).[67] Some of the same features occur in Hannah Mitchell's account of her life in Ashton in the 1890s, centred on the ILP and the Labour Church, or in Stella Davies's description of her years as a young telephonist in Manchester around 1914, with the Clarion Cycling Club in a comparable position.[68]

There was now a significant minority of white collar workers positively rejecting the established values of their own section of society, scorning the long cherished ideal of respectability, and seeking to make common cause with the working class, the proximity of which J. S. Harrison in 1852 and many since had so much dreaded.[69] But although the position of white collar workers has declined with the greater availability of female labour and the decreasing marketability of the respectability that had been their greatest asset, white collar values have in general proved surprisingly persistent.[70]

They are, however, expressed much less frequently in religious terms. Middle class church-going was falling sharply in London by the 1890s and in Liverpool by the beginning of the twentieth century.[71] It was less and less a necessary part of 'respectability'. Religious organisations lost their wider functions more gradually, though from the 1890s socialist societies and the new culture of popular rationalism fed on the RPA cheap classics were establishing themselves as alternative focuses of idealism and media of self-education, and commercial leisure was beginning to challenge the provisions made by the churches.[72] Their social role remained greatest among adolescents, for many of whom church-based clubs continued to be attractive.[73] With this exception, the churches now impinge on a committed minority, rather than performing a variety of characteristic functions in the life of the white collar stratum generally.

Notes

I would like to thank Paul Thompson and Thea Vigne for generously allowing me to make extensive use of and to quote from their interviews on family life and work experience before 1918.

1. The necessity for 'decent professional garb' to be worn by all employees who came into 'immediate touch with the client' is noted by G. S. Layard, 'A Lower-Middle-Class Budget', *Cornhill Magazine*, 1901, p. 660. As an article on commercial travellers in *Free Lance*, 2 March 1868, p. 96, put it: 'The accredited agent of merchant princes he reflects in his respectable person the honour and dignity of those he represents.' But even where clerks were not in direct touch with the client, employers were interested in their background and manner: see Charles Booth's interviews in 1895 with employers of clerical labour, recorded in Booth Collection (London School of Economics Library), B136, pp. 32, 36-8.
2. Clyde Binfield's definition of what was required of a draper's assistant. *George Williams and the YMCA*, Heinemann, London, 1973, p. 70.
3. J. S. Harrison, *The Social Position and Claims of Clerks and Book-keepers Considered*, Hamilton Adams, London, 1852, p. 4.
4. Ibid., pp. 6, 7-8, 13.
5. See D. Lockwood, *The Blackcoated Worker*, Allen & Unwin, London, 1958, pp. 19-33.
6. See the discussion 'On what may I marry?' in B. G. Orchard, *The Clerks of Liverpool*, Collinson, Liverpool, 1871, pp. 63-4.
7. There were 29 domestic servants per 100 households headed by a clerk or commercial traveller, as against 103 for merchants and brokers, 5 for printers, one of the most prosperous working class groups, and 2 for gas workers. C. Booth, *Life and Labour of the People in London*, 17 volumes, Macmillan, 1902-3, II [2nd Series], ii [Volume II], p. 189; II, iii, pp. 272-3, 449.
8. See Table 2.1.
9. Lockwood, op.cit., pp. 42-4; Booth, op.cit., II, iv, p. 169.
10. Booth Collection, B136, p. 26.

11. In 1891, 62 per cent of the clerks in Inner London lived in seven suburban districts containing 39.2 per cent of the total population. Booth, op.cit., II, iii, p. 489.
12. See Table 2.2.
13. Incumbents of lower middle class parishes noted the mobility of their parishioners and their lack of contact with neighbours. A Hammersmith vicar said: '"They do not neighbour one another": in a poor parish you have only to make a communication to one person and the whole parish soon knows of it: here even families living in the same house often do no more than pass the time of day with one another' (Booth Collection, B267, p. 9). A Tooting vicar attributed the mobility of the local people to a lack of ties 'ecclesiastical or otherwise' (ibid., B312, p. 121).
14. The results of some of the more recent work are summarised in H. McLeod, 'Class,Community and Region: The Religious Geography of Nineteenth-century England', M. Hill (ed), *Sociological Yearbook of Religion in Britain*, 6, SCM Press, London, 1973, pp. 29-73.
15. R. Mudie-Smith (ed), *The Religious Life of London*, Hodder & Stoughton, London, 1904, p. 342.
16. Ibid., pp. 192-3.
17. Bishop of London's Visitation, 1883 (Lambeth Palace Library).
18. Booth, op.cit., III, v, pp. 201, 210-12. Board School teachers, on the other hand, seem to have been a particularly devout group, to judge from comments in the London Visitation Returns for 1900, e.g. those by the vicar of St Philip's, Bethnal Green.
19. Booth, op.cit., III, i, p. 150.
20. Compare Booth's comments (ibid., III, i, p. 79) on 'the pathetic lives' of 'poorly-paid clerks' in Hackney with those of a Baptist minister in Upper Tooting (Booth Collection, B297, pp. 217-9) on his congregation of City and West End workers, among whom 'there is no effort to live and all have a margin', and where the average rental was £45 a year.
21. For a fuller statement of these generalisations, see H. McLeod, *Class and Religion in the Late Victorian City*, Croom Helm, London, 1974.
22. Ibid., pp. 170, 304-7.
23. See Tables 2.3-2.4. Note that there were differences within the 'white-collar suburbs' between some upper middle-class areas, where attendances were very high, and the more typical clerks' districts.
24. These figures come from Mudie-Smith, op.cit. For an explanation of how estimates of population were made, see McLeod, *Class and Religion*, p. 305.
25. I have developed this idea more fully in *Class and Religion*, pp. 8-11, 42-60, 282. See also G. Stedman Jones, 'Working-Class Culture and Working-Class Politics in London, 1870-1900', *Journal of Social History*, vol. VII, no 4, Summer 1974.
26. In one of the most famous of suburban murder cases, F. H. Seddon was hanged by his failure to inform her relatives, living about 200 yards away, of the death of the lodger he had allegedly poisoned. The Attorney-General saw this as evidence that he had something to hide. But if we are to judge him by the standards of Tollington Park rather than those of Belgravia his own explanation is just as plausible: that his daughter had been snubbed by the relatives on an earlier visit, and he was not going to subject his family to the possibility of being treated in this way—if they missed the funeral, well, that would teach them better manners in future. See F. Young (ed), *The Trial of the Seddons*, Hodge, Edinburgh, 1914, the whole of which is a fascinating social document.
27. R. Church, *Over the Bridge*, Heinemann, London, 1955, pp. 206-18, 134-5.

28. Ibid., pp. 75, 136-7.
29. Booth Collection, B267, pp. 5-7.
30. Church, op.cit., p. 118.
31. Paul Thompson and Thea Vigne's Interviews on Family Life and Work Experience before 1918, University of Essex (hereafter cited as 'Thompson and Vigne's interviews'). For fuller details of this project see P. Thompson, *The Edwardians,* Weidenfeld and Nicolson, London, 1975. I have taken the sixteen interviews where the respondent had been brought up in an English town and his father had been a white collar worker during a substantial part of the respondent's childhood, and have matched each of these with an interview where the respondent had been born about the same time and brought up in the same town, but with a craftsman father. The towns and interview numbers are: London 65, 161, 183, 300 matched with 296, 71, 245, 230; Guildford, 63 and 66; Potteries, 196, 224, 262 and 31, 232, 24; Liverpool 49, 74 and 98, 32; Manchester 47, 68, 135 and 81, 90, 52; Farnworth 153 and 54; Bolton, 78 and 134; Tyneside, 250 and 155. There is no very marked difference between the two groups in their political affiliation (predominantly Liberal), attitude to charity (most were 'proud') or style of child-parent relations. But craftsman fathers were somewhat more likely to spend most of their free time in the public house (five, as against two, were said to do this), somewhat less likely to be active members of a church or chapel (five, as against nine); and there was a really sharp difference in the degree of intimacy of relations with neighbours: eight of the working class respondents *emphasised* this intimacy, and only one said they had little relationship; none of the white collar respondents *emphasised* this relationship, while eight said there was very little.
32. Thompson and Vigne's interviews, no. 135, p. 52.
33. Ibid., no. 183, p. 48; no. 47, p. 14; no. 196, p. 37.
34. As did, for instance, Richard Church's parents (op.cit., p. 98), who are never described as going into pubs.
35. Of the sixteen white collar fathers in Thompson and Vigne's sample, ten were said seldom to go out by themselves—though some of these might have one private hobby. Where such a hobby was mentioned it was going to race-meetings (four cases), pubs (three), bowls (three), photography (one), watching cricket or football (one each), singing (one). Otherwise they sat at home reading, or shared their amusements with their wife and children.
36. Thompson and Vigne's interviews, no. 63, p. 14; no. 196, pp. 19-21, 30; no. 262, pp. 66-8.
37. Ibid., no. 74, p. 24; no. 78, p. 26.
38. Seven out of sixteen white collar respondents specifically mention that their families held concerts on Sundays.
39. Church, op.cit., pp. 22-3, 30, 104.
40. Similar ideals of 'respectability' and 'independence' were adopted by many south-east London engineers and Durham miners. See G. Crossick, 'Dimensions of Artisan Ideology in mid-Victorian Kentish London', paper read to the Urban History Group Conference 1973; R. Moore, *Pit-men, Preachers and Politics,* CUP, Cambridge, 1974, chapter 6. But there were important differences—probably in the extent of neighbourhood life, and in the political and religious expressions of their 'respectability'; certainly in the fact that 'workers by brain' often saw manual work as intrinsically debasing and unrespectable.
41. Thompson and Vigne's interviews, no. 68, p. 17.
42. See the criticisms of clerks by spokesmen for manual trade unions, quoted

in Lockwood, op.cit., pp. 101-5.
43. This seems to me an underlying theme of Richard Church's autobiographical volumes, *The Golden Sovereign*, Heinemann, London, 1957, and *Over the Bridge*.
44. Horace Mann's phrase in his comments on the religious census of 1851, (*Parliamentary Papers*, 1852-3, vol. LXXXIX, p. clviii).
45. For the social connotations of religion, see Orchard, op.cit., p. 63. After describing one section of Liverpool clerks who belonged clearly to the middle class, he then referred to 'a far more numerous body . . . the young men who (if in many cases well read, well mannered, and religious) still are not in society, place very little value on gloves, lunch in the office on bread and cheese, clean their own boots [etc.]'.
46. Cf. McLeod, *Class and Religion*, pp. 36-7; and the Bishop of London's remarks on the Labour Party, *Official Report of the Church Congress, 1911*, pp. 7-14.
47. When Booth was touring London in the late 1890s this association was still strong, but several witnesses were noticing a change. As a Baptist minister in the new middle class district of Herne Hill said (Booth Collection, B304, p. 29): 'Though servant-keeping and comfortable they are not natural church-goers, church-going is by no means a condition of respectability'.
48. Thompson and Vigne's interviews, no. 83 and no. 63.
49. For interpretation, see S. Yeo, 'A Contextual View of Religious Organisation', M. Hill (ed), *Sociological Yearbook of Religion in Britain*, 6, SCM Press, London, 1973, pp. 207-34.
50. G. Acorn, *One of the Multitude*, Macmillan, London, 1911, pp. 149-51, 173-9; N. Hancock, *An Innocent Grows Up*, Dent, London, 1947, pp. 128-33.
51. B. G. Orchard, *Liverpool's Legion of Honour*, Birkenhead, 1893, pp. 42-3. The following exchange between a draper and his prospective assistant comes from H. G. Wells, *The History of Mr Polly*, Nelson, London, 1910, p. 65: '" . . . You're a Christian?" "Church of England," said Mr Polly. "H'm," said the employer a little checked. "For good all round business work, I should have preferred a Baptist. Still—."'
52. Thompson and Vigne's interviews, no. 183 and 300. Pseudonyms have been used.
53. Two very clear-cut examples of the relationship appear in the autobiographies of men living in Battersea and working as clerks around the turn of the century: A. Mansbridge, *The Trodden Road*, Dent, London, 1940; W. J. Brown, *So Far . . .* , Allen & Unwin, London, 1944.
54. Even in London, which was predominantly Anglican, Nonconformists were slightly more numerous in the white collar suburbs. In most northern and Midland towns the differential must have been much greater.
55. C. Field, 'Methodism in Metropolitan London, 1850-1920', University of Oxford D.Phil. thesis, 1974, pp. 215-21, shows that the great majority of London Methodists belonged to the lower middle class or skilled working class, and that most chapels included a mixture of these two groups.
56. Thompson and Vigne's interviews, no. 250, p. 50.
57. Ibid., no. 153, p. 48; no. 183, p. 32. See also Moore's explanation (loc. cit.) of the fervent teetotalism of Methodist miners.
58. Field (op.cit., p. 217) quotes from a handbook for Wesleyan ministers published in 1898 these subsidiary objects of Bands of Hope: 'the regular attendance . . . upon public worship; the inculcation of the moral duties of industry, honesty, truthfulness, cleanliness, kindness; the discouragement

of the practice of smoking and the creation of disgust for all bad and offensive habits—Sabbath breaking, swearing, gambling and such like'. For the link between teetotalism and work: J. Briggs and I. Sellers, *Victorian Nonconformity*, Edward Arnold, London, 1973, pp. 66-7.
59. This function has been demonstrated by R. Q. Gray in his paper. I am arguing, however, that Christian moralism did not necessarily lead, at least at a superficial level, to an acceptance of individualist values or of the justice of the social order: it could have both conservative and radical implications, sometimes for the same individual.
60. J. Clifford, *Socialism and the Teaching of Christ*, Fabian Society, London, 1897. Cf. S. Koss, *Nonconformity in Modern British Politics*, Batsford, London, 1975, pp. 147-51. Such views were held especially by Nonconformists, but not exclusively so: they are similar to those of the Anglican Albert Mansbridge (op.cit.) or a Catholic Manchester goods checker (Thompson and Vigne's interviews, no. 47).
61. *On the Road*, May 1883, as quoted by B. J. Avari, 'British Commercial Travellers and their Organisations, 1850-1914,' University of Manchester M.A.thesis, 1970, p. 130.
62. Binfield, op.cit., pp. 72-3. Sensational statements were sometimes made about the irreligion of living-in shop assistants. See W. B. Whitaker, *Victorian and Edwardian Shopworkers*, David & Charles, Newton Abbot, 1973, pp. 42-3, 84; G. L. Anderson, 'A Study of Clerical Labour in Liverpool and Manchester, 1850-1914', University of Lancaster Ph.D. thesis, 1974, p. 173.
63. S. Bullock, *Robert Thorne, The Story of a London Clerk*, Werner Laurie, London, 1907. Thorne himself is rather more earnest.
64. W. J. Fish, *The Autobiography of a Counter-Jumper*, Lutterworth, London, 1929, pp. 72-3.
65. Brown, op.cit., pp. 41-60.
66. I. Sellers, *Salute to Pembroke: Pembroke Chapel, Liverpool, 1838-1931* (duplicated copy in Liverpool Reference Library). It seems to have had much in common with the City Temple under R. J. Campbell, as described in F. Brockway, *Inside the Left*, Allen & Unwin, London, 1942, pp. 12-26.
67. N. Swindin, *Engineering Without Wheels*, Weidenfeld & Nicolson, London, 1962, pp. 24-67.
68. H. Mitchell, *The Hard Way Up*, Faber, London, 1968, pp. 114-24; C. S. Davies, *North Country Bred*, Routledge & Kegan Paul, London, 1963, pp. 82-5.
69. See also Anderson, op.cit., pp. 281-313, which analyses the slow growth between 1890 and 1914 of the National Union of Clerks, and the campaign waged from 1908 by its organ, *The Clerk*, against the goal of 'respectability' and for a recognition of their membership of the wage-earning class.
70. For the decline of white collar status and relative earnings, as well as for continuing differences in attitudes between white collar and skilled manual workers, see Lockwood, op.cit., pp. 99-105, 116-7, 127-30, 217.
71. See Tables 2.3 and 2.4.
72. For descriptions and interpretations of these processes, see E. R. Wickham, *Church and People in an Industrial City*, Lutterworth, London, 1957; B. R. Wilson, *Religion in Secular Society*, Watts, London, 1966; S. Budd, 'The British Humanist Movement, c. 1860-1966,' University of Oxford D.Phil. thesis, 1969; McLeod, *Class and Religion*, chapter 8; S. Yeo, *Religion and Voluntary Organisations in Crisis*, Croom Helm, London, 1976.
73. See B. Martin, 'Adolescent Interaction in an Anglican Church,' *Social Compass*, vol. XIV, 1967, pp. 33-51, a very interesting study of the social functions of a church youth club, and relevant to the whole theme of upper working/lower middle class values.

Table 2.1: Social origins of men marrying in Anglican churches

Place	Time	Occupational category	Number of cases	Percentage with working class fathers
2 Birmingham parishes	1868-74	White collar workers	189	37.6
4 Birmingham parishes	1896-1905	White collar workers	345	47.5
3 Birmingham parishes	1901	Manual workers	306	86.3
Edgbaston	1895-1906	Elite occupations	84	7.1
23 Inner London parishes	1898-1903	White collar workers	937	44.4
23 Inner London parishes	1898-1903	Clerks	388	42.8
23 Inner London parishes	1898-1903	Commercial travellers	87	40.2
27 Inner London parishes	1896-1903	White collar workers	1289	40.3
..	..	..	Bank employees	30	6.7
..	..	..	Journalists, editors	16	12.5
..	..	..	Insurance employees	11	22.2
..	..	..	Stockbroker's clerks	11	22.2
..	..	..	Actors, comedians	17	23.5
..	..	..	Artists	15	26.7
..	..	..	Commercial travellers	129	31.0
..	..	..	Clerks	557	37.9
..	..	..	Teachers, tutors	50	38.0
..	..	..	Law clerks	31	45.2
..	..	..	Musicians, singers	32	50.0
..	..	..	Shop assistants, salesmen	158	50.0
..	..	..	Railway clerks	24	54.2
..	..	..	Insurance agents	13	61.5
..	..	..	Post office sorters	23	65.2

Notes
a. Marriage registers almost invariably record the groom's occupation; in about 97% of cases, those used also give his father's.
b. The Registrar-General is at present unwilling to allow Register Offices, where records of all weddings since 1837 are kept, to be used for historical research, so it is impossible to obtain a fully representative sample. I have only used registers available at the Greater London Record Office or the Birmingham Reference Library, except for those of St George's, Edgbaston, which are at the church. I wish to thank the Rev. Canon D. J. W. Bradley for permission to see these.
c. The 937 Inner London weddings analysed consist of all those in the years 1898-1903 where the groom was a white collar worker and his father's occupation was recorded in 23 parishes chosen at random from those whose registers

are in the Greater London Record Office.
d. The larger sample of 1289 weddings also includes those in 4 middle class suburbs.
e. 'Elite' occupations are: gentleman, officer in armed forces, land agent, merchant, manufacturer, broker, factory manager, Anglican clergyman, barrister, solicitor, architect, accountant, doctor, dentist, university teacher, surveyor, civil engineer. 'White collar' occupations are all those classified with commercial clerks in the 1891 census (see list in Booth, op.cit., II, iii, p. 273), together with those employed as school-teachers and private tutors, shop assistants, librarians, photographers, draughtsmen, or in entertainment, the arts and journalism. 'Clerks' are those recorded as clerk, commercial clerk or mercantile clerk.

Table 2.2: Addresses of couples marrying in three Birmingham parishes, 1896-1905

CHRIST CHURCH, SUMMERFIELD

	Husband is manual worker	Husband is white collar
Total sample	238	84
Giving same address	74 (31.1%)	13 (15.5%)
Others	164	71
Living in same street	44 (26.8%)	10 (14.1%)
Elsewhere in same neighbourhood	65 (39.6%)	19 (26.8%)
Same or adjoining suburb	36 (22.0%)	22 (31.0%)
Elsewhere in Birmingham	4 (2.4%)	4 (5.6%)
Outside Birmingham	15 (9.1%)	16 (22.5%)

Proportion of neighbourhood marriages in a low status area:
working class (141) 70.9%
white collar (21) 42.9%

Proportion of neighbourhood marriages in a high status area:
working class (10) 40.0%
white collar (37) 32.4%

CHRIST CHURCH, SPARKBROOK

	Husband is manual worker	Husband is white collar
Total sample	163	162
Giving same address	78 (47.9%)	55 (34.0%)
Others	85	107
Living in same street	15 (17.6%)	12 (11.2%)
Elsewhere in same neighbourhood	36 (42.3%)	22 (20.6%)
Same or adjoining suburb	21 (24.7%)	44 (41.1%)
Elsewhere in Birmingham	3 (3.5%)	15 (14.0%)
Outside Birmingham	10 (11.8%)	14 (13.1%)

Proportion of neighbourhood marriages in a low status area:
    working class (69) 62.3%
    white collar (46) 37.0%
Proportion of neighbourhood marriages in a high status area:
    working class (14) 50.0%
    white collar (58) 27.6%

ST GEORGE'S, EDGBASTON

	Husband in elite occupation	Husband is white collar
Total sample	86	62
Giving same address	6 (7.0%)	11 (17.7%)
Others	80	51
Living in same street	0	3 (5.9%)
Elsewhere in same neighbourhood	17 (21.3%)	11 (21.6%)
Same or adjoining suburb	19 (23.8%)	17 (33.3%)
Elsewhere in Birmingham	13 (16.3%)	8 (15.7%)
Outside Birmingham	31 (38.8%)	12 (23.5%)

Notes
a. Each of the categories relates to the distance between the addresses of bride and groom. For instance, 'Outside Birmingham' means that one lives in the parish in question, the other outside the city; 'Elsewhere in neighbourhood' means that the couple live in the same neighbourhood, but in different streets, and so on.
b. Birmingham is defined as the present Birmingham district (excluding Sutton Coldfield) together with Smethwick.
c. The 'neighbourhood' is defined as an area of less than half a mile squared, not crossed by a railway, waterway or major road, or broken up by a park or belt of factories.
d. Weddings where both bride and groom gave the same address have had to be excluded from the analysis. A number of reasons have been suggested for this practice, and it is impossible to tell which applies in any given case: that the couple were co-habiting at the time of marriage; that they lived in different flats in the same tenement block or lodging-house; that the groom had lodged with his fiancée's parents prior to marriage; or that they were claiming to live in the same parish in order to avoid paying twice for the reading of the banns.

Table 2.3: Church attendances in London as a percentage of estimated population, 1886-7 and 1902-3

1886-7				
	C of E	RC	Others	Total
City of London	42.5	0.1	24.7	67.4
Elite areas	21.3	5.5	9.5	36.3

	C of E	RC	Others	Total
White collar suburbs	16.9	1.4	14.9	33.3
Other suburbs	11.2	2.0	12.4	25.6
Inner ring	6.9	2.6	10.8	20.2
Metropolitan London	13.5	2.8	12.2	28.5

1902-3

	C of E	RC	Others	Total
City of London	41.6	–	47.3	88.9
Elite areas	14.1	3.8	8.4	26.3
White collar suburbs	10.1	1.4	12.5	24.1
Other suburbs	8.2	1.6	9.4	19.1
Inner ring	6.0	2.0	10.5	18.5
Metropolitan London	9.4	2.1	10.5	22.0

Sources: *British Weekly,* 5 November 1886-17 December 1886, 13-20 January 1888; R. Mudie-Smith, *The Religious Life of London,* Hodder & Stoughton, London, 1904.

The City of London was largely depopulated, but still contained some central churches and chapels. 'Elite areas' are defined as those metropolitan boroughs (Hampstead, St Marylebone, Westminster, Kensington, Paddington, Chelsea) with more than 50 indoor domestic servants per 100 households in 1901, together with Holborn. 'White collar suburbs' are those boroughs (except for Hampstead) where more than 8 per cent of occupied males were clerks in 1901: Stoke Newington, Lewisham, Camberwell, Hackney, Wandsworth, Lambeth. 'Other suburbs' comprise Fulham, Hammersmith, St Pancras, Islington, Deptford, Greenwich, Woolwich, and 'Inner ring' consists of Stepney, Poplar, Bethnal Green, Shoreditch, Finsbury, Southwark, Bermondsey. For fuller details of these censuses and of methods used in estimating population, see McLeod, *Class and Religion in the Late Victorian City,* chapter 2.

Table 2.4: Church attendances in Liverpool as a percentage of population, 1851-1912

	C of E	RC	Others	Total
1851	12.8	14.0	10.0	36.8
1881	9.8	11.3	12.1	33.2
1891	11.1	11.6	11.1	33.8
1902	9.7	11.3	9.5	30.5
1912	7.8	12.3	8.8	28.9
1902				
Abercromby	13.7	12.2	17.5	43.4
Garston	15.7	12.9	9.8	38.4

	C of E	RC	Others	Total
White collar suburbs	10.4	9.0	12.0	31.4
Working class: mainly Protestant	8.4	7.7	9.1	25.3
Working class: mainly Catholic	7.5	29.4	7.4	44.2
1912				
Abercromby	11.3	17.4	18.6	47.3
Garston	15.1	8.9	6.4	30.5
White collar suburbs	7.4	8.3	8.7	24.4
Working class: mainly Protestant	6.6	8.9	6.9	22.4
Working class: mainly Catholic	6.2	37.3	2.9	46.4

Sources: 1851 *Religious Census,* manuscript returns (Public Record Office, H.O. 129); (for comparability with later censuses, attendances at afternoon services and by Sunday scholars have been excluded); *Liverpool Daily Post,* 15 November 1881, 24 November 1891, 11 November 1902, 13 December 1912; *Catholic Times,* 30 October 1891, 20 December 1912. Because the *Liverpool Daily Post* only counted one mass, average attendances at all masses have been taken from the latter paper: for 1881 and 1891 figures for each church are available; for 1902 and 1912 a total for the city is given, and this I have had to distribute according to the average ratio of attendances at 11 o'clock mass to those at all masses. The units used are the Liverpool sub-registration districts as they were in 1912.

Abercromby was an area of declining population, including the 'West End', some of the 'central business district' and many of the central churches and chapels. Garston includes some of the wealthiest suburbs.
'White collar suburbs' are those in which more than 20% of a sample of householders with occupations listed in *Gore's Liverpool Directory, 1912,* were in white collar jobs: Toxteth East, West Derby East, Wavertree, Walton.
'Working class: mainly Protestant' comprises Everton, Kirkdale, West Derby West, Toxteth; and 'mainly Catholic' comprises Exchange and Scotland. (Exchange also included part of the central area.)
Because of the extension of the city boundaries in 1895 and 1902, the figures for 1891 and 1902 are not strictly comparable. The only suburban district to be included in both counts was Toxteth East, and the ratio there of attendances to population was: 1891, 37.9%; 1902, 36.2%; 1912, 26.9%.

3 SOCIETY, STATUS AND JINGOISM: THE SOCIAL ROOTS OF LOWER MIDDLE CLASS PATRIOTISM, 1870-1900

Richard N. Price

Those who have examined late-nineteenth-century jingoism would mostly agree that the phenomenon was appalling, excessive and puzzling; but no adequate explanation, no analytical understanding of its significance and meaning has yet been provided. Jingoism has been seen as an aberration, a regressive mutation that emerged from the resurgence of primitive and primeval forces. As a consequence, jingoism and the patriotic conservatism of which it was a part, have been analytically wrenched from the social world out of which they grew and transported into the mists of social psychology. This is particularly evident in the large body of contemporary literature that tried to explain jingoism. One commentator, for example, argued that jingoism was a result of the 'new mode' of raising children by sparing the rod, adulating their every action and granting their slightest wish. The behaviour of the jingo crowds was childish and exhibitionist: thus, the explanation must lie in their collective childhoods. It is difficult to imagine precisely who this author had in mind. There is no evidence that working class families were proto-Spockian at this period and he can only mean, therefore, the children of the middle and upper classes. It is indeed probable that the practice of child-rearing was changing but as an explanation of jingoism it is patently absurd.[1] By implication, however, such an analysis does focus on one central fact to which we shall return: that modes of behaviour were changing and that mass phenomena like jingoism must be seen in this context. One looks in vain for such an implication in the works of those incomparably superior thinkers, John Hobson and J. M. Robertson.

Both these men, being Liberals of the radical stripe, believed jingoism signified the welling to the surface of the primitive passions of man's innermost tribal nature. To Robertson, the nation's involvement in the South African War was the territorial tribalism of the Jago's Ranns and Learys writ large.[2] Hobson, following very closely the analysis of *The Crowd* by Gustave Le Bon, saw jingoism as 'a collective or mob passion which . . . makes the individual mind subject to a control that joins him irresistably to his fellows.'[3] Militarism and imperialism could be partly explained by the breakdown of 'civilised' values, and the supremacy of 'malice, passion, and pride.'[4]

But Robertson and Hobson were not shallow, superficial men even when analysing jingoism; nor were they totally unaware of the concrete basis for jingoism in the development of late-nineteenth-century society. Their analytical myopia lay in their Liberalism. For in spite of the considerable contributions both men made to the analysis of Imperialism, they remained classic Whigs when it came to democracy. As Liberals, they believed in the rule of a 'civilised,' 'cultured' and educated elite. For both men the sin of the imperial interest groups was that they manipulated public opinion in such a way as to threaten to open the floodgates of 'the abyss' and allow the uncivilised, uninformed masses to influence rational discussion and policy making.[5] 'No one,' Hobson wrote, 'seriously pretends [that the jingoism of the masses] is based upon any information or understanding of the actual issues. The ebullition of passion there is merely temperamental violence, without any real sub-stratum of intellectual conviction.'[6] It was not the actual jingoism of the masses that worried these men but the fact that if the masses were allowed to 'play the fool' on this issue who could tell where it would stop?

It would be a disservice, however, to deliver a totally negative judgement on these thinkers. They did not understand the meaning of jingoism because they only faintly plumbed its social structural context; their Liberalism viewed the people as 'masses' to be ruled and controlled. Paradoxically, it was this presumption that gives their analysis of imperialism its lasting, if one-sided, value. In pointing to the control of the organs of government and the media by those whose economic interest lay in consolidating the Empire, they rightly recognised the emergence of techniques of social control by modern elites. Whether the 'manipulation' of public sentiment was, or is, as easy as they assumed remains, of course, contentious. But the recognition that imperialism could serve to divert attention from domestic interests made their analyses pertinent and important. A jingo consensus in the country undoubtedly served the interests of late-nineteenth-century British capitalism in the struggle to retain its world economic role.

It was, however, mistaken to argue from this that jingoism as a vague and broad political ideology and as an expression of priorities and values was an irrationality. And it was a further misconception to argue that those who embraced jingoism were puppets responding to the manipulative tugs of the evil genie who created public opinion. It is the contrary case that will be argued here; for I want to suggest that the relevance of jingoism can only be understood by recognising that it was a response to social pressures and changes that marked the 1890s. But it must be emphasised at the outset that our focus is on the lower middle classes and them alone; the same kinds of explanations may not suffice for jingoists in other social groups, although the framework of analysis might very well be the same. Jingoists were to be found among all classes and we are not suggesting that only lower middle class groups were jingoes, although my suspicion is that they tended to be more susceptible to the appeals of jingoism than others. It is a lot easier, for example, to point to direct evidence of lower middle class patriotism in this period than to almost any other group. The presence of 'clerks' is noted in many of the outbursts of jingo hooliganism, and not only in the nineties; the spontaneous, patriotic demonstrations in the Stock Exchange on the occasion of the reliefs of Ladysmith and Mafeking; the disproportionate numbers of clerks in the volunteer regiments for the Boer War; all of this, and more, has been documented elsewhere and there is no need to repeat it here.[7] Whatever its quantitative extent, lower middle class jingoism was manifest, visible and widespread. And it is the reasons for this that we have to explain.

Let us start in a roundabout way with an analogy which some will find dangerous, even foolhardy. There is much in the concrete manifestations of jingoism, especially in its crowd form, that reminds us of a 'charivari'. The essence of charivari, as Natalie Davis and others have shown, is the collective assertion of values or a morality that has been violated or transgressed.[8] It involved the humiliation or mockery of its victims, and was the collective voice of those who generally went unheard. The parallels with jingo outbursts are interesting. In the first place, the very word 'jingo' establishes a linguistic continuity with the seventeenth century: the word had been a part of conjuror's gibberish and had lain dormant for 150 years before it was revived to describe the seemingly irrational crowds of the late 1870s.[9] In addition, jingoism had its saturnalian (the word is often used) side. All the London suburbs had their patriotic processions complete with bunting, floats, bright lights and flags in celebration of the victories in spring 1900.[10] The structure of the Mafeking Night crowds contained parallels with the forms of pre-industrial, patrician-sponsored sports and customs. In the City sovereigns were thrown to the crowds. From the West End balconies, the upper classes 'cheer as they were cheered. "Duke's son, cook's son . . . " all swung together in a democracy which will never be again.'[11] It is this element of carnivality that distinguishes jingo crowds from other 'reactionary' crowd actions like the Church and King mobs. And finally, and most powerfully, jingoism, like charivari, was socially and politically conservative. Both were concerned to re-assert a system of values that was breaking down or being threatened by external and internal enemies.[12]

But I would not wish to assert the jingo-charivari analogy too rigorously. I am fully aware of the clear differences between them. The social context was obviously different. Charivari was rooted in the tight societies of the villages, jingoism was an urban phenomenon. The targets of charivari were often those who had made marriages violative of moral tradition, the jingo targets were those who were thought to have made unpopular political choices. Jingoists did not legitimise their actions by appealing to a long-established framework of traditional behaviour. And jingo crowd actions did not have the ritualised forms of the charivari, although it would be a mistake to overlook the ritualistic elements that tended to recur. The soft, felt hat, for example, which approximated to the Boer slouch hat, was frequently taken as an 'enemy' identification mark.

But with these qualifications in mind, there is a sense in which a conceptual parallel between lower middle class jingoism and charivari is useful. Both phenomena were examples of what can happen when a section of society feels that the rules by which it lives are being violated or destroyed. And in the 1890s two broad currents climaxed to beleaguer the lower middle classes and help make a call to patriotic tradition appealing. On the one hand, the mid-Victorian framework of respectable morality was crumbling and, on the other hand, there was the crystallisation of socio-economic trends that sharpened the status anxieties and insecurities of the lower middle classes.

The decade of the 1890s was a climacteric to the 'late-Victorian revolt'. The hegemonical values of mid-Victorian respectability were clearly on the defensive, if not in steep decline. And although the beginnings of this dissolution can be clearly traced to the 1870s it was in the nineties that things noticeably began to come apart. Fundamental to the replacement of Certainty with Doubt was the changing role of Britain in the world economy. The challenge to Britain's world role not only caused people to look again at conventional assumptions about the organisation of society but also necessitated changes in values that were traditionally sacred. Unemployment, for example, could no longer be looked at as a *moral* issue: it involved the wastage of human labour that could be of vital importance in the struggle between the economic giants of the world. But of more immediate importance was the challenge to 'Victorian' morality and the concept of Respectability.

What this challenge involved, in its essentials, was the breakdown of the moral consensus that had emerged out of the evangelical middle classes in the earlier part of the century. The verities of religious faith, if not the form of that faith, were not only being questioned but were undergoing wholesale abandonment.[13] The challenge to 'respectable behaviour' was being made on all fronts, and the techniques of the challenge ranged from the scientific enquiry of a Havelock Ellis through the courageous, if foolish, confrontation of an Oscar Wilde. The concern with sexual and marital morality touched the respectable code of social behaviour at perhaps its most sensitive point; for whatever the ultimate message of works like *The Woman Who Did*, they clearly contained the germ of an alternative morality.[14] And, at the very least, they pointed up the moral insecurity of the decade.

Those sections of society who were beginning to abandon traditional moral standards as guides to social and family behaviour can be more easily identified than those who still retained a conviction of the importance of traditional respectability. But contemporary observers—who were very sensitive to shifts in popular moods—strongly imply that traditional morality was slowly and surely retreating into its strongholds among the burgeoning lower middle classes. Until we uncover more hard social facts about this group such a proposition can be only tentatively suggested. But, to argue from a surer foothold, it is clear that in terms of the 'paraphernalia of gentility' and respectability the lower middle class were making considerable strides and the differential between the lower and middle sections of the middle class was narrowing. By the 1860s 'the non-productiveness which had for long been the hallmark of the lady was spreading down into all but the lowest ranks of the middle class,' and from the seventies 'in comparison with the lower middle classes, the better-off sections of society were faced with a greater struggle to maintain and extend the differential standard.'[15]

The differentiation of the suburbs, the growth of villadom, the availability of mortgages all bore testimony to lower middle class achievement of status and respectability.[16] But the prospect of a solid niche in society for this marginal group was becoming a reality just at the very time when the values always associated with that achievement were under severe attack. It is surely no coincidence, therefore, that villadom (and however loosely defined the context is always lower middle class) is frequently identified as the repository of conventional morality.[17]

As early as the mid-1880s the discrepancy between the theory of respectability and its reality had been accompanied by the observation that:

If English morality could be judged by the standards of morals which exists among the lower section of the middle class, the small shopkeepers and other employees on the same level, there would be no reason not to congratulate ourselves most heartily upon it. Between the lowest class and the professional class there is a happy interspace of virtue.[18]

A decade later, this theme was being developed even more forcefully in an attack upon *The Blight of Respectability* which, it was claimed, fostered—in 'the frowsy atmosphere' of villadom—a hypocritical conservatism. This observer followed our earlier commentator in identifying lower middle class groups as good examples of the 'Respectables.' These people, he argued, 'are the censors of genius, the founders of public taste, the friends of morality . . . Every little shallow, mean-sided Respectable thinks himself capable of deciding that Shelley and Burns were "immoral" . . . British Respectability makes Britain the laughing-stock and butt of wits of the world . . . The Respectables' stupid blatant "patriotism" and bullying arrogance cause us to be hated in all quarters of the world.'[19]

As if to dramatise the loosening bonds of respectable morality, the 1890s saw a revival of a type of crowd activity that had not been seen since the Mohock, Hell-Fire rowdyism of the eighteenth century. One of the most perspicacious observers of the period, pinpointed the changed composition of rowdyism in the last quarter of the century:

The Staffordshire miner, the roughest perhaps of his class, would no longer be represented, even by Punch, as proposing to 'heave half a brick' at a new comer for the offence of having a strange face. As for setting the bull-pup at the parson's little boy, the suggestion is less likely to come . . . from the collier than from the mischievous undergraduate, the son of the collier's employer, who is home for his college vacation.[20]

The London crowd, this same commentator pointed out, from being the most emotional in the world had been socialised into the best conducted and least drunken whose occasional outbursts were nothing:

in comparison with the horseplay of the prosperous gentlemen in glossy, silk hats . . . who, having placed a new rose in their buttonhole, drive . . . to their suburban railway station every morning and who, if a stranger strays into their Stock Exchange deal with that unfortunate person as an Epsom mob treats a welsher.[21]

Rowdyism in the nineties came to be firmly identified with 'parading groups of young men in Inverness capes . . . who threw sovereigns about, and were celebrated in such songs as Leicester Square, [and] The Rowdy-Dowdy Boys . . . foolish youths . . . with no invention and less wit'.[22]

The significance of the new, middle class rowdyism lay in its deliberate hostility to 'respectability.' It consciously aimed to humiliate hypocrisy, gentility, and sedateness; and, at times, as during the Empire riot of 1894, it physically attacked the symbols of kill-joy propriety in its desire to establish the new moral freedom.[23] The jingo crowd was moved by precisely the opposite *mentalité* to that of the Empire crowd, but the presence of both kinds of rowdyism illustrates the breakdown in traditional values during the nineties. The purpose of the Empire crowd was to flout defiantly traditional respectability; the purpose of the jingo crowd was to assert, through patriotism, the good old values. Jingoism was the expression of a political morality and value system which briefly tried to halt the disintegration of social and political conventions by demanding the creation of a national patriotic consensus. The jingo crowd was concerned to enforce this consensus.

Although the 'scramble for Africa' was grounded in the demands and needs of competitive imperialism and, as such, was a necessary response to the economic well-being of British capitalism, the political rhetoric that justified imperial expansion was in general devoid of a clear expression of the rational needs and interests of the country. The need for an aggressive foreign policy in the Near East in the late 1870s, for example, was justified to the public in terms of self-interest and traditional influence; and the debate that ensued was one that had clear political, even class, dimensions. But the characteristic concepts of the jingo rhetoric in the nineties were mystical by comparison and cut across class, party and economic boundaries. Appeals to British rights that were never defined, to inherent British superiority that was never explained, to British valour that was extolled above all other virtues were not only unanswerable as Hobson and others realised, but were the necessary adjuncts of the popular political ideology that accompanied foreign policy in the period. In part, this consensus was created and represented by the new, mass-circulation and inter-class newspapers that found a reading public in the 1890s and especially by the *Daily Mail.*

It cannot be doubted that the prime target of the *Mail* was the lower middle class, although other groups were not excluded; the whole tone of the newspaper reeks of the concerns of villadom. The presence of cycling columns, fashion columns, home hints columns; the suggested menus with their invitation to be daring yet economical in cooking; marketing information on best buys of vegetables; all assume a readership which has time for leisure and status accoutrements, which is not without some domestic help but which is intimately involved in the realities of making ends meet. The newspaper's jingoism was renowned; its jingo rhetoric quintessential: of the potential re-conquest of the Sudan, it remarked 'a little blood letting is good for a nation that tends to excess of luxury'.[24] But the *Mail's* jingoism had a message. When it drew the analogy between the avaricious designs of Germany on Transvaal gold and the 'ingenuity and industry' of the German clerk who slaves 'to oust an Englishman from a situation' it forged a link between foreign and domestic threats which addressed itself directly to the problems of the large body of London clerks.[25] Through the tangled skein of such connections, jingoism ceased to be rhetoric and attained a reality and meaning that should not be underestimated.

The need for a national patriotic consensus to meet the growing threats to economic ascendancy and also to overcome internal divisions and problems was a constant theme of the nineties. Sir Walter Besant might regret the failure to fly the flag in the East End, and lament that love of country and Empire was not an explicit part of school curricula, but the fact was that imperial ideology and culture were all-pervasive. This was especially true in the life of the young whose school history books were arguing the necessity of subordinating class and individual interests to the sacred trust of Empire, whose popular magazines and books were full of the deeds of imperial valour, and whose organised recreations revolved around militarism and the flag.[26] As early as 1891 an Imperial Patriotic League had argued that the solution to economic competition lay in patriotically 'buying British.'[27] And at least one strike of clerks was broken in part because an appeal was made to their 'patriotic duty'—an appeal that was received with cheering.[28] In this sense patriotic unity was the conservative version of socialist collectivism that was gaining popularity as an answer to economic inefficiency. Patriotism argued for a collectivism of spirit and sacrifice for the nation and against the selfish individualism of the Little Englanders who refused to be subsumed in the unity of a national consensus:

> To appeal to the patriotism of the nation is one of the Jingo's objects in domestic policy. He realises quite plainly that the people must be educated to believe in their country and to be ready to make personal sacrifice for her.[29]

And the *Daily Mail* made a similar point on the results of the 1900 Election:

> Little Englandism has fallen because it supposed that the people of England were selfish . . . Imperialism has won because . . . it has been able to appeal to that instinct of unselfishness which leads men to . . . subordinate the petty desire for material comfort to the commands of duty.[30]

The ideal of a patriotic consensus never appealed much to the working classes. But for others, patriotic conservatism provided an opportunity to respond to the challenges that had been made against traditional morality and, as such, it struck a responsive chord amongst those who felt the greatest need to assert and be reassured of their own respectability. For the call for a patriotic unity (jingoism) which would sacrifice self to nation represented a new conservative political respectability and morality; and the jingo crowds (in which lower middle classes often played a leading role) acted as the enforcers of this new morality. It is in this sense then that the 'charivari' dimension of jingoism lies and it is in this sense also that jingoism can be seen as a rational, deliberate, and purposeful phenomenon. It is not sufficient, however, to explain lower middle class jingoism merely in terms of the decline of respectability. Beyond this lay the far more fundamental elements of social status, status anxiety, and the socio-economic pressures that typically afflicted lower middle class existence. In the 1890s such pressures were acute enough to provide the necessary social context for patriotic conservatism to breed and flourish.

The central fact of lower middle class life was the necessity to balance the obligatory accoutrements of status with the realities of economic marginality. 'Be our ideas ever so humble, it was still necessary to keep a certain standard of life. It would never do to let Mrs Brown think that we dined on lentils and porridge . . . how might Nell go forth shopping if the perambulator had a shabby hood?' asked Robert Thorne in Shan Bullock's novel of a London clerk.[31] At the very time that Thorne was pondering the essence of the lower middle class dilemma, over fifty per cent of clerks earned less than thirty-one shillings a week, and their position was worsening.[32] I shall make no apology in what follows for concentrating on the clerk as a representative example of the lower middle classes. There is a wealth of material known about them, they are universally recognised to be archetypal lower middle class workers, and they were, perhaps, the fastest growing occupational group of the period. Clerks, of course, were not a homogeneous group. There was a well-developed economic and social hierarchy which represented the increasing division of white collar labour and which, by its rigidity, intensified the status dilemma and anxieties of the group.[33] The highest paid earned £500 per annum and up, but such salaries were few and far between and with these people we are not concerned. The range of earnings was always great: dock clerks earned on average 24 shillings per week in the 1890s and in the 1870s £70 to £90 per annum was not an unusual wage.[34] But the general position is clear and well recognised; as Booth pointed out there was no difference between the artisan and the clerk in economic terms but a world of difference socially.[35]

The relationship between economic insecurity and the necessity to preserve their status position was a constant feature of lower middle class life, although the problems in preserving this balance became progressively more difficult. As early as the 1850s the necessity for a salary commensurate with status necessities was being argued in terms that were to change little over the next fifty years:

> Can it ... be reasonably expected, or even considered reasonable, that a man thus stationed should be quite content to marry with the ... certainty ... that his wife must be in the position of a mere domestic servant.[36]

'How then,' it was being asked in the late seventies, 'is a man to live and keep a wife on this miserable pittance, [of 30 shillings a week] and, at the same time dress decently?'[37] But earlier in the century the status necessities of lower middle class existence tended to be defended in terms of the superior kind of work that clerks did and their importance in job opportunity: 'We know that one of the capital sins charged upon clerks is the "appearance" they make in comparison to their means; but considered as a pecuniary speculation it pays as often as not.'[38] By the end of the century and beyond, however, 'appearance' took on a more ominous social significance. It represented the 'small margin of safety which my parents struggled to maintain between their respectable little home and the hungry ocean of violence whose thunder never left our ears'.[39] And Shan Bullock's London clerk soon learned that 'appearance' involved no advantage in terms of opportunities for promotion; rather, it served the purpose of social demarcation, of

> making the best show we could. The brass knocker, the bay window, the dining and drawing room, establish the fact ... that already we

had in view the great suburban ideal of being superior to the people next door.[40]

Both those above and those below them in the social scale helped to define the status-consciousness of the lower middle classes. It is this position in the vacuum between middle and working classes that helps to explain the curious ambiguity that pervaded lower middle class attitudes toward social mobility. The proximity in geography, income, and often origins to the working classes served to remind of the perils that awaited slippage down the social scale. Richard Church has described the 'intensity of the mood of thrift' that characterised his mother's determination to pay the mortgage on the house, buy a new piano or bicycle for the children. But he was unsure as to her final aim: 'Perhaps ... she was trying to draw her little household up to a [higher] standard of living ... Maybe [and note this is put as an alternative] she was propelled from behind ... by the spectacle of the ... grandparents in their squalid rooms.'[41] When they looked down, lower middle class people aspired to achieve a safer position on the social and economic pyramid, at least for their children. But when they looked up they also felt distinctly uneasy: 'My mother ... had an inferiority complex when she thought she was in the presence of anybody socially higher than herself.'[42] There was an acute awareness of the subtle differences within the middle class and if lower middle class people felt insecure about the seething mass of working classes around them they were equally aware of their insecurity *vis-à-vis* even those only slightly above them:

> They [i.e. a middle class builder's family] lived ... on a slightly higher social plane, they had more money to spend ... whereas we had to look after our coppers. They were probably [and note the hesitant subtlety of the distinctions being drawn] —although we were well dressed they were—better well-dressed if you understand what I mean. Otherwise their ... interests were more or less—much the same as ours but—on a slightly higher social plane.[43]

The net result of this circumspect duality was to heighten the drive for respectability and status but it also engendered an acuter sense of insecurity because of the difficulty of attainment. Thus, children were taught the importance of the 'proper' behaviour that was believed to characterise the upper social levels. The quality of men was defined by 'speech, behaviour, and dress'; sons were taught to raise their caps (and this was different from the working classes who, compelled to exhibit outward respect, merely *touched* their caps); the discipline and manners of the house were governed by what was known, or thought, to be done in 'nice households'; and security of employment was valued more highly than good pay.[44]

But none of this altered the reality that lower middle class clerks were marginal men tenaciously holding on to what they had but uncertain of their ability to climb the social ladder. An exaggerated assertion of middle classness by an insistence on the appearances and behaviour of a 'gentleman' had the effect of distancing them from the working classes without bringing them any nearer to the secure, stable middle classes. It did not, moreover, bring any respect from either the working or the upper reaches of the middle class. In fact, it had the opposite effect on the working class whose contempt for unmanly paper work was confirmed and legitimised by the pretension of appearance that characterised lower middle class life.

This statement of the economic and status dilemma of the lower middle classes is, to some extent, timeless. We can find, for example, echoes of the late nineteenth century ridicule of clerks in Albert Smith's ironic look at 'the gents' of the 1840s whose fundamental characteristic he defined as a 'constant wearing struggle to appear something more than we in reality are'.[45] And the position of low-level white collar workers today must be, in Britain at least, as fraught with fears and insecurities as it ever was.[46] But there are peculiarities to different periods: distinct elements combine to sharpen or blunt the status problems of the group and to pose new choices as to how these problems can be resolved. The 1890s was, I believe, such a period of crisis and choice when some new factors fused with older established trends to form a potent combination which can help us interpret and understand the character of lower middle class jingoism and patriotic conservatism.

In *The History of Mr Polly,* H. G. Wells has a long statement on the pathetic futility of lower middle class life-styles and aspirations. His remarks typify the combination of contempt and pity which characterised the image of the class in the later part of the century. Wells, who was certainly well-qualified to comment in this area (and, incidentally, was living proof that mobility was possible), was referring particularly to the small-shopkeeping class. But there is a relevance in his sensitive indictment of this group that extends to the whole class:

> Nothing can better demonstrate the collective dullness of our community, the crying need for an intellectual revival than the consideration of that vast mass of useless, uncomfortable, under-educated,

under-trained and altogether pitiable people we contemplate when we use that inaccurate and misleading term, the Lower Middle Class ... Essentially, their lives are failures, not the sharp and tragic failures of the labourer who gets out of work and starves, but a slow, chronic process of consecutive small losses which may end if the individual is exceptionally fortunate in an impoverished death bed before actual bankruptcy or destitution supervenes.[47]

Robert Thorne, Shan Bullock's London clerk, soon came to see the justice of the ridicule and contempt to which clerks were subjected by those below and above them. Reflecting a common accusation that clerking was unmanly, Thorne bitterly characterised his class as 'a small breed. We aren't real men. We don't do men's work ... No wonder bricklayers and omnibus drivers have contempt for us. We haven't even health.'[48] And to escape from this dilemma Thorne emigrated to New Zealand to work on a farm.

In addition, the increasingly suburban character of the Pooter lifestyle provided another target for those critics of respectability who during the nineties treated villadom as a synonym for hypocrisy.[49] But the 'respectability' of the clerk had not always been an object of ridicule. Until the last quarter of the century, 'respectability' had, on the whole, been recognised as the natural accompaniment of the job. In one of the earliest statements of the problems of the clerk, there is no hint of the status dilemmas that were to plague the nineties; the emphasis is on the intelligence and educated character of most clerks. Close parallels were drawn (and this was a common theme) between the work of clerks and their employers which established a similarity in status; and although the parlous economic situation of many clerks is lamented, the argument for more money is based upon the implicit assumption that clerks *were* superior.[50]

By the 1870s after a decade of expansion in the white collar sector, the descriptive tone of the clerks' predicament was more ambiguous. The distinctiveness of the clerk's work, their industry and morality were still argued, but in addition is the emergence of resentment at their pretension. B. G. Orchard, who wrote an interesting sociological analysis of Liverpool clerks, quotes an employer as saying:

They call themselves their masters' equals, and demand recognition as such. And in dress, assumption, everything within their power, they follow this up, affording themselves much gratification and realising substantial advantage from the nature of their vassalage ...

let them [then] consider this as a part of their remuneration.[51]

The image, role and function of the clerk were undergoing a wholesale re-evaluation. Just at the time when clerking was being flooded with new recruits, emphasis began to be placed less on the desirability of a liberal education, or indeed, on education itself (it was one of Orchard's complaints that educated men were performing ill-paid, lowly tasks) but instead on the need for a 'professionalisation' of clerical work. What this meant was, on the one side, a style of work discipline and moral behaviour that encouraged servility, and, on the other, fresh insecurities in terms of the work situation.

The first handbook for clerks, published in 1878, firmly linked clerkly 'respectability' with the demands of work discipline. The clerk, it was argued, must acquire 'patience, perseverance, courtesy, cheerfulness, and perhaps more than any other quality, a humble distrust of self and a deferential respect for the judgement of others' because the ability to perform routine clerical work is 'wholly incompatible with impatience, indolence or nervous agitation of the mind.'[52] To cultivate these qualities required the adoption of a life-style full of the 'rational recreations' and 'uplifting' experiences that were increasingly outmoded in the culture of the late nineteenth century. It was argued, for example, that clerks should shun the theatre because of the type of society to be found there, that habitual novel-reading was 'as hurtful to the mind ... as habitual dram-drinking is to the body'. But, significantly, among those recreations that were recommended for clerks was participation in the Volunteers. A certain kind of artificially respectable behaviour was also mandated: clothing must be 'quiet and unassuming' because it denoted 'a becoming modesty of mind'; and eccentric, individualist, manners or speech patterns were to be eschewed as 'provocative of contempt'.[53]
At a time, then, when many of the middle classes of society were actively abandoning the conventions of mid-Victorian morality, and questioning the relationship between personal character and social behaviour, the link was being forcefully reasserted for large sections of the lower middle classes. If the clerk, therefore, behaved with an exaggerated sense of his own 'respectability' this was not merely a reflection of his marginal class position but also a function of the ideology of their work culture—an ideology that was often imposed in formal sets of rules. Thus, in some banks, marriage was forbidden to clerks earning less than £150 per year because they would not be able to live like gentlemen. And the Southern Railway's conditions of service insisted that employees must have led a blameless life before joining the com-

Society, Status and Jingoism 103

pany, while indecorous behaviour off duty was punishable by instant dismissal.[54]

Before the 1870s it had not been necessary to defend the dignity and superiority of clerical work. In the old counting-house days clerks were often socially mobile and, at a time when it was a mark of distinction to write fluently, they were a relatively literate and educated group.[55] But the Elementary Education Act of 1870, the vast growth in the commercial sector, the dramatic increase of jobs for clerks, and the increasingly specialised division of labour—which was based on the new technology of office work—changed all that.[56] Clerks began to face the same kinds of problems and dangers as other workers but in the context of an ideology of work and status that created a constant tension between the objective reality and subjective perceptions of their situation. It is to the resultant change in the work situation of the clerk in the post-1870 world that we must now turn our attention.

After 1870 the structure of the clerical labour market underwent an important transformation. The low wages that had been a characteristic of clerical work before the 1870s were a reflection of the willing surrender of income to status. But after 1870, poor pay was more a function of the over-supply of white collar labour and the looming spectre of unemployment which threatened *both* income and status. It is, of course, impossible to estimate the exact degree of either phenomenon. The most we can do for the present is point to the constant references to the problem to suggest its extent and use fragmentary evidence to illustrate its dimensions. An advertisement for a clerk at £1 per week in the late eighties, for example, drew five hundred applications.[57] As early as 1873 it was claimed that clerks were suffering from the same kind of unemployment as the manual working class.[58] But whatever the precise extent of unemployment and oversupply, it is certain that the expansion in clerical employment (an expansion which was undoubtedly encouraged by the 1870 Education Act) resulted in new kinds of insecurities and vulnerabilities for clerks. It is significant, for example, that over-supply and unemployment produce the first discussions of the desirability of regulating the labour market— preferably in a gentlemanly way in cooperation with employers but, if necessary, by unionisation.[59]

In addition to the fears of being subject to the vagaries of market forces, there came the recognition that the whole nature of the clerk's relationship with employers was changing. Here, of course, we enter an area of intangibles and the most we can do is make intelligent speculation. But from the 1870s, a note of distinct ambiguity begins to dominate the discussion of employee-employer relations. It was still possible to argue that a special relationship existed (Booth was arguing in this way as late as 1897) but it was increasingly obvious that the economic relationship was fundamental and overriding. Complaints began to be made that employers deliberately bought the cheapest labour in spite of the crucial role clerks were traditionally believed to play in the prosperity or failure of business.[60] And by 1888 it was admitted, at least in the most 'advanced' circles, that 'the relations between employers and clerks have altered in the last decade . . . They have in fact become modernised, and they are now purely a matter of business.'[61]

By the 1890s these problems were becoming particularly acute and especially the question of an overstocked labour market. Not only was clerical work 'one of the readiest modes of earning a living which can be adopted by those lacking education'[62] but two sources of labour in particular began to attract attention: the German clerk and women. As early as the late seventies the threat from the German clerk had been noted, but by the nineties the phenomenon had become something of an obsession—although it was sometimes claimed that the threat was much overrated. Certainly the image of hundreds of Germans invading Britain to gain commercial experience, learn British commercial secrets, and under-cut British clerks was a vivid and recurring one.[63] And this image, as was indicated earlier, provided fertile ground for the aggressive patriotism of jingo politicians and newspapers.

The competition from women was more serious and exemplifies the real pressures to which lower middle class men were exposed during the nineties. Although the employment of women in the clerical sector began in the 1880s, the full impact was not felt until the nineties. Between 1891 and 1901 women increased from 5 to 11 per cent of the clerical labour force.[64] On a more intimate level, the Accounts Department of the Post Office Savings Bank had seen, in one decade, fifty percent of the jobs turned over to women. In the telegraphy department, too, a similar trend could be detected.[65] The sentiments of the men were well expressed by an editorial in *The Office* which curtly asserted that 'woman is entering too much in the field of labour where the man ought to be',[66] home was the proper place for women. At times, the issue was sharp enough to produce direct unrest, as was the case at the Post Office Savings Bank in early 1891. It had been rumoured for some time that the authorities planned to replace the men with women; and, in October 1890 a meeting of clerks was held to protest the favouritism reputedly being shown to female employees. When complaints were made to departmental heads, certain men were victimised. The issue boiled over in January 1891 when the men spontaneously refused to obey an order to work two hours overtime and were promptly locked out. After a strike of one week the men were enticed back to work with the promise that grievances would be investigated at the highest levels.[67]

The increased employment of women posed two major threats to the men; on the one hand, the direct displacement of men fuelled the already substantial fears of unemployment. How much of this there was is not clear, although it was reported to have occurred on a large scale in the City.[68] In addition—and this seems to have been the important issue in the Post Office—the stabilisation or reduction of the male labour force meant that 'their prospects of promotion, as compared with their male colleagues in other departments of the Civil Service is ... considerably less.'[69] The Post Office clerks had reason to be concerned. Since the 1870s the prospects for social mobility had become increasingly elusive and uncertain. Orchard, writing in 1871, had pointed out how infrequently the expectation of mobility had been gratified; a major complaint of the lower-level clerks before the Royal Commission on the Civil Service had been the obstacles to promotion from the lower to the higher grades and unrest on this issue was still apparent in 1909.[70] Houlston's handbook for clerks specifically warned against clerks trying to step out of their station. Of course, we do not yet know how much reality there had ever been to the mobility of clerks up the social scale but it does seem to have been the case that those avenues that might have existed (or were assumed to have existed) were systematically closed off at the latter end of the century. As Lockwood has pointed out, by the late nineteenth century clerks were divided into two classes: those in banking, insurance, and mercantile offices who were able to maintain a middle class standard of life and those, the greater proportion, whose salaries never rose much above that of the artisan. This division implied an increasingly rigid social stratification. The growing 'professional' nature of the work meant that the top managerial positions were suitable jobs for the sons of the upper middle classes. In the railways, for example, promotion slowed down as expansion ceased and amalgamations rationalised the whole system; and, in addition, the higher grades tended to be filled by those with university or public school backgrounds.[71] Similar factors were also operating on the waterfront and provided a stimulus to the unionisation of clerical workers and foremen in the London docks.[72] Furthermore, there was always the reality of *downward* mobility which had been noted by Mayhew and was rediscovered in the 1880s. The docks, always a refuge for the unemployed, received a constant influx of middle-aged shop assistants who had been fired to make room for younger men. And cyclical trade depressions, as Wells pointed out, always destroyed numbers of small shopkeepers.[73] It is not possible to establish with quantifiable accuracy the extent to which these dangers were greater during the later nineteenth century than at earlier periods. But, in the context of the Great Depression, when the fears and tensions of unemployment, oversupply of labour, and scarcity of social mobility opportunities all came together they served to bring to fever pitch the insecurities of such lower middle class groups.

There is one additional factor that must be mentioned in our sketch of the pressures that served to beleaguer the lower middle class during the nineties: the rise of an aggressive, working class movement. With the revival of social unrest in the 1880s, all discussion of social problems and poverty revolved around the working classes. The beginnings of the active involvement of the state in social questions, the official investigations into the structure of working class life, the campaign for Old Age Pensions and the like, all had as their reference points the potentially dangerous labouring classes. Furthermore, the spread of socialist and labour societies that rejected the class mutuality of mid-Victorian political and economic convention, the fierce battles on the industrial relations front, all served to draw attention to the working classes to the inevitable detriment of other groups. Lower middle class sentiment towards these problems is hard to gauge and like much else that has been suggested in this essay needs detailed, specific attention, but the social questions of the time can hardly have served to increase their sense of social and status security. There is some evidence that old-fashioned attitudes towards social problems were strongest amongst the lower middle class; certainly, this would accord both with the work culture of clerks and others and with those observers who saw the suburbs as the bastions of traditional moral conventions.[74] But whatever the case, the point is to suggest that to the lower middle classes it must have seemed as if the advances being made by the working classes bore an inverse relationship to the perils and dangers that surrounded their own plight.

Ultimately, there were two responses that lower middle class groups could present to the forces that in the 1890s were serving to accentuate and reveal their marginal socio-economic status. They could either accept their role as black coated proletarians or they could defensively reassert their differential respectability. In the event, the resolution of this choice was never clear-cut, but it is equally clear that the balance tended more towards the second alternative than the first. This was true even though the early years of the decade saw a flurry of unionisation among white collar groups which extended even to such unlikely candidates as newsagents. Most of these organisations were short-lived and all were very small. And, in a sense, this was surprising given the long history of agitation for better conditions that can be found in the clerk's history from the 1870s.[75] But always, the exhortations to throw aside the artificial flower of 'respectability' fell upon the stony ground of what Bernard Shaw (himself a clerk) termed the highest possible development of the qualities of 'sheepishness . . . docility . . . cowardice'.[76] It is perhaps significant that most of the early union activists were also socialists and, indeed, the contribution of the lower middle class to the early history of the socialist societies was in all probability greater than has yet been realised.[77] In fact, by 1914 some white collar unions were more militant and class conscious than most unions of manual workers. But the uneasy balance between proletarian economics and respectable social status could not be resolved, even for union men. The National Union of Clerks, the clerks' biggest union, which demanded a minimum wage of 35 shillings in 1909 did so within the context of 'respectability': 'The clerk has to appear like a gentleman to pretend to live like a gentleman, and to have the manners of a gentleman.'[78] Indeed, the vocabulary of unionisation illustrates the equivocal, half-hearted recognition of proletarian status; the rhetoric is negative, seldom referring to the rights of labour, but more often to the necessity to assert 'manhood', to throw aside the 'flabby, jelly-fish' attributes of 'gentility'.[79]

We have, inevitably, wandered a long way from jingoism; but this has been necessary in order to show how the patriotic conservatism of the period was related to class structures and status anxieties. We could go further and speculate about jingoism's relationship to the broader social structural and political shifts of the late nineteenth century. The transformation of late-nineteenth-century conservatism, for example, was not only based upon the suburbs but was integral to the emergence of imperialism as a political party issue.[80] And this transformation was a reflection of the expansion of the white collar sector which, in its turn, was a consequence of the increased importance of commercial and financial imperialism after 1870. And the jingo clerks of London—the cogs in the machinery of the export of capital—were, in a vulgar sense, merely acting upon their natural economic interest. But the relationship was not that simple or direct because jingoism was in essence defensive and protective. As far as the lower middle class was concerned, jingoism was a consequence of the tensions and pressures that were created by the expansion of the commercial sector. This expansion destroyed the uniqueness of clerical work, introduced oversupply and unemployment, stimulated a new division of labour, a new office technology, and new kinds of social relations with employers. Thus, imperialism was both the begetter and the albatross of the modern lower middle classes. And jingoism was the result, for the tensions and problems that existed within this section of society made the patriotic message attractive. For these groups patriotism, far from being the last refuge of a scoundrel, was the ultimate assertion of respectability. It was an answer, albeit transient, to the shattering economic, social and cultural attacks that had been directed against the ethics and attainment of respectability. It allowed one to 'belong' not merely in an immediate sense to a crowd group or to the winning side, but also to a code of values that emphasised selfless duty, sacrifice, and obedience (the necessary virtues of the clerk). And, hardly least, it allowed an association, admittedly tenuous, with the presumed beliefs and values of social superiors. In short, patriotism provided one answer to the status insecurities of 'funny little people . . . groping in the dark'[81] to understand forces and pressures which they feared but did not, as yet, know how to control.

Notes

I wish to thank the Northern Illinois University Dean's Fund for a research grant that made the research for this article possible and William Beik and Barbara Price for their useful comments.

1. Francis Freshfield, 'The Development of the Jingo', *Westminster Review*, vol. 154, October 1900, pp. 392-397. On child-rearing see Paul Thompson, *The Edwardians*, Weidenfeld & Nicolson, London, 1974, pp. 300-301.

    Mention should be made of the only attempt by a modern historian to explain jingoism. A. P. Thornton, in *For the File on Empire*, Macmillan, London, 1968, ch. 20, has argued that the roots of jingoism lie both in the self-righteous Liberal belief of Britain's moral and political superiority and in the conservative, romantic vein in the British character that allowed emotive appeals to be made to the collective energy of society. But he views it as a lower class phenomenon, as a 'random emotionalism' and his argument does not explain why jingoism emerged when it did although it may help explain the bi-partisan nature of the thing.
2. 'Most men are still morally and psychologically on the plane of the Middle Ages, with but a veneer of modern science to disguise them.' J. M. Robertson, *Patriotism and Empire*, Grant Richards, London, 1899, pp. 24, 31-35.
3. J. A. Hobson, *The Psychology of Jingoism*, Grant Richards, London, 1901, pp. 9, 17.
4. Robertson, op.cit., p. 71.
5. C. F. G. Masterman, *From the Abyss*, R. B. Johnson, London, 1902, pp. 2, 7.
6. Hobson, op.cit., p. 98.
7. Hugh Cunningham, 'Jingoism in 1877-78,' *Victorian Studies*, vol. XIV, No.

4, June 1971. Richard Price, *An Imperial War and the British Working Class*, Routledge & Kegan Paul, London, 1972, Ch. IV.
8. Natalie Zemon Davis, 'The Reasons of Misrule: Youth Groups and Charivari in Sixteenth Century France,' *Past and Present*, No. 50, February 1971. E.P. Thompson, '"Rough Music": Le Charivari Anglais,' *Annales*, 27 annee, No. 2, March-April 1972.
9. *Oxford English Dictionary*. Holyoake is credited with reviving the word, see Cunningham, op.cit., p. 429.
10. Price, op.cit., pp. 168-169. *Clapham Observer* 17, 24 March, 26 May 1900.
11. Shaw Desmond, *London Nights in the Gay Nineties*, R. M. McBride, New York, 1928, p. 94. Robert W. Malcolmson, *Popular Recreations in English Society, 1700-1850*, Cambridge University Press, Cambridge, 1973. In addition to the portrayal of Mafeking Night as a classless occasion, it is interesting to-note the differences that were frequently drawn with Armistice Night which did not see the 'swollen bull-doggism of Mafeking Night.' And, also, the presence of other symbols of popular rituals such as the Guys of Kruger that were carried around not only by youths but also by 'grey-headed and grey-bearded men.' Thomas Burke, *The Streets of London*, B.T. Batsford, London, 1940, p. 136. There is room for an investigation of the popular political significance of Guy Fawkes rituals in the nineteenth century.
12. In this respect, note Thompson's suggestion of the 'charivari' legacy to Ku Klux Klan lynch law. Thompson, op.cit., p. 308.
13. Hugh McLeod, *Class and Religion in the Late Victorian City*, Croom Helm, London, 1974, p. 246.
14. On this whole question see Peter T.Cominos,'Late Victorian Sexual Respectability and the Social System,'*International Review of Social History*, vol. VIII, Pt.2, 1963. Samuel Hynes, *The Edwardian Turn of Mind*, Princeton University, Press, Princeton, 1968, pp. 182-183 where the argument is made for the ultimately conservative morality of much 1890s literature. Also, as examples of the attack on conventional morality see Grant Allen, 'The New Hedonism,' *Fortnightly Review*, N.S., vol. 55, 1894; H.D.Traill, 'The Abdication of Mrs. Grundy,' *National Review*, vol. XVII, 1891.
15. J.A. and Olive Banks, *Feminism and Family Planning*, Schocken, New York, 1964, p. 83.
16. W.S. Sanders, *The Suburban Homes of London*, London, 1881, for the differentiation of the suburbs. Richard Church's lower middle class parents were buying their own house; see Richard Church, *Over The Bridge*, Dutton, New York, 1956, p. 73.
17. Clapham, with its large lower middle class population, was defined in one authoritative account as the capital of suburbia, T.W.H. Crosland, *The Suburbans*, John Long, London, 1905, p. 79.
18. H. Anstruther White, 'Moral and Merry England,' *Fortnightly Review*, N.S., vol. XXXVIII, July-December 1885, p. 775.
19. Walter Matthew Gallichan, *The Blight of Respectability*, London University Press, 1897, pp. 3, 6, 56.
20. T.H.S. Escott, *Social Transformations of the Victorian Age*, Scribner's, New York, 1897, p. 154.
21. Ibid., p. 155.
22. Burke, op.cit., pp. 134-135.
23. This riot was aimed at the 'violations' of the new moral freedom by the Moral and Social Purity Union and the LCC who had insisted that a screen divide the promenading prostitutes and the stalls at The Empire Theatre; supposedly active in the crowd was Winston Churchill. See Gareth Stedman Jones, 'Working-Class Culture and Working-Class Politics in London, 1870-

1900,' *Journal of Social History*, vol. VII, No. 4, Summer 1974, pp. 495-496; Mrs. Ormiston Chant, *Why We Attacked The Empire*, Marshall & Son, London, 1895; *Christian World*, 1 November 1894, p. 806.
24. Ibid., 22 February 1896, p. 2. See also the comments on Jameson's Raid and Jubilee Day, 24 February 1896, p. 2, 24 June 1897, p. 4.
25. Ibid., 25 February 1896, p. 1.
26. Price, op.cit., p. 130; Valerie Chancellor, *History for their Masters*, A.M. Kelley, New York, 1970, p. 137;J.O.Springhall, 'The Boy Scouts, Class and Militarism in Relation to British Youth Movements,' *International Review of Social History*, vol. XVI, 1971, Pt.2, pp. 127-130, 138-139 where the lower middle class composition of the Boy Scouts is noted.
27. *Evening News and Post*, 18 September 1891, p. 1.
28. *Daily Graphic*, 6 January 1891, p. 8.
29. H.W. Wilson, 'The Policy of Jingoism,' *National Review*, vol. 33, 1898, p. 637. This is the best contemporary statement of the significance of jingoism.
30. 6 October 1900, p. 4.
31. Shan F. Bullock, *Robert Thorne, The Story of a London Clerk*, T. Werner Laurie, London, 2nd ed., 1909, p. 22.
32. David Lockwood, *The Black Coated Worker*, Routledge & Kegan Paul, London, 1958, pp. 43-44.
33. 'Even socially, Men clerks and the Others did not mix much.' Bullock, op. cit., p. 143. 'Clerks, by One of Them,' *Chamber's Journal*, vol. LIV, 8 September 1877, p. 571.
34. *Royal Commission on Labour, 1892-1894*, vol. XXXIV, (C. 6708), 1892, ques. 1459; B.G.Orchard, *The Clerks of Liverpool*, J. Collinson, Liverpool, 1871, pp. 37, 44.
35. Charles Booth, *Life and Labour of the People in London*, Macmillan, 1893, vol. VII, pp. 277-278. It is the social difference that becomes all important when we are dealing with status anxieties. Thus, although there is a fundamental accuracy to Hobsbawm's grouping of the lower middle with the upper working classes when we are concerned with objective social structural shifts, the subjective perceptions of the different classes make that division very important. Eric Hobsbawm, *Labouring Men*, Weidenfeld & Nicolson, London, 1964, pp. 273-274.
36. J.S. Harrison, *The Social Position and Claims of Book-Keepers and Clerks Considered*, London, 1852, p. 7.
37. *The Clerk's Grievance*, Wm. Pole, London, 1878, p. 3.
38. *The City Clerk*, November 1867, pp. 3-4.
39. Church, op.cit., p. 51.
40. Bullock, op.cit., pp. 249-250.
41. Church, op.cit., pp. 73-74.
42. Paul Thompson and Thea Vigne's interviews on *Family Life and Work Experience before 1918*, University of Essex, Interview No. 183, p. 41. I wish to express my gratitude to Paul Thompson and Thea Vigne for kindly allowing me to examine the lower middle class sample of their valuable collection of interviews.
43. Ibid., Interview No. 196, p. 39. The father of this family was a foreman baker and later an insurance agent.
44. Ibid., Interviews No. 4, n.p.; No. 183, p. 56.
45. He also noted that the gent was a natural jingo. Albert Smith, *The Natural History of the Gent*, D. Bogue, London, 1847, pp. 3, 86.
46. The *Guardian*, 22 May 1975, p. 6 for a speech by Anthony Wedgwood Benn on the dangers and problems of white collar unemployment. Note the recent formation of a self-employed association.

Society, Status and Jingoism   111

47. H.G. Wells, *The History of Mr. Polly*, Readers Club Edition, New York, 1941, pp. 199-200.
48. Bullock, op.cit., p. 276.
49. It is interesting to note the close association that was made between clerks and suburban life: 'It has been said by a more or less keen observer that suburban men are all clerks . . . It is more than probable that 75 per cent of the male denizens of suburbia have some business in offices or other places of trade.' Crosland, op.cit., p. 44. This book is one of the best examples of the ridicule poured on suburban life during this period.
50. Harrison, op.cit., p. 4.
51. Orchard, op.cit., p. 54.
52. Houlston's Industrial Library No. 7, *The Clerk. A Sketch In Outline of His Duties and Discipline*, Houlston, London, 1878, p. 16.
53. Ibid., pp. 34, 46.
54. *The Clerk's Journal*, 1 May 1890, p. 1; Charles Edward Parsons, *Clerks, Their Position and Advancement*, London, 1876, pp. 23-25.
55. Lockwood, op.cit., p. 106.
56. Between 1871-1881 numbers of clerks increased by 80.6%. The adoption of Pitman's shorthand, the typewriter, and duplicating machines began to make a real impact during the 1880s. Lee Holcombe, *Victorian Ladies At Work*, Archon Books, Hamden, 1973, pp. 210, 144.
57. Fred Hughes, *By Hand and Brain*, Lawrence & Wishart, London, 1952, p. 13. The Parliamentary Committee of TUC received 1,000 applications in response to an advertisement for a short-hand typist in 1903. The job paid £150 p.a. See V.L. Allen, *The Sociology of Industrial Relations*, Longman, London, 1971, p. 159.
58. *The City Service Gazette*, 8 January 1873, p. 3. For exactly the same argument at the present day see the *Guardian*, loc.cit.
59. On the need for some way to regulate the labour market see *The Clerk's Newspaper*, 14 July 1877; Parsons, op.cit., p. 34; *The City Service Gazette*, loc.cit. Note that it was also at this time that the Civil Service Supply Association was formed as a discount store for clerks and other white collar workers.
60. *City Service Gazette*, loc.cit.
61. *The Clerk's Journal*, 1 September 1888, pp. 1-2.
62. Parsons, op.cit., p. 19.
63. Lockwood, op.cit., p. 26; *Clerk's Journal*, 1 December 1888, p. 12; J.J. Findlay, 'The Genesis of a German Clark,' *Fortnightly Review*, N.S., vol. 66, July-December 1899, pp. 533-536; *The Office*, 15 May 1889, p. 100.
64. Holcombe, op. cit., p. 210.
65. *Daily Graphic*, 8 January 1891, pp. 8-10; *Daily Mail*, 13 February 1897, p. 3.
66. *The Office*, 9 August 1890, p. 169.
67. Ibid., 4 October 1890, p. 265; 10 January 1891, pp. 13-17, 17 January 1891, p. 25; *Daily Graphic*, 5 January 1891, p. 8, 6 January 1891, p. 8, 7 January 1891, p. 10.
68. *The Office*, 9 August 1890, loc.cit.
69. *Daily Graphic*, 7 January 1891, loc.cit.
70. *Civil Service Inquiry Commission*, First Report, (C.1113), 1875, ques. 946-947, 1122, 1146-1147; Bullock, op.cit., p. 144. See also *Capital and Labour*, 26 January 1881, p. 61, for discontent among Post Office telegraphists over barriers to promotion.
71. Lockwood, op.cit., pp. 22-25, 63.
72. *Royal Commission on Labour*, op.cit., ques. 7356.

73. In Liverpool it was claimed that 50% of shop assistants underwent this kind of unemployment. Ibid., vol. XXXIV, (C.6894), 1893-4, ques. 30836-30838.
74. Thus we can note the comment of the lower middle class journal, *The Christian World,* 3 November 1887, p. 1 on the unemployed: '[they] more truly represent the loafers and the so-called "Socialistic" agitators of the metropolis. A deputation to the Board of Works has figured among the incidents of the last few days, but the behaviour of the spokesmen was not such as to command sympathy or respect.' We must not assume, however, a blanket hostility to the working class. It is very probable that in those towns where the social structure tended to homogeneity, with a very small middle class, subtle class distinctions were less significant and the lower middle class in these places tended to identify much more with the working class.
75. *Civil Service Inquiry,* loc.cit.; Booth, op.cit., vol. VIII, pp. 12-13: *The Office,* 5 January 1889, p. 3. As early as 1861 a Clerk's Association had been formed in Liverpool, Orchard, op.cit., p. 4.
76. *The Clerk,* January 1908, p. 7.
77. Hughes, loc.cit. S.G. Hobson was a clerk. On this question see the very suggestive article by Deian Hopkin, 'The Membership of the Independent Labour Party, 1904-10: A Spatial and Occupational Analysis,' *International Review of Social History,* vol. XX, 1975, Pt. 2. Logie Barrow of Kingston Polytechnic has some interesting findings on lower middle class participation in the Clarion Clubs.
78. *The Clerk,* January 1909, p. 4. This wage demand was also designed to preserve the differential with manual labourers. From the early 1890s this element in wage demands appears; see *Royal Commission on Labour,* op.cit., ques. 1491-1492: 'We have to keep up an appearance, and in every way conduct ourselves above the labourer.'
79. *The Clerk's Journal,* 1 September 1890, p. 1.
80. See James Cornford, 'The Transformation of Late-Victorian Conservatism,' *Victorian Studies,* vol. 7, 1963-4. A recent article by Arno Mayer, 'The Lower Middle Class as Historical Problem,' *Journal of Modern History,* vol. 47, No. 3, September 1975, has drawn attention to the importance of studying the lower middle class because of their crucial role as a bastion of political conservatism. This important article appeared too late to be fully incorporated into this paper but its thesis and commentary can be seen to be in basic accord with the argument put forward here.
81. Bullock, op.cit., p. 181.

4 THE SOCIAL ECONOMY OF LATE-VICTORIAN CLERKS

G. L. Anderson

Of all the lower middle class groups which expanded with the structural shift in the late-Victorian economy from manufacturing to services, clerks were by far the most numerous and important. In 1861 only 91,733 men and virtually no women were employed as clerks; by 1891 there were 370,433 men and 18,947 women but by 1911 with 561,155 men and 124,843 women, clerks represented one of the largest and fastest-growing occupational groups in society.[1] The majority of these clerks were employed in commerce, banking and insurance and were responsible for servicing that network of financial and commercial institutions which developed after 1870 in response to the growth of multilateral trade and the export of British capital. Moreover, the clerks' economic role in staffing the service economy was matched by their social role as the most numerous of the expanding new suburban middle class in the cities. However, despite their economic and social importance, clerks have too easily come to be regarded merely as archetypal stereotypes of their age and even as cliché figures, a development largely caused by the popular image of the clerk being derived from such contemporary literary sources as Dickens and the Grossmiths. Unfortunately historians, until recently anyway, have failed to provide a more objective treatment of the lower middle class and have strangely neglected clerks along with other emerging white collar groups in the nineteenth century.[2]

The main purpose of this essay is, therefore, to examine an important and previously neglected occupational group. It is not intended, however, even if it were feasible within the present limitations of space, to provide a 'total' picture of clerks' economic and social lives. There is little here of the domestic and leisure activities of clerks. Rather the essay sets out to explore their work and market situation and suggests that in the period after 1870, coinciding with the Great Depression and the downturn in British economic performance, many clerks in the face of new economic pressures were placed in an increasingly marginal position.

Not all clerks, of course, experienced these economic pressures to the same extent, or even at all, because clerks did not represent a uniform or homogeneous occupational group. There were, in fact, innumerable gradations of clerks covering a very wide spectrum of ability, career prospects, job type, status and remuneration. Moreover these differences occurred within firms and industries as well as between them. There was, therefore, a wide gulf indeed between such sought-after positions in the office hierarchy as corresponding clerkships, which involved a close working relationship with the employer and a thorough understanding of most aspects of a firm's business and the routine clerkships which normally involved a familiarity with only part of the business procedure. Similarly those occupying routine but established clerkships were in a much more secure position, both in actual and status terms, within the office hierarchy than those apprentices and office boys, many of whom were employed on a short-term basis, at the bottom of the structure. In addition to the status gulf within offices, there was a world of difference between those routine clerks in a variety of industries, who were trapped in a limited salary range with little hope of promotion within their own firms and were beyond the age or without the credentials when upward mobility between firms was possible, and those 'quasi-professional' clerks in banking and high commerce. In terms of income and career prospects, at least, the lower clerks were not very distinguishable from many working men, particularly those of the respectable skilled type, though the so-called 'intellectual' quality of their work and their own pretensions separated them socially from that class.[3]

However, the clerks engaged in banking, insurance and the top commercial firms were in a quite distinctive position above the working class and on a par with the lower professions such as school teaching. These prestigious clerkships offered to the fortunate few the chances of mobile careers in well-established firms. Therefore, a situation in a well-known London-based insurance company such as the Royal Exchange Assurance (REA) conferred upon its occupant both the prestige associated with working in the City and the opportunity of entering management. The career opportunities were mainly a function of the growing departmentalisation of insurance work in the nineteenth century. It was common for the heads and deputy managers of particular departments to be recruited from the clerical ranks. This was the case in the REA where only a few highly specialised employees were recruited from outside.[4] Among bank clerks there was a similar tradition of mobility. Indeed, it was widely believed that they held a 'unique position in the business world, from which they can look proudly down on those who toil on, week after week, over a commercial or law office desk'.[5] Banking was acknowledged as a profession in which any clerk, if he was sufficiently talented, persevering and attentive might secure a managership. Needless to say, such desirable clerkships were reserved for the well-connected few. The banks were a closed world, closed that is to outsiders who had no personal contacts within them; situations were rarely advertised but were filled by personal recommendation and introduction. Those who entered this world might well find employment in the countrywide network of joint-stock banks. There the opportunities for advancement were excellent and young men, after first serving long apprenticeships of between three and four years, emerged as full clerks and could anticipate successful careers ending in management. In the Liverpool-based North and South Wales Bank, a typical provincial joint-stock concern, nearly a third of the clerks were attaining branch managerships by the mid-Victorian years. This was natural in a growing organisation in which there was a large number of branches and consequently a high ratio of managers to clerks. Even those clerks who did not secure managerships experienced upward occupational and income mobility as well as job security and only the careers of the inefficient, the insubordinate and the dishonest, or those who left to take up appointments elsewhere, did not unfold in the normal way.[6]

However, even for these well-placed clerks, the growing scale of office organisation and the trend towards amalgamation before 1914, may have served to slow down the rate of entry into management. In the REA, for example, the opportunities for clerks reaching managerial level were greater in the middle of the century than after 1900. In 1840, therefore, with only forty-eight staff divided between six departments, opportunities were excellent but had declined somewhat by 1900 when with only seven departments the staff had expanded to one hundred and forty-nine and were frankly very limited by 1914 when there were three hundred and fourteen staff in eight departments.[7] It must be said, however, that this changing work situation does not seem to have perturbed the REA's clerks who were apparently satisfied with 'the decent pay, the good hours, the permanency of tenure, the likelihood of a pension and the security derived from belonging to a corporate body'.[8]

Bank clerks also continued to derive satisfaction from the prestige associated with their profession, yet, here too, the rise in the scale of organisation associated with the amalgamations in late-nineteenth-century banking may have disturbed the earlier pattern of mobility into management. This was the view of R. H. Mottram who entered Gurney's, the Norwich-based country bank, at the turn of the century. Mottram was following in the footsteps of his father who had worked for half a century at Gurney's and who had risen to the distinguished position of chief clerk at their Norwich office. However, while his father's career had been shaped at a time when 'the ladder on which they set their feet ... was an escalator, at least after 1850', career conditions by Mottram's day had deteriorated.[9] Earlier in the century a young man like Mottram following a well-placed father might have expected to be singled out for special attention in his future career. However, the relationship which his father had developed with the Gurneys was now less effective in shaping Mottram's career, especially as Gurney's small-scale, personal organisation gave way to a larger and more anonymous one, after the firm was absorbed by Barclay's in 1896. Mottram described his expectations and subsequent disillusionment at that time:

> I had been born and lived over the bank and saw it from that angle, his [father's] angle in fact. I had been fetched home by a telegram from Switzerland, where I was completing my education according to a well-conceived plan of his. Having become at a relatively early age the right-hand man of the partners of old Gurney Bank, to such an extent that all the older generation called him by his Christian name, he thought that by having me learn French and German I should step, more or less, into his shoes, especially for the discounting for foreign bills and dealing with the new internationalism which he dimly discerned beyond his provincial horizon. He was just twenty years wrong. He had been so long at the top of things that he could not see the things nearer to him in time and space. So engrossed was he in the business, he hardly noticed that the office had doubled in size and personnel.[10]

For other clerks the situation after 1870 was changing even more to their disadvantage. In particular, although the basic research has yet to be undertaken in this area, it seems certain that clerks' chances of entry into the employer class were diminishing. Throughout the nineteenth century the prospect of such upward mobility was deeply entrenched into the ideology of clerks and for the first two-thirds of the century the opportunities of achieving economic independence were real enough. Therefore, as late as 1895, one clerk's journal could suggest that 'few who start as clerks mean to remain clerks, a clerkship is only the stepping stone to higher things'.[11] It was in the ports and commercial centres, and particularly among the brokers, merchants and shipowners, that clerks had the best chance of achieving independence. Therefore, B. G. Orchard could dedicate his unique study of Liverpool clerks to that class 'from whose ranks not a few, after serving with capacity, zeal and faithfulness, rise to the position of employers'.[12] Indeed Orchard believed that 'half the partnership firms in Liverpool twenty years old contain a partner who was once a clerk'.[13] More recently Gordon Jackson has revealed a similar pattern of recruitment in eighteenth-century Hull and Francis Hyde has shown that Victorian Liverpool was indeed a city in which men of small means might make their fortunes in trade.[14]

Needless to say many of the clerks who achieved independence in this way possessed important economic and social advantages. Often they were the sons of merchants who merely served a clerical apprenticeship in order to acquire the necessary experience before entering their fathers' businesses or setting up on their own. The success of these young men was, to some extent, guaranteed by the business and social connections which existed between merchant families at the level of the local community. The careers of Alfred and Charles Booth, sons of a prominent Liverpool Unitarian grain merchant, were determined by their background. It was no accident that both served their clerical apprenticeships in the office of Lamport and Holt, another important local Unitarian merchant house, or that later the Unitarian merchants, Rathbone and Company, provided Alfred with a position in their New York office. With this experience, in addition to capital inherited from their father and credit facilities extended by the Rathbones and Holts, the Booth brothers were able to establish their own business.[15]

Even without the advantages of young men like the Booths, who were, in effect, 'employers-in-training', clerks of talent and determination could still achieve economic independence. John Holt, for example, who was born in a Lincolnshire village and managed to secure an apprenticeship in the office of a Liverpool coal-dealer, possessed no actual resources other than a strong desire to succeed. In addition he showed an early awareness of the lack of opportunities implicit in a routine clerkship. 'What am I to do?' he wrote to his father, 'If I stay where I am I have the prospect of a £60 salary which to my ambitious nature is beggary. No! it is money I want and money I must have if I go through fire and water for it . . . It is not the gold, but the independence it brings and the cares it drives away . . .'[16] It was only by taking a risk, incidentally against his employer's advice, that Holt achieved success. In 1862 he accepted a position as secretary to the British Consul in Fernando Po and after initially managing it, ultimately gained control of the latter's merchanting business. By 1875 he was able to extend his West African operations to Liverpool.

Such success stories were more likely in the commercial conditions before 1870 than after. The pre-1870 trading world was one in which technological backwardness in transport, uncertainties in the speed and reliability of information regarding markets and sources of supply and, consequently, high costs, combined to create a commercial transaction in which a number of intermediaries intervened between the producer and the final consumer in order to spread the risks. In this situation many brokers and small merchants grew up, especially in those ports involved with the major produce trades between England and the United States, whose function was to bring buyers and sellers together, act in an advisory capacity, supervise the purchase and sale of produce and store materials.[17] As they were not normally responsible for the provision of funds or even for guaranteeing bills of exchange, the capital needs of such enterprises were small, consisting of probably no more than an office, a small staff and warehouse space. It was against this background, in which the emphasis was on the provision of commercial information, that the more able and enterprising clerks, with a wide knowledge of conditions in their own trades, were able to set up in business.[18]

However, in the last third of the century a number of technological and institutional changes occurred which served to gradually undermine this commercial transaction. Most significantly, the wider use of iron steamships in inter-continental trade lowered transaction costs and increased the speed of supply. The Atlantic Cable, laid down in 1866, plus the establishment of futures markets in the United States and England resulted in the further reduction of risks, price fluctuations and transaction costs. Manufacturers were now in a position to bypass intermediaries and deal directly with the producers.[19] There was now much less need for the large numbers of small brokers and merchants who had grown up in the ports. In Liverpool, for example, while there were some 300 commission merchants, approximately 320 cotton brokers and over 1,000 general merchants in 1870, by 1914 these had declined to just over eighty commission merchants, some 190 cotton brokers and less than 330 general merchants.[20] Needless to say, apart from the institutional changes in commercial transactions, the long-term price fell in the last decades of the century and the resultant squeeze on profits would have seriously weakened the position of many of the small brokers and merchants. Furthermore, the rise in the scale of business organisation meant that the days of the 'small man' were numbered. In the face of both internal and external competition new and larger units of capital became a feature of late-Victorian commerce and shipping. In Liverpool by the 1890s only Cunard, itself a giant organisation, had not joined the amalgamations of steamship companies.[21] While clerks undoubtedly experienced upward career mobility within these large bureaucracies, their chances of setting up their own businesses in this new economic environment were clearly limited.

Apart from organisational and technological changes, another reason why the office was becoming a more unlikely starting-point for career success was because the new channels of upward mobility were now on the marketing and selling side of commerce. Interestingly, by the 1900s, the career literature for white collar workers was differentiating between 'creative' (i.e. selling) and clerical occupations. Clerks were warned that 'the office is a good place to start off, but should only be regarded as such'[22] and that the 'pitfall which besets the majority of clerks is that they are liable to drift unconsciously into a groove'.[23] To escape from such a groove required a combination of 'pushfulness', willpower and an ability to recognise the opportunities in selling and marketing. The new models of success exhibited these qualities. Hudson Kearley, for example, who later as Lord Devonport became Chairman of the Port of London Authority, first started as a £60-a-year clerk in a London tea merchant's office. He soon realised, however, that the best opportunities were in the firm's salesroom and, although his father could not afford the necessary premium of not less than £300 for such a position, his employer was sufficiently impressed by Kearley's determination to give him special consideration and allow him in. Within three years, Kearley had established the firm which ultimately grew into International Stores.[24] Success stories such as Hudson Kearley's were obviously exceptional but there were still plenty of openings in export, retail and wholesale establishments in the large cities for buyers, salesmen and commercial travellers.[25] There can be little doubt that much of the interest in salesmanship at this time reflected the central role of the salesman in the fiercely competitive markets, both at home and overseas. The aggressive techniques of salesmanship, given the widely publicised success of American and particularly German commercial travellers, fitted more securely into that mix of Social Darwinism, national and commercial rivalry which characterised the late-Victorian period, than did the more passive qualities associated with clerking.[26]

Changing career patterns and fewer opportunities for mobility in the work situation were matched by an equally serious, if more temporary, development in the clerical labour market: increasing evidence of distress and unemployment. Although Victorian clerks were far less vulnerable to the effects of poverty and unemployment than the casual labourers and factory operatives below them, after 1870 an increasing number were no longer absolutely certain of full and regular employment or completely protected from the impact of poverty.[27] However, because clerks did not resort, as far as one can tell, in any numbers to the more traditional survival agencies for the poor and unemployed, such as the Poor Law, private charities or trade unions, much of their distress remains hidden.

Indeed, distress when it occurred was often deliberately concealed from a society in which there was little sympathy for those unable to maintain their social position and economic independence and much stigma attached to poverty. Some sense of the private suffering which must have occurred among clerks was accurately observed during the severe trade depression which affected Liverpool in the winter of 1879. The *Liverpool Argus* suggested:

> Even these days when benevolent organisations are so numerous and when such publicity is given to their operations it is not always the cases of greatest distress which become most widely known and it is feared that many of the clerks of Liverpool who have been thrown out of employment by the long continued depression of trade, have during the past few months been enduring privations as great as the labouring classes. Many are prevented by natural sensitiveness from asking for any assistance beyond the narrow circle of their own friends, who are often unable to render help.[28]

Sometimes in rare outbursts of frustration and resentment, clerks described their private experiences of poverty and unemployment. Thus one poor clerk compared his own forgotten economic struggle with that of the working man, who seemed to attract public concern, in this self-pitying way:

> I don't growl at the working man, be his
>   Virtue strict or morality lax,
> He would strike if they gave him my weekly wage,
>   And they never ask him for income tax.
> They take his little ones out to tea in a
>   Curtained van when the leaves are green.
> But never flower, field nor fern, in the
>   Leafy lanes have my children seen.
> The case is different, so they say, for I
>   Am respectable—save the mark!
> He works with the sweat of his manly brow

And I with body and brain—poor clerk![29]

Even the young clerks' culture of the large cities, on the surface devoted to games, entertainment and the latest fashion, may only have served to conceal the reality of distress. This was particularly true of the less well-placed clerks. In London, for example, while the better-paid clerks might find comfortable accommodation in the boarding houses of Bloomsbury, Kensington or Bayswater or commute from the cleaner if remoter suburbs, many of the poorer clerks, in the thirty shillings a week range, were forced to inhabit the seedier lodging houses of the central areas. There they were vulnerable to exploitation by landladies who were themselves often struggling on the economic margin. In addition to their rent the young clerks were obliged to pay heavily for 'extras' such as meals, washing, boot cleaning, light and heat. The escape from the shabbiness and loneliness of the cheap lodging houses lay in the bright world of the music hall, public house and night club or in the more 'acceptable' games activities such as football and cricket. However, the appearance of many young clerks in the cheaper London coffee houses with their shiny coats, frayed collars, shabby cuffs and haggard looks, betrayed the difficulty in trying to reconcile poverty with gentility.[30]

The actual extent of distress among clerks, while less easy to evaluate, is not entirely lost from sight. A number of voluntary associations, catering mainly or solely for clerks' economic and social needs, operated during the second half of the nineteenth century. Among them was the YMCA, which in addition to its wider and more well-known missionary and educative functions, provided clerks, as well as related white collar occupations such as drapers' assistants and commercial travellers, with a number of important welfare facilities.[31]

In London, for example, an employment bureau for clerks was operating under the auspices of the YMCA from January 1891. The *Daily News*, when reviewing the need for a national labour exchange, regarded the YMCA's employment bureau along with the Salvation Army's labour scheme, as a pioneer agency in the field.[32] The YMCA bureau worked on the simple principle whereby young, and in some cases not so young, men entered their names on a register for a month on payment of five shillings, half of which was returned at the end of the month if no situation had been obtained. Employers were charged half a guinea in the event of their employing men on the register. The significance of the London bureau lies less in the number of clerks who were actually found situations than in the number who applied for help. It was, therefore, an important barometer of the amount of otherwise hidden distress among clerical workers. In 1891, the first year of its operation, 491 men were found situations out of 617 names on the register. However, in excess of 13,000 clerks and others, seeking work, were interviewed throughout the year at Exeter Hall, the headquarters of the London YMCA.[33]

An identical picture of fairly widespread job searching and unemployment among clerks and related groups emerges from the activities of the provincial YMCA. In Manchester, from the mid-1870s, an employment bureau similar in principle to London's was operating. Here again, there was always a preponderance of applications over men actually placed in situations. For example, in 1876 out of 500 applications for employment 270 men were placed; in 1888 out of 400 applications 116 were placed, while in 1894, a bad year, only 134 were placed out of 821 applications.[34] This disparity between numbers applying and numbers placed can be explained partly by the general employment situation and partly by YMCA policy which ensured that only those men were placed in the employment book who were genuine cases of distress, had acceptable references and had in no way proved unsatisfactory to their previous employers. Apart from its employment bureau, the Manchester association also established a special relief fund for distressed clerks and their families in the winter of 1879 and maintained it throughout the depression years until the 1890s.[35]

By far the most interesting, and in some respects the most important, of the practical economic facilities developed by the Manchester association was an emigration department established in 1882, whereby young clerks and others were given letters of introduction to Canadian farmers under whom they served a form of rural apprenticeship before setting up as farmers themselves.[36] Between 1882 and the end of the century some 2,359 clerks were given letters of introduction, mainly to farmers in Manitoba. However, the interest shown in emigration by this means was far greater than this figure suggests, for there were over 13,000 applications for letters of introduction during this period, yet another indication of the pressures existing in the clerical labour market.[37] Despite the wide disparity between those requesting help and actually given it, a reflection of the YMCA's determination to send only the most suitable men to Canada, the emigration department undoubtedly acted as a useful safety-valve for an increasingly competitive white collar labour market in England during the last decades of the century.

Apart from the YMCA a group of narrower, friendly-society type institutions, catering solely for clerks, was also established in this period.[38] By the late-Victorian years there was a fairly extensive network of these clerks' associations operating throughout the country, of which the most important were those in Liverpool, London and Manchester with large and growing memberships of between 2,500 and 3,500. In addition there were smaller associations in provincial centres such as Cardiff, Newcastle, Sheffield and Leeds with memberships numbered only in hundreds. Typical of the latter was the Sheffield Clerks' Association, established in 1896 and which by the turn of the century had a membership of around 150. It provided assistance to Sheffield's relatively small number of sick and unemployed clerks in the form of medical attendance, sickness benefits, annuities and relief for members' widows and children. More significantly, it also acted as a well-organised labour bureau for all unemployed male clerks in the area between the ages of eighteen and forty-five.[39]

It was, however, in the larger commercial cities, where clerks figured more prominently in the local occupational structure, that clerks' societies assumed a more significant role. The Scottish Clerks' Association, for example, established in Glasgow in 1886, rapidly expanded in the late depression years (its membership rose from 215 in 1886 to nearly 1,700 in 1896) and quickly developed a network of branches in other Scottish towns including Edinburgh, Dundee and Aberdeen.[40] Its expansion coincided with the growth of economic distress in Scotland in which 'while the industrial grades of the labouring classes have suffered, the commercial and professional class, to which clerks belong, have not escaped'.[41] Certainly by the early 1890s upwards of 320 enquiries for work each year were being handled by the Association's employment department though never more than 140 situations a year were being filled. In 1894, a typically dull year for trade, in which Scottish business was seriously affected by the coal strike, the Association noted that 'towards the end of the year it became apparent that the number of unemployed clerks was increasing, and the number and value of vacant situations was decreasing'.[42] In this situation there was considerable pressure on the small number of vacant situations and the Association was forced to contend with 'the keen competition of the large number (of clerks) outside of the membership who are without the advantages of its support, and the personal influence exerted on all hands to secure the few appointments available'.[43]

Evidence from the activities of other large clerks' associations during the depression years merely reinforces the Scottish experience. In Liverpool and Manchester, the two largest clerks' associations in the country were providing a similar range of unemployment and sickness benefits from as early as 1861 and 1855. Both these associations, however, witnessed their most significant expansion with the onset of the depression years in the early 1870s. Therefore, the membership of Manchester's Association increased from 1,500 in 1872 to 3,079 in 1890 and 6,347 in 1912.[44] Similarly the Liverpool Association grew from 403 in 1861 to 1,033 in 1873, 3,222 in 1894 and 5,714 in 1914.[45] As elsewhere, the employment department was the most widely used and important of the facilities provided by these associations. In Liverpool its use varied inversely with economic prosperity, clerks having greatest resort to it during slumps in trade and finding employment through more traditional means when economic recovery occurred. In Liverpool, therefore, although only forty clerks found situations through the Association in 1870, from the onset of the depression a few years later down to 1914, with the figures falling and levelling off after 1905, upwards of 400 to 500 situations were being found each year. Moreover, nearly half of the situations filled by the Liverpool Association were temporary (between 1881 and 1914 there were 4,875 temporary compared to 5,173 permanent situations), thus denying to those clerks, at least, one of the advantages which historically they possessed over the working class: security of employment.[46]

There was no single cause of the increase in unemployment and distress among clerks after 1870. A number of long and short-term factors combined to create this new element of insecurity in clerical employment. Some clerks, of course, lost their jobs, as some had always done, for non-market reasons. Sickness was the biggest cause in this respect. Clerks were particularly vulnerable to pulmonary tuberculosis, or more commonly consumption, which was partly associated with ill-ventilated and overcrowded workplaces, and offices were not included in any of the factory and workplace legislation before the First World War.[47] Some clerks were also discharged because of embezzlement or conflict with their employers. Furthermore, it seems likely that the scale of embezzlement was much larger than the number of prosecutions would indicate. After all, many employers probably refused to prosecute and simply discharged their clerks in order to preserve the 'good name' of their firms or even to protect their employees from the social stigma attached to their crimes. What is certain is that an embezzlement was enormously destructive both of clerk/employer relations and of the culprit's job prospects. R. H. Mottram vividly described the effect of an embezzlement at one of Gurney's small village banks. The process of checking, counter-checking and duplication which followed the embezzlement left Mottram acutely aware of 'the curious personal and unintentional reflection upon us all'.[48] What made it worse was that the man had been a friend and workmate, capable at his job and marked out for promotion. 'The fact that he was so average', suggested Mottram, 'seemed to make an abyss yawn beneath all our feet'.[49] The guilty man, without references and with a reputation in ruins, might quickly sink into the real abyss. There can be little doubt that many of the last-resort casual occupations which consisted of men, including clerks, who had 'skidded' from genteel positions contained embezzlers and the like.[50]

Given that sickness and embezzlement had always affected clerks' security of employment, the causes of the increase in distress after 1870 must lie elsewhere. Deteriorating economic conditions in the Great Depression period were partly responsible. On this basis the increase in clerks' unemployment between the 1870s and 1890s can be seen as merely reinforcing the general pattern of an increase in unemployment among other workers.[51] And clerks, like industrial and manual workers, if not to the same extent, were certainly vulnerable to economic fluctuations. In the severe cyclical downturn in 1879, for example, even the better-placed Liverpool clerks who 'regarded their situations almost as beyond the reach of the casualties of commercial life'[52] were warned that the differences between themselves and working men were mainly ones of degree not kind and that the habits of thrift and prudence cultivated by working men applied with equal force to them. Apart from the temporary employment effect of cyclical movements, there were the longer-term effects of the fall in prices, the impact of foreign competition and the slight fall in the rate of increase of world trade after 1870.[53] Clerks and their employers stood in the teeth of this increasing competition. From the scanty evidence provided by the clerks' associations it appears that the bulk of unemployment was caused by the failure of firms or the rationalisation, i.e cutting, of office staff through depression of trade. Having been discharged on to the labour market, clerks may also have experienced difficulties in re-entering the labour force. Most clerks probably had no experience other than that acquired in a particular office or trade and may have been unsuited, given the wide variations in business methods, for employment elsewhere. They were more likely than other workers, therefore, to suffer from 'search unemployment'.[54] 'Clerks are not in the position of tradesmen', one clerks' journal observed, 'who may lose employment and still find work at the same rate of wages in other localities. If clerks lose their situations it may be a long time before they again obtain employment even at less and altogether inadequate remuneration'.[55] In a 'search unemployment' situation, the clerks' associations fulfilled a vital role by providing members with unemployment benefits, circulating employers with details of members' qualifications and processing the information, usually derived from a wide range of newspaper advertisements, concerning job vacancies.

A more fundamental cause of unemployment among clerks was the changing relationship between the elasticity of demand for clerical labour and the elasticity of supply. While the growth of the service economy after 1870 increased the demand for clerical labour the supply of such labour was expanding more rapidly.[56] The source of this increase can be traced to the routine and unskilled nature of much clerical work. All that was required of the low grade clerks, especially in the large bureaucratic offices of central and local government and to a lesser extent of commerce, was a degree of numeracy and literacy and such basic attainments became more general in the latter part of the century. The 1870 Education Act may have had some influence on this development but was perhaps more effective in producing better disciplined factory workers than clerks. Only the most menial forms of clerical labour, the office boys and messengers, who were often employed on a temporary basis, were the products of this system.[57] It was more likely from the lower middle class and the respectable working class, where the level of education had always been higher, that the new recruits to clerking came attracted by 'the light labour and continuous employment not to speak of that broadcloth gentility'.[58] The attractiveness of the work and the low level of required skills, coupled with a weak tradition of trade unionism and the wide status and income differences between them ensured that clerks were in no position to effectively control entry into their labour market.[59] In this sense they were in a quite different position from those nearest to them in economic and social terms, the skilled workers. For whereas the craft apprenticeship was regulated by a particular trade in order to maintain its bargaining position, standards and wages, the commercial apprenticeship was controlled by employers not by the clerks. The abuse of the apprenticeship system by some employers was regarded as a cause of oversupply in the labour market. Therefore, according to one observer:

> The true source of evil is the perennial one of the selfish and unscrupulous conduct of those wealthy firms who carry on the mechanisms of their business by the help of apprentices supervised by one or two professional clerks. After five years' service at a nominal salary of £20 a year, a young man is offered the princely stipend of £40 a year.

This he probably spurns and joins the increasing body of candidates for office elsewhere, whilst his place and work are relegated to his junior.[60]

Two other sources of uncontrolled entry were recognised as having an impact on the labour market: female and foreign clerks. Of these, female clerks have had the most lasting effect in that their numbers have expanded with the growth of the service sector since the First World War to the point that they now outnumber male white collar workers. However, before 1914 their effect on male clerks can be exaggerated. Certainly both in absolute and relative terms they were increasing rapidly but the bulk of that increase occurred after 1890 and more especially after 1900. It came too late to have had any significant effect on the unemployment and distress among clerks between the 1870s and 1890s. Even after 1890 female clerks did not have a serious displacement effect, at least in the commercial sector, because they fulfilled an essentially different work function within the office than men. Their employment was associated with the increased division of clerical labour and the introduction of new office skills: shorthand and typewriting.[61] At first male clerks also sought the acquisition of these skills, especially shorthand, in the mistaken belief that they would somehow professionalise clerical work and solve their declining market situation.[62] This did not happen and eventually the skills became recognised as simply aids to commerce. Indeed shorthand clerkships came to be regarded as blind alley occupations which severed clerks' links with promotion elsewhere.[63] It was against this background that most female clerks formed a distinctive group within the clerical labour force below the male clerks. Their low wages, and they could earn as little as ten shillings a week and rarely more than £2, reflected the pressure of oversupply on their section of the labour market. In this respect they should be seen as undercutting each other more than they competed with men.

The problem of foreign clerks, although a shorter-term phenomenon, raised much deeper anxieties. There was throughout this period a substantial number of foreign commercial clerks in England (rising from 2,498 in 1871 to 6,171 in 1911) of which the majority were German.[64] It was this German influx, coinciding as it did with a loss of confidence in the Great Depression and the threat of German commercial and national rivalry, which caused the greatest concern. The German clerks, like all Germans, were viewed with that peculiar mixture of envy, hatred and grudging admiration which characterised British attitudes in the period from 1870 to 1914. In this sense the German clerks were seen as the vanguard of a new type of competition in which commercial strengths were inseparable from cultural and racial ones.[65] In particular the German clerks were regarded as possessing a superior commercial education and especially a greater knowledge of foreign languages. There is no doubt that the apparently superior commercial training of German, and other foreign, clerks and travellers was a major reason for the wide interest shown in commercial education in England in the latter part of the century. The educational model, which many English observers sought to emulate in this area, was that which had been developed in Germany and the United States.

Moreover, it was thought that the German clerks, equipped with their language and other work skills, were taking the best situations (foreign correspondence clerkships for example) in English offices.[66] In addition, they were accused of working for little or no remuneration, thus rendering English clerks uncompetitive and further depressing their wages.[67] Neither was the impact restricted to England for in sensitive foreign markets, such as Latin America, British merchants were giving way to the more dynamic business houses often started by young Germans who had previously been employed as their clerks.[68]

The impact may have been overstated, however, for by no means all the German clerks arriving in England were successful. A proportion of them found only poverty and disenchantment. Some failed to hold white collar jobs and were reduced to labouring, begging and even crime. Others were forced through economic necessity to return home usually under the aegis of organisations such as the German Benevolent Association and the Society of Friends in Distress. For those who remained there was a wide gulf indeed between the colony of successful merchants and well-placed clerks and

> the poor starving majority, the troops of underpaid clerks and copyists, teachers of music and languages in search of lessons and other needy fresh arrivals, not to speak of the swindlers and professional beggars.[69]

In addition, after 1900, with the ratio of foreign to native male clerks having stabilised (at 1.7 per cent) the threat of foreign clerks, in numerical terms anyway, was no longer a growing one.

The threat of German clerks can be most sensibly viewed against the background of the Great Depression, in which German strengths and British weaknesses were too often and too easily exaggerated. In this sense, the real impact of German clerks was more psychological than actual. They represented a convenient scapegoat for English clerks many of whom were being affected by a series of more profound and to some extent irreversible changes. The increase in unemployment and distress meant that clerks, like other workers, were no longer protected from the sharp edge of capitalism. The slowing down in career mobility and the cut-off of entry into the employer class also placed many clerks in a marginal position. Taken together these developments signified the break-up of that self-contained and relatively secure commercial world which had existed down to 1870 and of which clerks had been a part.

Notes

1. Figures from L. Holcombe, *Victorian Ladies at Work*, David and Charles, Newton Abbot, 1973, p. 215.
2. For many years the only treatment of Victorian clerks was D. Lockwood, *The Blackcoated Worker*, George Allen and Unwin, London, 1958, chapter one. Recently clerks along with other white collar groups have been variously analysed by Holcombe, op.cit., R. Price, *An Imperial War and the British Working Class*, Routledge and Kegan Paul, London, 1972 and H. McLeod, *Class and Religion in the Late-Victorian City*, Croom Helm, London, 1974.
3. On the differences between clerks and skilled workers see R. Q. Gray, 'Styles of Life, The Labour Aristocracy and Class Relations in Later Nineteenth Century Edinburgh,' *International Review of Social History*, vol. xvii, 1973.
4. B. Supple, *The Royal Exchange Assurance*, Cambridge University Press, Cambridge, 1970, p. 375.
5. *The Clerks' Gazette*, 31 July 1895.
6. See G.L. Anderson, 'The Recruitment, Apprenticeship and Mobility of the Mid-Victorian Clerk: A Study of the North and South Wales Bank, 1850-1875', *The Welsh History Review*, vol. 7, No. 3, 1975, pp. 341-356.
7. Supple, op.cit., p. 376.
8. Ibid., p. 378.
9. R.H. Mottram, *Bowler Hat. A Last Glance at the Old Country Banking*, Hutchinson & Co., London, 1940, p. 26.
10. Ibid., p. 25.
11. *The Clerks' Gazette*, 29 June 1895.
12. B.G. Orchard, *The Clerks of Liverpool*, J. Collinson, Liverpool, 1871, p. 5.
13. Ibid., p. 41.
14. See G. Jackson, *Hull in the Eighteenth Century*, Hull University Press, Hull, 1972, p. 101 and F. Hyde, *Liverpool and the Mersey*, David and Charles, Newton Abbot, 1971, p. 46.
15. See A.H. John, *A Liverpool Merchant House: Being a History of Alfred Booth and Company*, George Allen and Unwin, London, 1959, pp. 20-25.
16. *Merchant Adventurer: John Holt and Company*, Liverpool, 1951, p. 13.
17. See S. Marriner, *The Rathbones of Liverpool, 1845-1873*, Liverpool University Press, Liverpool, 1961, p. 81, for an account of the broker's function.
18. For evidence of clerks' mobility into the brokerage trade see T. Ellison, *The Cotton Trade of Great Britain*, Effingham Wilson, London, 1886, part II, chapter III and G. Broomhall and J. Hubback, *Corn Trade Memories*,

Northern Publishing Company, Liverpool, 1930, pp. 59-221.
19. This assessment of the impact of technological changes and decreasing risks on the role of intermediaries in commercial transactions is derived, in part, from S. Marriner, op.cit., ch. 9, L.E. Davis and D.C. North, *Institutional Change and American Economic Growth*, Cambridge University Press, Cambridge, 1971, pp. 193-197 and S. Nishimura, *The Decline of the Inland Bills of Exchange in the London Money Market*, Cambridge University Press, Cambridge, 1971.
20. The figures are from Gores' Trade Directories of Liverpool.
21. For the growth of large shipping firms see F. Hyde, 'Cunard and North Atlantic Steamship Agreements' in B. Ratcliffe, ed., *Great Britain and Her World*, Manchester University Press, Manchester, 1975, p. 272.
22. G. Newnes, *£300 a Year Business Positions. Where they are and how to get them*, George Newnes Ltd., London, 1912, p. 51.
23. Ibid.
24. Ibid., pp. 15-16.
25. Ibid., pp. 33-49.
26. For a Social Darwinian view of the success of the Germans as salesmen see P. Magnus, 'Schools of Commerce', *Contemporary Review*, 1887, pp. 847-866. For the importance of marketing and the role of the commercial traveller against the background of the Great Depression see D.H. Aldcroft and H.W. Richardson, *The British Economy, 1870-1939*, Macmillan, London, 1969, pp. 155-159.
27. There is little information comparing unemployment rates between clerks and other workers. However, see M.J. Cullen, 'The 1887 Survey of the London Working Class', *International Review of Social History*, vol. XX, 1975, pp. 48-60 for an interesting analysis of the relationship between unemployment, wages and rents among thirty-five trade groups including clerks.
28. *The Argus, Weekly Review of the Political, Literary and Social Sciences*, 22 February 1879.
29. *The Clerks' Journal*, 1 July 1889.
30. There was an acknowledged need for large-scale residential accommodation for single clerks in London along the lines of Rowton House which by 1897 was providing working men with rooms for sixpence a night. See R. White, 'Wanted: A Rowton House for Clerks', *The Nineteenth Century*, October 1897, pp. 594-601.
31. The literature on the English YMCA is limited but for a good general history written around the personality of its founder George Williams see C. Binfield, *George Williams and the YMCA*, Heinemann, London, 1973. Dr Binfield, however, is more interested in the Nonconformist world of which the YMCA was a part than in the practical facilities developed by the organisation.
32. *Daily News*, 21 January 1891.
33. Ibid.
34. The figures are derived from the abstracts of the Manchester YMCA's annual reports found in *The Bee-hive*, journal of the Manchester YMCA.
35. See also *The Bee-hive*.
36. Clerks, along with other settlers, could acquire 160 acres of free government land for a ten dollar registration fee under the Dominion Lands Act of 1872. See P.B. Waite, *Arduous Destiny: Canada, 1874-1896*, McClelland and Stewart Ltd., Toronto, 1971, pp. 61-64.
37. The figures are derived from the abstracts of the Manchester YMCA's annual reports found in *The Bee-hive*.
38. For a list of the major clerks' associations at this time see D. Lockwood, op.

cit., p. 34. In fact the list was much longer than this. Many societies, some lasting only a few years, catered for clerks in particular trades or professions.
39. I am grateful to Mr. Peter Aspinall for supplying me with this information on the Sheffield Clerks' Association. The Victorian clerks' associations anticipated the twentieth-century role of employment agencies in the white collar sector. See, for example, E.H. Conant, 'An Evaluation of Private Employment Agencies as Sources of Job Vacancy Data' in *The Measurement and Interpretation of Job Vacancies*, National Bureau of Economic Research, New York, 1966, pp. 519-547.
40. *The Clerks' Gazette*, 27 February 1897.
41. Ibid., 30 April 1895.
42. Ibid., 28 February 1895.
43. Ibid.
44. *Details from Annual Report of Manchester Warehousemen and Clerks' Association 1912* (Registry of Friendly Societies).
45. Details from Annual Reports of the Liverpool Clerks' Association for respective years (courtesy of the Liverpool Clerks' Association).
46. Ibid.
47. For the debilitating effects of office work see C.T. Thackrah, *The Effects of the Arts, Trades and Professions on Health and Longevity*, Longman and Co., London, 1832, p. 176 and for the exclusion of offices from workplace legislation see J. Hallsworth, *Protective Legislation for Shop and Office Employees*, G.G. Harrap and Co., London, 1939.
48. R.H. Mottram, op.cit., p. 175.
49. Ibid., p. 176.
50. For evidence of 'skidders' see G. Stedman Jones, *Outcast London*, Oxford University Press, London, 1973, p. 63 and G.L. Anderson, op.cit., p. 354.
51. The unemployment rate increased from 5% in the period 1851-73 to 7.2% during 1874-95 before falling back to 5.4% during 1896-1914. See S.B. Saul, *The Myth of the Great Depression, 1873-1896*, Macmillan, London, 1969, p. 30.
52. *The Argus*, 8 February 1879.
53. See W. Ashworth, *A Short History of the International Economy since 1850*, Longman, London, 1975, p. 192 and S.B. Saul, op.cit., for the economic background to the Great Depression period.
54. Economists are perhaps more familiar than economic historians with the nature of job search behaviour among workers. Some workers may, of course, quit their work in order to search full-time for jobs with better opportunities. Such behaviour is more likely in periods of prosperity than recession. The job searching of most late-nineteenth century clerks, given the state of the labour market, was likely to have been involuntary. See L.G. Reynolds, *Labour Economics and Labour Relations*, Prentice-Hall, New Jersey, 1974, pp. 122-125 for a brief assessment of workers' search behaviour.
55. *The Clerks' Gazette*, 31 December 1875.
56. In simple economic terms the late-nineteenth century clerical labour market worked in the following way. While the clerical labour demand curve shifted right (from D to D_1) the clerical labour supply curve shifted even further right (from S to S_1). In this situation, assuming everything else is held constant, we might theoretically expect money wage levels to fall. In fact, however, we know that money wages rarely fall and should, therefore, look for evidence of stagnation. There is strong evidence that clerks' money wages between 1870 and 1914 were stagnating. Taking the commercial sec-

132 *The Lower Middle Class in Britain 1870-1914*

tor there is no evidence of any upward movement of wages in this period. Liverpool clerks in 1871 struggled along on £80 a year (see B.G. Orchard, op.cit., p. 65), the bulk of the situations filled by the Liverpool Clerks' Association down to 1914 were in the £50-£100 range (see the Annual Reports of the Liverpool Clerks' Association) and according to the 1909 national survey of the earnings of male clerks the average salary of commercial clerks was still £80 and only 23% earned more than £160 (see D. Lockwood, op.cit., p. 42).

57. The office boys and messengers were a kind of white collar residuum. They were paid as little as five shillings a week and often had no job security. At the end of the century, along with other boy workers, they were the subject of much debate and concern. See, for example, R.H. Tawney, 'The Economics of Boy Labour', *The Economic Journal,* December 1909, p. 517 and C. Jackson, 'Report on Boy Labour' in *The Royal Commission on the Poor Laws,* 1909, xxxvlll, p. 87.

58. *The Argus,* 4 January 1879.

59. A number of factors inhibited the growth of clerks' unions before the First World War. They can be briefly enumerated as (i) the strength of respectability and the feeling among clerks that trade unions were working class organisations; (ii) the impact of women who have less commitment to unionism because they do not normally anticipate long working lives; (iii) the variations between clerks based on income, status and career structure; (iv) the small-scale size of the workplace and the 'particularism' which was a feature of clerical work. The last reason was the most vital. In modern economics, as clerical work conditions have come to approximate more to the bureaucratic model, clerks have joined unions in large numbers. Even before 1914 clerks in the large bureaucracies of central and local government had a strong tradition of unionism. Only the National Union of Clerks succeeded in recruiting among commercial clerks and its membership remained small (12,680 in 1914). For brief historical surveys of a number of clerks' unions see D. Lockwood, op.cit., pp. 155-194.

60. *The Argus,* 4 January 1879.

61. From the 1880s a number of organisations such as the Society of Arts and the Union of Lancashire and Cheshire Institutes offered commercial examinations in a range of subjects including shorthand and typewriting. It was at this time, also, that evening classes in office skills became popular. See M. Sadler, ed., *Continuation Schools in England and Elsewhere,* Manchester University Publications, 1907 and F. Hooper, *Commercial Education at Home and Abroad,* Macmillan and Co., London, 1901.

62. In the late nineteenth century shorthand was so highly regarded that a large number of shorthand writers' societies, with associated journals, emerged concerned with publicising its qualities. See G.L. Anderson, 'A Study of Clerical Labour in Liverpool and Manchester 1850-1914' (unpublished Ph.D. thesis, University of Lancaster, 1975), pp. 254-260.

63. *The Shorthand Writer,* November 1896 and March 1903 and *Office Hints,* January 1909, emphasise the shortcomings of shorthand clerkships while *The Shorthand Writer,* February 1897, drew attention to the fact that female clerks did not really compete with men.

64. In 1891 out of 4,096 foreign commercial clerks, 2,101 were German and in 1901 out of 5,195 foreign commercial clerks 2,170 were German.

65. *The Clerks' Gazette,* 30 April 1895, and *The Clerks' Journal,* November and December 1889, emphasise the racial superiority of the German clerks.

66. The debate over German usurping English clerks was given official support by the survey of the London Chamber of Commerce in 1887. For comment

see *The Times*, 13 July 1887 and *The Clerks' Journal*, March 1888 and June 1889.
67. The little or no remuneration which German clerks were prepared to accept aroused comment in *The Bee-hive*, December 1889, *The Clerks' Gazette*, 31 October 1895 and *The Manchester Guardian*, 20 November 1886. In London the German clerks' scare was sufficient to give rise to The City Clerks' Alliance, formed in 1890, which canvassed the Lord Mayor about the German problem. See *The East London Advertiser*, 13 December 1890.
68. D.C.M. Platt, *Latin America and British Trade, 1806-1914*, Adam and Charles Black, London, 1972, p. 136.
69. L. Katscher, 'German Life in London', *The Nineteenth Century*, vol. 21, 1887, p. 740. Interestingly the Liverpool Clerks' Association, which was close to the real causes of clerical unemployment, believed that the impact of foreign clerks was much exaggerated. See *The Office*, 5 January 1889.

5 RELIGION, CULTURE AND SOCIAL CLASS IN LATE NINETEENTH AND EARLY TWENTIETH CENTURY EDINBURGH

R. Q. Gray

This paper is concerned with the distinct social identity and innovative cultural role of the middle strata of society in Victorian and Edwardian Edinburgh. Any attempt to discuss these social groupings faces conceptual and terminological problems, and the first part of the paper briefly indicates the position adopted here. The common tendency, both contemporary and historiographical, to refer to such middle layers of society as the 'lower middle class' is in my view misleading; it obscures the problem of the diffusion of dominant values, by inserting these subordinate sectors of society into a vaguely defined, upward stretching 'middle class'. (It is quite true that the middle strata were often seen, and saw themselves, as the lower middle class; the historian's concern is to *explain* their social consciousness, not to treat it as a self-evident analytical principle.) This paper therefore begins from the distance that separated the middle strata from the ruling class, and its implications for the formation and transformation of consciousness in Victorian society.

Middle Strata and Bourgeoisie: Problems of Definition

The two main groupings of the middle strata—small business proprietors and white collar employees—both occupied socio-economic positions distinct from the productive relations of capitalist industry, the dominant mode of production in Victorian Britain.[1] Thus, although white collar employees worked for wages, they were not generally engaged in the direct production of surplus value, and did not belong to the proletariat (the class exploited by the extraction from it of surplus value) in the Marxian sense; while small business proprietors (the classic petty bourgeoisie) were distinguished not just by their petty property and scale of operation, but also by the fact that their businesses generally involved the sale to customers of the proprietor's own labour (this could be so even where some wage labour was also employed). The positions of the middle strata are thus distinct, both from the productive relations of capitalist industry and from each other. Given this element of heterogeneity the loose term middle strata seems preferable to any attempt to assign these groupings to a social class; themselves heterogeneous (ranging from the lower fringes of the bourgeoisie to the upper fringes of the working class), they are distinct from the two major classes of capitalist society.[2] While their relations of production provide the basic criterion for establishing the distinctness of the middle strata, that criterion should not be applied mechanistically. Many employers who were, in a formal sense, 'pure' capitalists were none the less more closely tied to the middle strata than to the ruling bourgeoisie; similarly, professional men, depending on their family connections, property holdings, clientele, etc., might be assimilated to either the ruling class or the middle strata.

The trends which were expanding the middle strata were especially marked in Edinburgh.[3] As a capital city it contained administrative and cultural institutions employing large numbers of white collar workers; the local concentration of banking and insurance, and the growing role of finance capital in the Scottish economy,[4] likewise created clerical employment. As in other cities, urban development was supported by a proliferation of small businesses in retailing, services, and some sectors of industry. The concentration in Edinburgh of wealth and fashion added to the demand for such industries and services. The same features of the city made for complex differentiations in its bourgeoisie. A metropolitan high society analogous to that in the West End of London was based on wealth produced elsewhere; much of the administrative and political bourgeoisie (of which sections of the legal profession were a key part) was assimilated, by origin and outlook, to this metropolitan society. There was also an industrial and commercial bourgeoisie, based on local economic activities. The second and third quarters of the nineteenth century saw significant social, political and religious conflicts between these groupings. These differences were residentially identified, in the contrast between the 'aristocratic' Georgian New Town (the counterpart of London's West End) and the prosperous suburban districts developing from the mid-nineteenth century.

The identification of the various bourgeois groupings itself raises conceptual problems, which cannot adequately be discussed here. The ruling class in capitalist social formations may be briefly defined as those who own, or effectively dispose of, economically strategic holdings of capital, together with those (such as the top layer of the professions, top civil servants, etc.) linked to them by interest, ideology, and a common mode of life; these latter groups constitute a 'political' ruling class performing important directive functions in society as a whole.[5] In Victorian Britain sections of the ruling class had a pronounced local character, and exercised hegemony through a network of local institutions dominated, often in complex ways, by the local bourgeoisie; in the central state apparatus, on the other hand, big landowners played an important role.

For research purposes, it is impossible to draw an adequate distinction between the ruling class and the middle strata by reference simply to occupational descriptions; both business and professional categories are heterogeneous in this respect. It will therefore be necessary to use such indicators as residence and life-style to delineate different social levels in the urban community. This is, it should be stressed, a matter of indicators, not of definition; it is an economical alternative to the detailed reconstruction of property holdings, kinship connections, and other determinants of class position.

This paper explores the formation of distinct sub-cultures in the middle strata, the innovative pressures exerted by this process, and its implications for the cultural hegemony of the bourgeoisie. Religion played a crucial, if diverse, part in that hegemony, and much of the discussion will be concerned with the socio-cultural significance of religious adherence.[6]

The Pattern of Religious Adherence

The religious scene in Edinburgh was dominated by presbyterianism, which took three main forms: the Established Church of Scotland, the Free Church and the United Presbyterians.[7] The Free Church had broken away in 1843 over issues of patronage and appointment of ministers, the culmination of a long-standing conflict between Evangelicals and Moderates within the Established Church. In urban areas the Free Church took with it the most dynamic, and most rigorously Calvinist, forces in the Church of Scotland. The bourgeois religious response to the challenge of urban growth was largely the Free Church, and to some extent the United Presbyterians. The United Presbyterian Church, formed in 1847, was an amalgam of groups which had seceded at various earlier dates from the Established Church. It differed from the Free Church mainly in not seeing itself as the true legitimate Established Church, and this issue of 'Voluntaryism' long kept the two bodies apart; in 1900, however, they merged to form the United Free Church.

According to the religious census of 1851 the three presbyterian churches each accounted for about a quarter of the church sittings in Edinburgh and Leith.[8] The attendance figures, however, suggest the greater dynamism of the Free Church and the United Presbyterians; they both claimed about three quarters of the available accommodation filled at their best attended service, while the Church of Scotland claimed only 43 per cent filled.⁹ There were also a number of sects and denominations, embracing a doctrinal and social range roughly equivalent to that of English Nonconformity (though the dominance of presbyterianism in Scotland, and the unique position of the Free Church, complicate any comparison). None of these were individually of great relative significance, but added together they comprised 19 per cent of church sittings. Dissent therefore had, in aggregate, a significant presence in the city.¹⁰ The most important denominations were the Methodists, Congregationalists, and Baptists, with five, six and seven places of worship respectively. Finally the Episcopalians accounted for 5 per cent and the Catholics for 2 per cent of sittings.

There are no figures for church attendance subsequent to the 1851 census. But the *Post Office Directory* list of places of worship suggests that the pattern remained broadly similar (see Table 5.1).¹¹ This indicates that the presbyterian churches, already well provided with premises in the city centre, concentrated their building in the newly developing suburbs; it is again the Free Church and the United Presbyterians which are more dynamic. The formation of new suburban congregations apparently reflected a real demand, rather than the reckless denominational aggrandisement that sometimes characterised nineteenth-century church-building. The founders of Mayfield Free Church petitioned the presbytery in 1875 for the establishment of a preaching station: 'the suburb is already large & is rapidly extending ... a large proportion of the inhabitants are connected with the Free Church'.¹² The Barclay Memorial Free Church quickly attracted 'families drawn from the newer districts in the neighbourhood', and subsequently acted as mother church to the new congregation at Warrender Park.¹³

Direct evidence for the social composition of different denominations is unfortunately limited. Table 5.2 analyses three churches for which information is available at a date allowing access to the census enumerators' books.¹⁴ The table suggests the strong business and white collar representation in all three churches. There are, however, some interesting differences. Although too much weight should not be placed on a comparison of office-bearers (stewards) in one case with membership samples in others, the Methodists appear to be more socially homogeneous; the two other churches have, for example, appreciable manual working class adherence. The incidence of servant-keeping also suggests the presence of a somewhat higher social stratum in the Church of Christ; but that this is only a short step removed from the non-servant-keeping group is indicated by the predominance of teenage girls among the servants concerned. The relative social position of the business and white collar adherents of these churches is brought out by a comparison with the eldership of Bristo Street United Presbyterian Church in 1881.[15] This included three clergymen, three lawyers, two large master printers, one tea dealer, five retailers, three white collar employees (a teacher, a cemetery superintendent and a city missionary), and a museum attendant. Seven of the eighteen elders (including two of the white collar group) had one servant, and seven (including three of the retailers) had two or more. Residence provides a further contrast with the membership as a whole. Of professional, business, and white collar elders, one lived in the New Town, ten in the suburbs, and five in the outer central districts (i.e. residentially mixed areas already developed at the mid-nineteenth century, characterised by concentrations of retail businesses, services, etc. around the main roads out of the city). Of members in the same occupational categories, none lived in the New Town, ten lived in the outer central districts, three in the suburbs, and two in working class districts.[16] As this pattern suggests, suburban development prior to the 1880s tended to consist of spacious and select streets of villas. Development thereafter (often of tenement flats rather than villas) catered for a wider social range and was, it will be argued, an important aspect of the religious and cultural patterns emerging among the middle strata.

Table 5.3 analyses officers in the Boys' Brigade, one of a number of para-religious organisations which were an important feature of late-nineteenth-century religious movements. It should be noted, first, that more than half the officers could not be found in the enumerators' book for the address stated. Apart from random errors, this may reflect a tendency for inactive companies of the Boys' Brigade to record out-dated information about their officers. In eleven such cases the household head had the appropriate surname, was married or widowed, and was of an age to have adult sons; it is reasonable to suppose that these officers had moved from the parental home, were absent on census night, etc. Despite these difficulties, the information is sufficiently interesting to merit analysis. Participants in the Boys' Brigade appear to be socially diverse with, if anything, a weighting toward the upper end of the social scale; servant-keepers outnumber non-servant-keepers, and those with two or more servants outnumber those with one. But the overall pattern obscures a number of interesting social and denominational differences. Five of the professional category were in fact students (predominantly divinity students), four of whom were living in the households of their servant-keeping parents. In the households headed by businessmen it likewise tended to be co-residing adult sons who were active in the Boys' Brigade. But officers in the white collar, intermediate and manual categories were more likely to head their own households. This may indicate that for the sons of relatively wealthy parents the Boys' Brigade was a transient interest (possibly even a social obligation in some congregations); while for the other social groups it was a more permanent commitment.

Some social correlates of a denominational breakdown of the various companies are summarised in Table 5.4. The main interest of this analysis is its confirmation of the greater dynamism and social penetration of the Free Church and United Presbyterians. Companies connected with these churches have higher participation by the white collar and intermediate categories, and this is borne out by the patterns of residence and servant-keeping. Officers of the Church of Scotland and Episcopalian companies account for four of the five New Town households, while five of the seven officers connected with these denominations lived in households with two or more servants.

Table 5.5 analyses a Mutual Improvement Association, another para-religious organisation typical of the period, and clearly indicates the appeal of such activities to white collar employees. The most interesting feature of the figures is the high concentration of manual workers among the members' parents, while analysis of the heads of neighbouring households reveals that four of the seven households headed by business proprietors and white collar employees had at least one manual worker neighbour. These families lived predominantly in the outer central area around Tollcross. It is also interesting to note that manual worker members were more likely to head their own households; this may repeat, at a different social level, the contrast between permanent and transitional commitment noted in the Boys' Brigade.

The emphasis on religious organisations of the middle strata reflects the survival of data, and should not lead us to misrepresent its significance within the broader cultural pattern. As Hugh McLeod suggests elsewhere in this volume, various kinds of religion formed one part of a spectrum of alternative sub-cultures in the middle strata, some of which may have been distinctly unrespectable. As Sir James Marwick recalled of his days as a law apprentice:

> They were too prone to frequent the tavern when they had any money to spend; and when they knew that I was supplied with funds from home, I was waylaid as I left the office and compelled to give them 'a drink'.[17]

The only hard membership data for a non-religious activity is for the committees of bowling clubs in Edinburgh and Leith. Like some of the religious organisations, these were drawn from the middle strata (four professional men, nine business proprietors, twelve white collar employees, one retail employee and two skilled manual workers); two of these households kept two servants, and three kept one teenage servant.[18] Many of the commercialised forms of cultural activity developing during the period probably also catered for the middle strata; but such activities by definition leave no individual record of their participants.

It is therefore possible to identify cultural institutions associated particularly with the middle strata, separate from both the dominant bourgeoisie and the manual working class. The distance between the dominant groups of local society and the lesser professionals, small and medium businessmen, and white collar employees implies that the reproduction of dominant ideology in the middle strata should be seen as historically problematic. Treatments of hegemony in British society have generally analysed the implantation of dominant ideology in the working class; but the exercise of hegemony over the middle strata (whose own social function is often that of subaltern intellectuals, the NCOs of the apparatus of bourgeois hegemony)[19] is a critically important feature of the social formation.

The social separation of the middle strata also has implications for the study of the working class. It is often argued that the middle strata severed their contacts with the labour aristocracy, and that this led to a strengthening of working class consciousness in the 1890s and 1900s.[20] I have also suggested that there may be important differences between sections of the middle strata, with small masters, technical and supervisory employees promoted from the shop-floor, etc. being relatively closer to the labour aristocracy.[21] The fragmentary nature of the material makes it difficult to test these hypotheses. It is however worth noting that two predominantly artisan recreational activities in 1871 also had significant representation from the middle strata;[22] in 1891 no record was found of any organisation with a comparable social mix. Residential patterns in these organisations support a thesis of increased social separation. Table 5.6 shows the association between suburban residence and segregation from the working class in 1891. This reflects the widening of the social range of middle class suburban housing from the 1880s when districts like Warrender Park began to offer tenement housing of a distinctively white collar character. Prior to that date the middle strata probably lived mainly in the more mixed outer central districts. In 1871 both manual and non-manual participants in the activities men-

tioned above lived predominantly in such districts. The data for the
Mutual Improvement Association in 1881 (Table 5.5) may represent a
point of transition. Again the members lived mainly in the outer central
districts; but participation in this church-linked activity by the white
collar sons of skilled workers may constitute the beginning of a process
of differentiation of white collar from manual labour, which was intensified by the emergence of new suburbs.[23]

Religion and the Culture of the Middle Strata

Religious institutions and values constituted only one element in the
cultural identity emerging in the middle strata in the 1880s and 90s. It
is however the best documented element, and an examination of the
functions of religious affiliation may throw light on more general features of their life-styles and attitudes.

Although the following discussion will emphasise the role of various
ancillary social activities, this should not be taken to imply a reductionist dismissal of the relevance of religious belief itself. (Such belief could,
of course, also be shared by people unconnected with any form of organised religion.) This dimension is difficult of access, especially as we are
concerned with the views of congregations rather than of preachers. At
the level of formal doctrine there was a range of denominational—and
in the larger churches probably also of congregational—variation; this
was partly a variation in the extent to which doctrine, of whatever sort,
was insisted upon. The Free Church and the United Presbyterians belonged, of course, to the Calvinist tradition, though the meanings of that
tradition to the mass of adherents are impenetrable; there were significant modifications during the period, especially from the 1880s when
'as an intellectual system Calvinism collapsed'.[24] Some Nonconformist
churches reflected an earlier reaction against Calvinism, upholding free
grace against predestination, and emphasising ethical conduct and a biblical faith with the minimum of doctrine.[25] Such views appealed to
Annie S. Swan's father, a potato merchant and later small farmer, who
was a pillar of Leith Evangelical Union Church during the third quarter
of the century.[26] The growing role of partly inter-denominational
bodies such as the Boys' Brigade, YMCA, Christian Endeavour, etc.
suggests a general pressure in the direction of a doctrinally eclectic
Protestantism; the typical form of such organisations, combining attachment of units (e.g. Boys' Brigade companies) to congregations with a
cross-denominational federal structure, can be seen as a compromise between the doctrinal indifference of their popular appeal and the retention of some denominational identity.[27]

Doctrinally eclectic Protestantism provided a source of ethical guidance and imparted significance to otherwise mundane lives:

> The older I grow the more strongly do I feel that religion is a matter of daily living—of practice, not precept; and that unless the Spirit of Christ animate us in all our relations one to the other, we name His name in vain. And what a lovely spirit it was, unsullied by any trace of selfishness, gentle, forbearing, long-suffering, just to the last degree![28]

The quality of religious belief in the middle strata is perhaps best captured in Annie Swan's account of her father: 'If it was not a faith that could move mountains, at least it was a shield and standby in the day of trouble, or when times were hard.'[29] Such a faith was adapted to the conditions faced by these sections of society: often tedious, sometimes hard, generally frustrating, and without the resources of collective resistance available to working class people.

Religious adherence could also have a more immediate material bearing on the life-chances of the middle strata. The social network of the church could provide business contacts. (This is perhaps reflected in the business membership of the Church of Christ, which includes three coal merchants, two of them brothers and partners, two bakers, and four lodging-house keepers.) Conversely, religious leadership could go with business success. In some congregations (especially of the Free Church and the United Presbyterians) such success was measured by the standards of leading business circles in the city.[30] (The Bristo Street elders, for example, would seem to have enjoyed success at this level.) But the levels of success of lesser business circles were probably relevant for other churches. For white collar employees, or socially ambitious manual workers, the churches could provide access to educational and cultural facilities.[31]

The dimension of social identity and companionship is perhaps the most distinctive feature of religious adherence in the middle strata. The running of the church itself could be an absorbing interest, as it was for Annie Swan's father:

> He helped to build that little church, was one of its office-bearers, and loved it with every fibre of his being . . . Our social life was all bound up in that little church, our friends were there, and we loved everything connected with it.[32]

Even in congregations with a predominantly bourgeois leadership, routine activities connected with the church, and ancillary organisations, could draw in a wider social range. Church choirs, for example, were central to the functioning of the church; the improvement in 'praise' is frequently noted in histories of Free Church congregations, although it had caused bitter controversy in the 1860s.[33] Such bodies as the Boys' Brigade have already been mentioned; the emergence of variously named mutual improvement associations, literary societies, etc. (in fact social clubs for young people) was another development of the period. The congregational year books of the 1900s contain a fairly standard list of ancillary activities. At Warrender Park United Free Church in 1904 the list includes a praise sub-committee (i.e. choir, which gave an annual recital as well as singing at services), sabbath school, bible classes, home mission, junior musical association, and literary society; Braid United Free Church in 1910 had lectures, literary and social evenings, a visit to the *Scotsman* newspaper offices, rambles and excursions.[34] The Free High Church Young Men's Union in 1878 offered a programme of 'Pleasant Evenings for Working People' devoted to such topics as 'water: good and bad', 'witchcraft' and 'the ruins of Pompeii'.[35]

This aspect of religious activity seems to have been best developed (or at any rate best recorded) by the Methodists. The success of their mission was widely attributed to this side of its work. For example it provided informal Sunday evenings

> with a view to filling the blank in the life of the lodger—shop assistant, clerk, teacher, or student . . . Books, papers, and music are provided, together with light refreshments, and the meeting closes with family worship.[36]

Other activities included a literary society and a rambling club.[37] The social life centred on religious institutions probably provided, among other things, one of the few socially approved meeting-places between the sexes. 'Three ladies hold office, and they seem made for the place, with clear heads and decided wills, . . . and always on the right side.'[38]

Cultural Innovation and Ideological Hegemony

The adaptation of the Free Church and United Presbyterians to the situation and needs of suburban small businessmen and white collar workers produced a different type of church from that envisaged by its founders. The religious culture of the middle strata should not be seen merely as passively reflecting the values of the dominant class; hegemony never operates in this simple way, but must be seen as complex, dynamically modified to incorporate innovative forms produced by subordinate groups.[39] The transformation of the presbyterian churches during the second half of the nineteenth century must be examined in this perspective.

In the conception of its founders the Free Church was to be a national church, and, in the Calvinist tradition, to impose Godly order on the whole community, not merely its own members. The Free Church originated in the Evangelical Party within the Church of Scotland; as its name implies, this group emphasised the evangelical mission of the kirk in combating irreligion, sin and moral disintegration among the urban masses. The social, moral, political and religious dimensions of such problems were fused in a single image of urban social danger; the conversion of the masses was seen as the necessary condition of a well ordered society.[40] The social mission of the church was to evangelise the masses, to impress upon them a sense of their own sinfulness and 'neglect of the means of grace'; but at the same time it was to exert coercive control over the unregenerate through the apparatus of education, charity, poor relief, etc.[41]

This approach still pervades the language of the 1860 report of Bristo Street United Presbyterian Church. 'When we reflect upon the unworthy use we have made of the many precious privileges that we have possessed, we have reason to humble ourselves in the very dust.'[42] Members were exhorted to give 'of their substance as God has prospered them', to support the congregation's city missionary, who reported 'still not a little ungodliness and neglect of the means of grace . . . still some avowed infidels are to be met with; and also a few of those who desire not the presence of a City Missionary'.[43] The transformation of the presbyterian churches is reflected in the quite different language of the 1890s and 1900s.

> The Committee of the Missionary Society have again the pleasing duty of presenting their Annual Report . . . the work has been quiet and unobtrusive, but not the less effectual on that account.[44]

This change in attitude may certainly be related to such things as the secularisation of modes of thought and a more optimistic view of man and society. But these modified forms of thought corresponded to other, less obvious changes. The greater stability of capitalist society after about 1850 gradually diminished the sense of social danger and urgency. At the same time it was becoming apparent that the practical requirements of a viable urban mission did not accord with the conception of the Free Church leadership. Meanwhile the social and cultural role of the churches was being transformed by the initiative of the middle strata. These aspects are connected: as it became manifest that the urban working class could not be converted *en masse*, the middle strata provided a reservoir of potential practising Christians, and such trends as the emergence of the labour aristocracy made for greater confidence about the containment of social danger.

Although it was the growth of a concentrated urban proletariat that aroused the strongest fears of irreligion, missionary effort may have been more successful in reaching the middle strata; they were also prominent in providing the personnel of missionary work, especially in such organisations as the Boys' Brigade. The Free Church Mission in the predominantly working class district of Fountainbridge formed the nucleus of a new congregation at Barclay Church, located on the edge of the more mixed district round Tollcross, and adjacent to the expanding suburban districts of Bruntsfield and Warrender Park.[45] The shortage of church accommodation earlier in the century, to which some contemporaries attributed the supposed decline in religious observance, may well have been a significant factor for the middle strata. The Methodist Mission, with its Sunday evening 'at homes' for lodgers, literary and rambling societies, was fairly explicit in its appeal to this section of society; it claimed considerable success, with a growth of membership from 50 in 1889 to 608 in 1896.[46] The impact of such developments modified the evangelical approach of the presbyterian churches in two respects. It meant a recognition of the key role of ancillary social activities in attracting the support of the middle strata, and a less doctrinaire denominational approach. The most successful missions were those that provided a non-doctrinal Protestantism, together with some sense of cultural participation. As the spread of movements like the Boys' Brigade indicates, denomination was no barrier to the adoption of successful innovations pioneered elsewhere.

Many of the cultural activities especially characteristic of the suburban religious pattern originated in mission work, and were then incorporated into regular congregations. Religious music, for example, was used in Sunday schools before it was accepted at presbyterian services;[47] its acceptance probably owed something to its popular appeal and the sense of participation choirs made possible, as well as to the aesthetic influences on the bourgeois intelligentsia more often mentioned in this context.[48] The young men's associations, literary societies, etc. grew out of former Sunday school classes:

... if I were to call it a class now, I daresay the whole of the young men would disappear. It is now an Association or Society, conducted entirely by themselves ... They conduct the prayer, praise, and addresses themselves. I seldom interfere. They read, generally one, sometimes two essays on religious topics, every Sabbath evening.[49]

Another teacher noted that it was the 'imperfectly educated' pupils who lost connection with the church as they got older.[50] At Newington United Presbyterian Church a group of young men asked permission to use the session room for their literary society; at Mayfield Free Church former members of the Boys' Brigade formed an old boys' union in 1909.[51] In one Mutual Improvement Association women were officially admitted after a number had in fact joined.[52] Such societies, which functioned as social clubs for young church members, thus arose from a spontaneous development, rather than from any plan on the part of the church leadership.

By the 1900s the middle strata appear to dominate the eldership, and not merely the membership, of some Free Church congregations. The only source of occupational information at this date is the *Post Office Directory*; this does, however, serve to bring out the point that most of the elders were of the relatively obscure social level not listed there, or listed without trade or profession, and it is reasonable to suppose from their addresses that these were mainly white collar workers. Elders at Warrender Park in 1900 included six professionals, eleven businessmen, three white collar workers, and fifteen untraceable. Ten years later the number of professionals had fallen to three, the businessmen to four, white collar had risen to six, and untraceable to twenty.[53] At McCrie-Roxburgh (1904) and Braid (1910) there a similar preponderance of white collar and untraceable elders.[54] The broadening of the eldership would appear to be a trend: of those not listed or listed without any trade or profession, all but two at Warrender Park in 1910 had been ordained since 1900, and all but one at McCrie-Roxburgh had been ordained since 1895. There may also be a shift in the character of the business groups involved: four of the six businessmen at Warrender Park in 1900-1 owned businesses outside the immediate suburban district, compared to only one out of three ten years later; four of the seven businessmen at Braid were shopkeepers, builders, etc. in the suburb itself. This local suburban business grouping is very different from that found in the eldership of Bristo Street United Presbyterian Church thirty years earlier.[55]

The formation of the middle strata thus had a considerable impact on the character of religious institutions. The church-centred sub-culture was, however, only one of a number of alternative, loosely overlapping suburban sub-cultures. The pressures of church membership were less compulsive for these sections of society than for their social superiors, but for those who were members, the church played a larger part in their lives.[56] Religious institutions must thus be set in the context of other cultural innovations associated with the growth of the middle strata.

The family may be one case of such innovative pressure. Generalisations about 'the Victorian middle class woman' are at no period entirely applicable to these strata. They often had experience of employment before marriage, and they might assist in the husband's small business, augment the family income by taking lodgers, or support themselves as spinsters or widows; they employed little or no domestic service and probably always did some housework; the style of housing within their reach, and other economic constraints, would certainly preclude the elaborate social rituals that defined the symbolic role of the wife in 'Society'.[57] These groups may thus have been the first to develop more intimate, less formal family relationships. The shift to such relationships perhaps underlies Annie Swan's recollection of her father:

> In the light of maturer knowledge and experience, I now realise that much of that sternness was assumed to hide his real nature. He was afraid of himself. Many Scots of the old school were like that, hence the strange bleakness of much of the family life.[58]

And she remembers her mother's love of reading and strange inarticulacy:

> I have often thought of all that must have been repressed and hidden in that still nature, of what she had to suffer from us all, and her endless patience.[59]

The same author's book on *Courtship and Marriage and the Gentle Art of Home-making* (1893) is in many ways a plea for a less elaborate and less distant pattern of family life adapted to the conditions of the middle strata. She argues for intelligence and outside interests in women; for joint financial decision-making; for a casual pattern of entertaining at home, very different from the rigid etiquette of Society; for the father to take an active role in playing with children and so on.[60] Her own career had, indeed, been somewhat unconventional: she married the village schoolteacher while still living on her father's farm, having already sold her first stories; subsequently her husband studied medicine in Edinburgh supported by her literary earnings—an arrangement which she says occasioned much malicious gossip.[61] But her innovations remained within certain limits: she saw the role of the wife, much more than of the husband, as supportive and long-suffering, but compensated for by 'motherhood . . . the crown of marriage'. Employment is seen as an alternative, rather than as an adjunct, to the role of wife.[62] In the context of the 1930s, when she published her autobiography, she occupied a somewhat conservative position; she deplores the explicitness of modern fiction and argues that she and her sisters had managed to 'warstle through' despite Victorian reticence on sexual matters.[63]

The career of writers like Annie Swan is bound up with the emergence of cultural forms catering for a popular mass market. Most of her output consisted of serials for the *People's Friend*, a Scottish weekly based on a formula of practical advice (recipes, household hints, tips on preparation for the civil service clerical examinations), miscellaneous information about the wonders of nature and of modern technology, and romantic serials.[64] This fiction was itself written to a formula: it had to have a happy ending, to punish vice and reward virtue, and as a rule to depict 'people of high degree'.[65] Some aspects of this formula— for example, the upholding of popular morality—can probably be traced back to much earlier popular traditions. Popular fiction appealing to the middle strata may have become more clearly distinguished from other cultural forms (as the serial stories in working class newspapers always had been). Dickens, Hardy and many other writers first sold their work in serial form. In the 1880s and 90s this practice seems to have died out; the *People's Friend* carried a serial by Trollope in 1881, but there were no comparable serials subsequently.[66] Annie Swan, on the other hand, gained her first success with *Aldersyde*, published as a complete novel in 1883, but thereafter shifted into serial-writing where the main demand for her type of fiction was concentrated.[67]

Other cultural forms seem to reflect a similar process, often in the context of the capitalisation of leisure facilities. Moss, the Edinburgh music hall entrepreneur, made the music hall respectable, while retaining its essential formal features.[68] His other projects included the Waverley Market New Year Carnivals, a similarly bowdlerised version of the culture of the fair, whose 'healthy, harmless, and filling' entertainment included such items as 'Mr. W. FREDERICK'S TROUPE OF *Cats, Rats, Mice, and Canaries* BOXING CATS, SLOPER CAT, and WONDERFUL CLOWN CAT', 'The Only Lady Electrician in the Universe', 'Horde of

ARABS', etc.[69]

Large-scale business investment in leisure and communications media was thus associated with a transformation of popular forms, rendering them more acceptable to respectable audiences. The downward transmission of elements of high culture was another aspect of the same process. The growth of cheap editions was one of the innovations of the second half of the nineteenth century.[70] Scraps of information about important writers, artists, etc. often feature in lecture programmes (such as those provided by the church literary societies), and in publications like the *People's Friend*. Through this process of diffusion cultural forms were interpreted in particular ways;[71] the tendency was often to personalise, to make simple moral identifications, and to look for confirmation of a given set of values. Non-doctrinal Protestantism emphasised the personality and example of Christ and other biblical figures. Similarly, Robert McEwan, a sponsor of classical concerts for popular audiences, discovered that the way to gain attention was to 'tell the audience about the composer—his life and times . . . in speaking about Beethoven, refer to his noble and unselfish character'.[72] One meeting of the Methodist Mutual Improvement Association discussed the merits and demerits of characters in *Hamlet*.[73]

Hegemony is less a matter of the diffusion of particular cultural products than of the way in which these are organised to form 'a given cultural world'.[74] All cultural activity is in this sense cultural production, and it is important to recognise the active role of the middle strata in the developments discussed above—a role often obscured by caricatures of their deference and passivity.[75] Such innovations involved important shifts in the forms of hegemony; the middle strata emerged as a solid bloc of support for a modified version of the dominant values, while the growth of heavily capitalised leisure and communications facilities represented an important new form of concentrated cultural power. Thus the cultural innovations examined above were set within definite limits, the most fundamental of which was the acceptance of the individualistic values of hegemonic ideology; it was from this, and from the absence of sustainable alternatives (such as those to be found in working class cultures), that the deferential and imitative aspects of the culture arose. Success or failure was seen as individually determined, and measured by the standards of those on whom the clerk or small tradesman was personally dependent; these groups lacked the ideological resources to see the structural determinants of their position. This consciousness no doubt corresponded to the social realities of promotion, salary increments, or the modest prosperity to which successful retailers could look forward. The caricatures do have some reference to reality, as is indicated by the laboured and pretentious essays read to church societies:

> Let us toil on, not blown about by every wind, not discouraged by dissappointments [sic] or losses but press forward keeping our eye fixed on our goal, whatever that may be. Don't stop in the way but push on, because the moment we stop other people will push us to one side and outreach us ... don't be grumbling about this, that, and the next thing but be in earnest, be energetic, be industrious and so improve our position.[76]

The mutual criticism, which was one of the stated objects of the magazine quoted, was bland in the extreme:

> The article on Industry is brimming over with sage and practical advice ... Let each of us strive to carry out these precepts ... combining with them a fear and reference [sic] for God.[77]

And one member of the Methodist rambling club found it necessary to 'call my muse to my aid' before describing an excursion.[78] This inflated sense of self-importance no doubt underlay much of the participation in church societies.

> In the first solemn moments the Chairman announced to his hearers the purpose of the meeting, and then put the question in definite form to them, and answered it in the affirmative.[79]

The cultural activity of the middle strata thus lent itself to the kind of caricature which has often served as a substitute for serious analysis of their social position and ideology. Their acceptance of dominant values, practised at their distinctive social level, produced the behaviour which has been a recurrent theme of literary caricature: imitation, pretension and occasional impotent rebellion. These strata tended, moreover, to adopt a rigid, partly archaic, version of hegemonic values, in contrast to the greater flexibility (itself a measure of the strength of their hegemony) of the ruling class. But this image, despite its reference to real social phenomena, should not be allowed to obscure the innovative role within bourgeois hegemony of the middle strata. (Sometimes the apparently archaic could carry a real innovation; Annie Swan, for example, referred back to the virtues of a simpler, less pretentious rural society to support new patterns of family life.)[80] Acceptance of dominant values was combined with innovation in certain limited areas.

The occupational activities of elementary teachers—a group unusual among the middle strata in their early development of organisations to further their specific interests—are a clear case of this phenomenon. The one extant issue of a magazine for Edinburgh pupil-teachers referred to the need for many fundamental reforms of the educational system, but remained remarkably vague as to what these might be, beyond asserting the value of 'the teaching profession . . . second to none in importance, in dignity, and in usefulness'.[81] Articles in the magazine show a similar mixture of limited criticism and deferential acceptance. One contributor criticised 'the drill-sergeant's eternal exercise of parsing' on the ground that children should be 'trained to *think* . . . not to learn a few facts'. Others were less critical of dominant definitions of culture and education, for example in the view that through literature pupils could be purified and ennobled, and in the recommendation of Annie Swan's books as containing nothing 'calculated to do harm to her readers', while 'showing the worth of comparatively humble lives . . . the nobility so to speak of the masses'.[82]

The subordination of the middle strata cannot be understood if hegemony is regarded as a static system, rather than as a historically problematic set of socio-cultural practices. The social identity of the middle strata (especially their sense of separation from, and superiority to, manual labour) was produced at a social level quite different from that of the dominant bourgeoisie. This involved a specific version of the hegemonic ideology divergent from that of the ruling class in its rigidity and archaism in some respects, its limited social innovation in others. It is just because the hegemonic ideology could encompass these divergent versions that it was powerful and could effectively subordinate the middle strata. In this respect their acceptance of hegemonic values was deeper, and harder to shake, than that of parts of the working class. The conditions of working class life (including those of the labour aristocracy) enforced a collective struggle, which always carried with it an oppositional potential, albeit often a weakly articulated one.[83] The conditions of the middle strata enjoined, if anything, individualism, and the more critical aspects of their social posture were decisively limited by this hegemonic value.

Notes

1. Recent Marxist writers distinguish the dominant mode of production from

the social formation determined by, but not reducible to, that mode of production (thus the social formation includes subordinate modes of production, politics, ideology, culture, etc.). The expansion of the middle strata was an aspect of the social formation determined by the capitalist mode of production, but they were not themselves involved in capitalist relations of production: see S. Macintyre and K. Tribe, *Althusser and Marxist Theory*, published by the authors, Cambridge, 1974, pp. 10-11.
2. For the concept of middle strata see, e.g., A. Hunt, 'Class Structure in Britain Today', reprinted in *Class Structure*, Communist Party pamphlet, London.
3. For a fuller discussion of Edinburgh's economy and social structure see Ch. 2 of my book *The Labour Aristocracy in Victorian Edinburgh*, Clarendon Press, Oxford, 1976.
4. See J. Foster, 'Capitalism and the Scottish Nation', in G. Brown (ed.), *The Red Paper on Scotland*, Edinburgh University Student Publications Board, Edinburgh, 1975, p. 148.
5. Hunt, loc.cit.
6. A.A. MacLaren, *Religion and Social Class: the Disruption years in Aberdeen*, Routledge, London, 1974; and H. McLeod, *Religion and Class in the Late Victorian City*, Croom Helm, London, 1974, both provided valuable insights and comparative information in the writing of this essay.
7. This paragraph is based on: W. Ferguson, *Scotland: 1689 to the present*, Oliver & Boyd, Edinburgh and London, 1968, pp. 336-40; MacLaren, op.cit., Ch. 2.
8. *Census of Great Britain 1851: religious worship and education (Scotland)*, PP 1854 LIX, 301. These figures unfortunately combine Edinburgh with the neighbouring burgh of Leith.
9. Cf. MacLaren, op.cit., p. 37.
10. See J.C. Williams, 'Edinburgh Politics, 1832-52' (University of Edinburgh Ph.D. thesis, 1972), pp. 12-30.
11. Table 5.1, and all subsequent facts and figures, refer to Edinburgh only; Table 5.1 is therefore not comparable to the religious census (see above, footnote 8).
12. *Mayfield 100, 1875-1975*, Mayfield Church Publications Committee, Edinburgh, 1975, p. 10.
13. *The Barclay Church, 1865-1915*, Pillans & Wilson, Edinburgh, n.d., pp. 8-13 (in National Library of Scotland: hereafter NLS).
14. I am indebted to the Registrar-General for Scotland for permission to use census material in Tables 5.2-5.6 and the accompanying text. The Church of Christ was apparently an independent Nonconformist chapel; I found no information about it apart from the list of members.
15. Bristo Street United Presbyterian Church, *Annual Report*, 1881 (in Edinburgh Public Library: hereafter EPL).
16. This classification of streets is inevitably somewhat arbitrary; it rests on the author's personal knowledge of the city, nineteenth-century street maps, and judgements based on the style of architecture, etc. in doubtful cases. The great majority of the addresses could, however, be quite unambiguously classified.
17. Sir James Marwick, LL.D., *A Retrospect*, privately printed, Glasgow, (c. 1905), p. 25 (NLS).
18. Re-analysis of data summarised in Gray, op.cit., p. 106; the present re-analysis excludes cases whose home addresses could not be traced.
19. See A. Gramsci, *Selections from the Prison Notebooks*, Lawrence & Wishart, London, 1971, p. 13.

20. E.g. Gray, op.cit., pp. 116-20, 169.
21. Ibid., pp. 108-111.
22. Ibid., p. 106.
23. Questions of occupational mobility and recruitment to white collar employment, which cannot be tackled here, are also relevant to this hypothesis.
24. Ferguson, op.cit., p. 336.
25. See Brighton Street Evangelical Union Congregational Church, *History of the Church and Report of Its Services*, J.B. Fairgrieve, Edinburgh, 1894 (NLS).
26. Annie S. Swan, *My Life*, Ivor Nicolson & Watson, London, 1934, pp. 19-20.
27. See, e.g., Edinburgh and District Union of Christian Endeavour Societies, *Fifth Annual Report*, 1898 (NLS); Edinburgh YMCA, *Twentieth Annual Report*, 1875 (NLS).
28. Annie S. Swan, *Courtship and Marriage and the Gentle Art of Home-making*, Hutchinson, London, 1893, p. 142.
29. Swan, *My Life*, p. 26.
30. Cf. MacLaren, op.cit., esp. Ch. 6.
31. Ibid., Ch. 7; and cf. above, Table 5.5.
32. Swan, *My Life*, pp. 19-20.
33. See, e.g., *Mayfield 100*, pp. 53-4; *Barclay Church*, p. 17. For the liturgical controversies, see Ferguson, op.cit., pp. 338-9.
34. Warrender Park United Free Church, *Year Book*, 1904 (NLS); Braid United Free Church, *Annual Report*, 1910 (EPL). See also, e.g., Bristo Street United Presbyterian Church, *Reports*, 1884-1905 (EPL); McCrie-Roxburgh United Free Church, *Year Book*, 1904-5 (EPL).
35. Minutes of the Free High Church Young Men's Union, 14 October 1878 (MS in EPL).
36. Wesleyan Methodist Mission, Edinburgh, *Report*, 1896, p. 20 (EPL).
37. Ibid., pp. 23-32. For the social life of the Methodist Church itself see *Wesleyan Methodist Quarterly Magazine: Edinburgh Circuit*, January-March, 1891 (EPL).
38. Methodist Mission, *Report*, 1896, pp. 32-3.
39. See M. Jacques, 'Trends in Youth Culture', *Marxism Today*, April 1975, pp. 111-4; R. Williams, 'Base and Superstructure', *New Left Review*, no. 82, 1973, pp. 8-12.
40. See MacLaren, op.cit., pp. 168, 200.
41. Ibid., Chs. 6, 7.
42. Bristo Street U.P. Church, *Report*, 1860.
43. Ibid.
44. Ibid., 1895, 1905.
45. *Barclay Church*, p. 5.
46. Methodist Mission, *Report*, 1896, p. 6. Cf. O. Anderson, 'Women Preachers in Mid-Victorian Britain', *Historical Journal*, vol. 12, 1969, p. 473.
47. J.R. Fleming, *A History of the Church in Scotland, 1843-73*, T. & T. Clark, Edinburgh, 1927, p. 123.
48. E.g. by Ferguson, op.cit., pp. 338-9.
49. Edinburgh Sabbath Teachers' Union, *Twenty-first Annual Report*, 1862, quoting report from teacher (NLS).
50. Ibid.
51. *Newington United Presbyterian Church Jubilee Memorial, 1848-98*, R.W. Hunter, Edinburgh, 1898, p. 44 (NLS); *Mayfield 100*, p. 55.
52. J.B. Barclay, *Bristo Place Mutual Improvement Association, 1877-1932*, Macrae & Paterson, Edinburgh, n.d., p. 8 (NLS).
53. Warrender Park Year Books.
54. McCrie-Roxburgh and Braid Year Books.

55. Cf. McLeod, op.cit., pp. 147-55.
56. Ibid., Chs. 5-7.
57. See L. Davidoff, *The Best Circles: society, etiquette and the season*, Croom Helm, London, 1973; and cf. Mr Pooter's comic attempts to carry out some of the rituals described by Davidoff: G. and W. Grossmith, *The Diary of a Nobody*, 2nd Penguin edn., Harmondsworth, 1965, pp. 19, 65-7, 224-5.
58. Swan, *My Life*, p. 15.
59. Ibid., pp. 21-2.
60. Swan, *Courtship and Marriage*, pp. 22, 34-7, 39-40, 104, 108.
61. Swan, *My Life*, pp. 40-8.
62. Swan, *Courtship and Marriage*, Chs. 2, 9, pp. 126-7.
63. Swan, *My Life*, pp. 281, 32.
64. The National Library of Scotland holding of the magazine runs from 1881; the formula is fixed by the end of the 1880s, and undergoes little change down to 1914.
65. Swan, *My Life*, pp. 285-6.
66. *People's Friend*, 5 January 1881.
67. Swan, *My Life*, pp. 41, 283.
68. G. Baird, 'Edinburgh Theatres, Circuses and Cinemas' (unpublished typescript, 1963), pp. 28-31 (EPL).
69. Moss's Waverley Market New Year Carnivals, *Programmes*, 1888, 1890-91 (EPL).
70. R. Williams, *The Long Revolution*, Pelican edn., Harmondsworth, 1965, p. 187.
71. Williams, 'Base and Superstructure', pp. 14-6.
72. R. McEwen, Preface to *Nelson Hall concerts: a list of programmes*, n.p., n.d., p. 16 (NLS).
73. *Wesleyan Methodist Quarterly*, January-March 1891, p. 14.
74. Gramsci, quoted by J. Semprun, in L. Baxendall (ed), *Radical Perspectives in the Arts*, Pelican edn., Harmondsworth, 1972, p. 202; cf. Williams, loc. cit.
75. E.g. Grossmith, op.cit.
76. *The Lantern*, vol. VIII, 1881-2.
77. Ibid.
78. *Our Rambling Club*, G.R. Hamilton, Edinburgh, 1898, p. 9 (NLS).
79. Ibid., p. 2.
80. Swan, *Courtship and Marriage*, pp. 80-6; and see also her very successful novel *Aldersyde*, Oliphant, Anderson & Ferrier, Edinburgh, 1883.
81. *Pupil-teachers' Monthly*, November 1887 (NLS).
82. Ibid.
83. Cf. Gramsci, *Prison Notebooks*, p. 327; for an attempt to interpret the development of the Edinburgh working class in these terms see Gray, op. cit., esp. Chs. 8-10.

Table 5.1: Places of Worship in Edinburgh

	1850-51		1910-11	
	Central	Suburban	Central	Suburban
Church of Scotland	27	2	28	17
Free Church, United Presbyterian[a]	41	2	41	27
Baptist	4	1	5	3

Religion, Culture and Social Class in Edinburgh 155

	1850-51		1910-11	
	Central	Suburban	Central	Suburban
Methodist[b]	1	—	4	—
Congregational	4	—	5	2
Episcopalian	9	—	20	4
Other Protestant	7	—	19	1
Roman Catholic	2	—	3	5

Notes
a. United Free Church from 1900.
b. One Primitive Methodist in 1910-11, otherwise Wesleyan.
Source: Edinburgh and Leith Post Office Directories (Leith excluded).

Table 5.2: Membership of Churches

	Bristo St UP 1881 (5% sample)	Methodist Stewards 1891	Church of Christ 1891 (33% sample)
Professional	3	2	1
Industrial business[a]	3	3	—
Wholesale, retail, services business[a]	7	2	10
Clerks etc.	1	1	3
Other white collar	2	3	3
Intermediate[b]	4	1	2
Manual	10	2	15
Domestic servants[c]	3	—	4
Unoccupied women, annuitants, etc.	4	—	2
	37	14	40
Not traced	12	3	14
Servant-keeping among professional, business, white collar households[d]			
No servants	11	5	5
One servant	4	4	9
Two or more servants	1	—	1

Notes:
a. Self-employed, small masters, and large employers combined.
b. Mainly retail employees; also foremen, police, minor officials etc.
c. Female servants; 6 untraced cases in Church of Christ are probably also domestic servants (women with addresses c/o).
d. Excluding households of hoteliers and lodging-house keepers.
Source: census enumerators' books, names and addresses listed in Bristo St United Presbyterian Church, Report, 1881 (EPL); Wesleyan Methodist Quarterly Magazine: Edinburgh Circuit, January-March 1891 (EPL); Church of Christ, Roxburgh Place, Edinburgh, Roll of Members, 1891 (EPL).

156 The Lower Middle Class in Britain 1870-1914

Table 5.3: Boys' Brigade Officers, 1891[a]

Occupations of officers	Occupations of heads of officers' households								
	Own h/h	Widows	Lodgers	Professional	Business	White collar	Intermediate	Manual	Annuitants, etc.
Private means	1	—	—	—	—	—	—	—	1
Professional	13	7	1	—	2	—	—	—	3
Industrial business[b]	3	1	—	—	—	2[b]	—	—	—
Wholesale, retail, etc.[b]	5	1	—	—	—	3[b]	—	—	1
Clerks, etc.	9	3	—	1	1	2	1	1	—
Other white collar	5	3	—	—	—	1	—	—	1
Intermediate	5	3	—	1	—	—	—	—	1
Manual	5	3	1	1	—	—	—	—	—
	46	21	2	3	3	8	1	1	7
Not traced	68								

Servant-keeping among professional, business, white collar, heads of households[c]

No servants	8
One servant	8
Two or more servants	12

Notes
a. See notes to Table 5.2 for occupational classification.
b. Including 4 sons (2 industrial, 2 wholesale, retail, etc.) employed in father's business.
c. Including households headed by widows, according to occupation of oldest co-residing employed relative of household head; households headed by annuitants, etc. and lodgings are excluded.
Source: census enumerators' books, names and addresses of Boys' Brigade officers listed in Post Office Directory, 1890-91.

Table 5.4: Denominational breakdown of Boys' Brigade officers, 1891

	Free Church, United Presbyterian	Church of Scotland, Episcopalian	Other, unidentified
Occupations of officers:			
Professional	3	6	4
Business	3	1	4
White collar	9	3	2

	Free Church, United Presbyterian	Church of Scotland Episcopalian	Other unidentified
Occupations of officers:			
Intermediate	4	1	—
Manual	1	2	2
Private means	1	—	—
	21	13	12
Servant-keeping among professional, business, white collar household heads			
No servants	5	—	3
One servant	6	2	—
Two or more servants	3	5	4
	14	7	7
Resident in:			
New Town	—	4	1
Outer central	3	1	2
Suburban	10	2	4
Working class	1	—	—
	14	7	7

Source: See Table 5.3: denominations identified by meeting-places of companies. See notes to Table 5.2 for occupational classification.

Table 5.5: Membership of St David's Free Church Mutual Improvement Association, 1881[a]

Occupations of members:		Occupations of heads of members' households:								
		Own h/h	Widows	Lodgers	Professional	Business	White collar	Intermediate	Manual	Annuitants, etc.
Professional	1	—	—	—	—	—	—	—	1	—
Industrial business	1	1	—	—	—	—	—	—	—	—
Wholesale, retail, etc.	2	—	—	1	—	1	—	—	—	—
Clerks, etc.	12	1	2	2	—	—	—	—	7[b]	—
Other white collar	3	—	1	—	—	—	1	—	1[b]	—
Intermediate	3	—	—	—	—	—	—	—	3[b]	—
Manual	5	2	2	—	—	—	—	—	1	—
	27	4	5	3	—	1	1	—	13	—
Not traced	1									

Servant-keeping among business, white collar heads of household:

No servants	5
One servant	2
Two or more servants	—

Notes

a. See notes to Table 5.2 for occupational classification.
b. One household contained 4 members (3 intermediate and 1 white collar); 2 households each contained 2 members (all clerks). Such households have been counted separately for each member.

Source: census enumerators' books, names and addresses listed in 'The Lantern: a magazine in connection with Free St. David's Mutual Improvement Association', vol. VIII, 1881-2 (MS magazine in EPL).

Table 5.6: Residence and neighbours of professional, business and white collar members of organisations, 1891

	Households with manual neighbour[a]		Households with both neighbours non-manual[a]	
	Outer central	Suburban	Outer central	Suburban
Methodist Stewards	2	1	2	5
Church of Christ	3	—	4	8
Boys' Brigade[b]	3	2	3	14
	8	3	9	27

Notes

a. Based on occupations of heads (or oldest occupied person in household; where no such person existed nearest relevant household was taken) of two households adjacent to member's.
b. By occupation of heads of members' households.

6 HOUSING AND THE LOWER MIDDLE CLASS, 1870-1914

S. Martin Gaskell

It would not be unfair to say that in the period 1870 to 1914 the lower middle classes were primarily responsible for the creation of the pressures and problems in both the housing market and reform movement. On the one hand, the chief characteristic of housing development in the later nineteenth century was not the consequence of poor construction and consumate overcrowding as it had been earlier, but rather the result of the continuance of unimaginative layout and unplanned expansion catering predominantly for the needs of the lower middle class. On the other hand, the culmination of nineteenth-century housing reform movements in the early twentieth century Garden City ideal found a ready response within the lower middle class for it reflected the social aspirations of that class and was financially feasible at that level. The emphasis in both the open housing market and the housing reform movement in this period was on urban extension and suburban growth, and this was stimulated to a large degree by social pressure from and the economic condition of the lower middle class.

Almost by definition that class largely consisted of people who had risen from the ranks of the working class, and this fact was clearly demonstrated in their residential patterns and housing requirements. They had, of course, a model for this process of spatial stratification in the efforts of the wealthier and better established middle class. Throughout the nineteenth century, and increasingly since the 1830s and 1840s, carriage-owning middle class families had been removing themselves to ever greater distances from the town centres. The prevalence of such rural retreats increased as the social segregation of the industrial cities strengthened, and as urban centres became areas devoted wholly to commerce and industry. With the complete separation of the prosperous suburbs from industry and from working class housing, so the very wealthy, as distinct from the merely prosperous, could be more selective in their choice of sites. Distance from the city meant little to them provided roads were good. The result was that around Manchester between 1830 and 1850, for example, those estates with rural settings and preferably on high ground with distant views were ripe for exclusive suburbanisation. A series of miniature arcadias arose beyond the extremities of the built-up area, to the north at Cheetham Hill, Higher Broughton and Buile Hill in Pendleton and to the south at Victoria Park and Whalley Range.[1] From the 1830s onwards similar patterns of development occurred around most of the major provincial centres. In Sheffield, later development occasioned the creation of a series of villa estates during the second half of the century stretching round from Kenwood Park to Ranmoor Hill.[2] All these estates had much in common, not only in the character of their designs but also in the nature of their organisation and development. They were laid out in fairly spacious fashion with tree lined roads and gardens of generous size.[3] Their prime concern was the securing of privacy and seclusion for their inhabitants.

By 1870 this process of housing expansion was not only well established but increasing with the growing ability of a greater proportion of the middle class to share in the benefits of suburban life. At the same time improvements in transport were to make commuting a viable pattern of life for a growing proportion of commercial and professional people. From the early days of the railways the select few had been able to travel daily well beyond the bounds of the city. In Manchester the successful cotton magnates had by-passed the first ring of suburban development at Victoria Park or Whalley Range and escaped to the rural retreats of north Cheshire.[4] In London the city businessman could choose to ignore the developed inner suburbs, such as Kensington and Hammersmith in the west, and travel swiftly to the distant countryside of the Thames Valley or the North Downs.[5] Suburban railway development began properly, however, in the 1860s, and with the expansion of lines around London and other provincial cities this brought residential building to detached and widely scattered communities. Still, neither on the trains nor on the horse omnibuses were fares yet generally cheap enough for families whose budgets were limited.[6] By 1870 the larger cities, and London in particular, were becoming ringed by suburban communities, but these were still both distinct and exclusive. The next thirty years were to see the development of a system of urban transport which catered for a much greater proportion of the population, and which consequently stimulated the development of residential estates on the edge of cities for occupation by tradesmen, clerks and the better paid artisans.

By the latter part of the nineteenth century the 'aristocracy' of the middle class had established itself in arcadian environments which produced a pattern of low density garden suburbs that was to be a model for future developments. At that time, however, the mass of the commercial and professional class could not afford to be so selective in their choice of suburban sites: 'They snatched the crumbs from the rich man's table, colonising any part of the outskirts not already bespoken by the very well-to-do.'[7] Moreover, though the low density suburban environment of the elite remained the ideal residential pattern for the lower middle class, and indeed a very potent influence for the future, in the conditions of the late nineteenth century it was a virtually unobtainable ideal. For the majority the pattern of social advance in the nineteenth century was to move gradually outwards into property that was newer and probably more soundly constructed. The slow rise from working to lower middle class was marked not by any dramatic residential transformation but rather by a slow improvement in the same type of house property. And as the lower middle class gradually moved outwards in the later nineteenth century towns this was the pattern of housing that they took with them. It was with variations on the terraced house theme that the tide of suburbia pressed outwards.

As this tide advanced, established middle class suburbs became surrounded and crowded out by property inferior both in size and quality. The process which was to be called 'the spoiling of the suburbs' was first in evidence along the main roads out of the larger towns and cities.[8] These had been the most eligible sites for the establishment, on building plots of an acre or more, of the comfortable suburban retreats of the wealthy. Such estates and suburbs would remain in their original condition for a longer or shorter time according to the particular characteristics of the locality. As the town increased in size, the lower middle class were pushed further out by the erection of places of business in the commercial centre. This caused them to seek out what the *Building News* in 1886 described as 'those trim semi-detached villas and terraces that soon make their appearance when the demand arises'.[9] As a mass of newcomers sought to enjoy those facilities which had formerly been reserved for the few, the original inhabitants found that the exclusive nature of the suburb could not be maintained and houses began to be let for professional purposes—schools or private asylums--and adjoining meadow land appeared on the market for the purpose of building smaller properties. Gradually the area would be transformed, with rows of houses fitted on to vacant ground as best they could, and with the occasional row of shops and public house fronting the main road where a villa had been demolished. The roads that were once kept in good condition for the carriages were no longer maintained, and ancient watercourses on which the drainage depended were no longer cleansed. As the plots were taken up here and there at random by men of small means—without proper restrictions as to design or value, or skilled supervision to ensure that such restrictions were enforced—then no pre-arranged plan was made or adhered to, and the neighbourhood sank to the level of the lowest class that first erected houses there, whatever might have been its natural advantages.

The process of social and structural metamorphosis took place at different rates and with differing emphases around most large towns and cities at the end of the nineteenth century, and the mechanics of this lower middle class colonisation can be demonstrated by reference to the process that was clearly evident during the last quarter of the century along the western approaches to Manchester. There, along Liverpool Road, Eccles Old Road and Lower Broughton Road, had been built large villas and terraces for the established middle class.[10] By the end of the century these estates had been invaded and overtaken by the second wave of middle class migration, as the expanding lower middle class sought modest villas and larger terraced houses further away from the city and its concentration of working class housing. In the first decade of the twentieth century, the more distant suburbs, such as Seedley and Weaste, were the areas of most rapid growth within the conurbation. Though they remained basically residential suburbs, the housing developed then was of a lower standard than previously. The fields and large estates gave way in the south to a myriad of small roads and terraces of houses built for artisans and clerks, and in the north to groups of trim semi-detached and terraced villas designed for the commercial and professional classes.[11]

It was pressure of this nature, emanating primarily from the lower middle class, which led, in the last three decades of the nineteenth century and into this century, to the rapid expansion of large towns and cities beyond existing municipal boundaries. In most urban areas prior to 1870 physical expansion, with the exception of isolated middle class estates, took place almost entirely within borough boundaries. After 1870 this began to change and generally the following three decades each saw the doubling of population in adjoining parishes, and from this point the growth of the suburbs continued and blossomed. Throughout the country the lower middle classes were finding the means to promote this growth. They were permitted to do so as a result of increased mobility; they were motivated in doing so by the increasing congestion of urban centres and the cheaper land and building in the suburbs, and they were encouraged to do so by the social aspirations which associated the idea of the suburb with respectability, a higher status, and an essentially middle class way of life.

As a result, this lower middle class pressure outwards was felt not just in urban areas where the development of that social group was a relatively new phenomenon, but also in those areas with a well established social spread. Thus Sheffield, whose social complexion was so different from Manchester's for example, nevertheless experienced a similar outward advance of the lower middle class. There, in 1901, it was noted that the last ten years had been a period of activity in the building trade such as was unlikely to be seen again.[12] The gardens along the Crookes Moor Road had already begun to give way to the speculative builder by the middle of the 1870s,[13] but it was the last decade of the century which saw the transformation of many of the Sheffield suburbs as 'people were forced to leave their old and once quiet houses for purer air and room to live'.[14] The railway brought the manufacturing classes into Millhouses and pushed further development out along the Abbeydale Road.[15] Builders saw the opportunity of disposing of houses to 'a better class of artisans or people of position in the East End Works', and a good class of terraced houses and solid villas spread from London Road onwards.[16] At Woodseats and Heeley whole districts were being transformed from quaint hillsides into red blotches, while the Ecclesall Road was being converted into respectable villadom.[17]

Of course, this process, which can be examined on a relatively small scale in provincial cities, was multiplied in both scale and intensity in the metropolis. There, throughout the last decades of the nineteenth century, the rapidly expanding lower middle class of the city had been settling in the less expensive parts of the middle class suburbs and were, by the early twentieth century, beginning to pioneer the formation of new districts themselves. In addition, as pressure on land forced people outwards, the lower middle classes found themselves forced into a very different type of suburb which was less attractive and less salubrious, and where clerks lived in close proximity to artisans and were surrounded by working class and industrial property. Such development was common to the east of London in places like West Ham, Leyton, Walthamstow and Tottenham.[18] But for all who could possibly afford it, and whose work did not demand residence in such areas, the urge remained to escape to somewhere with at least the semblance of *rus in urbe*. This they did in increasing numbers in the years before World War I so promoting the rapid growth and often the final infilling of an already established suburban framework around London. To the north, the lower middle classes were well catered for by the low fares of the Great Northern and the North London Railway which allowed them to move from their first stage of settlement in places like Hackney, Islington and Holloway to houses indicative of improving social status in such places as Wood Green, Hornsey, Southgate, Hendon and Willesden. For example, in Hendon the 1901-11 population growth was 73 per cent and most of this was accounted for by the provision of housing of modest standards.[19] Similarly south of the river, increasing middle class affluence was marked by the steady progression from the still developing areas of Balham or Tooting, served by the LCC tramways, out along the variety of suburban railway routes to pioneering lower middle class housing estates, such as Raynes Park and Merton Park, until it had spread through a built-up belt stretching from Surbiton through Sutton and Cheam to Bromley and Sidcup. In the first two decades of this century many of these suburbs catering primarily for the lower middle class more than doubled their population.[20]

However, an examination of these developing suburban areas around both London and provincial cities quickly reveals their lack of homogeneity in development. Though the lower middle class was responsible for pioneering new suburbs and was often the dominant class, there were very few areas limited to one particular level of social development. In this they differed from the upper middle class which had been able to move far away to areas of seclusion, and which, even with the advancing tide of lower class development, was able to maintain restrictions in order to guard the privacy of their enclaves. On the contrary, as housing developed to meet the needs of an expanding lower middle class it tended to progress sinuously through and around existing communities. As a result, in lower middle class development, it is difficult to isolate extensive areas of any one particular social character. It is more common, in fact, to find housing of this kind grading away at the fringes of districts already in the process of social decline or elevation.

This pattern can be demonstrated both in the case of specific streets and for developing urban areas. It was clearly the case in the examination of suburban growth in Manchester where lower middle class housing on the one hand engulfed earlier housing of a higher class, and which on the other was itself pressed by developing industrial building and working class housing. This typical confusion and contiguity of development is mirrored equally in the social patterns of established suburban areas. This pattern cannot be analysed in any refined manner through the printed census returns, but it can be examined through the records of occupation and rental contained in rate books. A detailed study of the suburban expansion to the south and west of Sheffield reveals a pattern of lower middle class infilling on a considerable scale, but in small units.

This was true of the manner of development as well as of the pattern of built-up areas established by the turn of the century. Along the main roads out of the city, such as Ecclesall Road and Abbeydale Road, lower middle class housing had completed the line of development between the working class dwellings on the edge of the built-up area and the earlier middle class suburban communities established approximately a mile distant from the city, and at the same time had pressed the extension of suburbia beyond these out into the country.[21] Away from the main roads lower middle class housing fitted even more closely between totally different types of development. On the fringes of the great middle class estates at Broomhall and Kenwood the housing shaded with varying degrees of rapidity into terraces of respectable but relatively humble dwellings which abutted in turn, often with surprising suddenness, on to established works in the valleys and densely congregated back-to-back housing.[22] Occasionally the transition in social standards was sharp and uncompromising, as, for example, where a protected middle class estate outran its potential and the land had to be sold without the original restrictive covenants.[23] But commonly the lower middle class housing provided a band of three or four streets indicative of social transition from prosperous artisan to comfortable middle class respectability.

This pattern of small scale infilling of middle class residential property was paralleled in established areas of development in London. Only in the newer, more distant suburbs did the lower middle class element ever dominate and manage to impose a particular character on a district. In the inner suburbs, and particularly in the railway suburbs of East London, the pattern was very much that recorded by Charles Booth in 1889.[24] His descriptive maps showed no particular residential segregation of his social category A (professional classes and shopkeepers). Apart from the latter, who tended to live along main roads, the majority of that category were found in odd streets where the houses merged closely with those of categories B and C (respectable and hardworking artisans). This pattern was confirmed two decades later in the detailed social survey of West Ham by Howarth and Wilson.[25] In the southern part of the borough, in Canning Town, Plaistow and Hudson's Wards, industry of various kinds and industrial housing was well established, but the Survey revealed numerous instances of where housing of varying degrees of respectability had been fitted into the existing pattern over the past two decades.[26] In Hudson's Ward, for example, the older section, such as Outram, Seaton and Frank Streets, was mainly inhabited by workers of the most irregular type, yet beyond the Gasworks around

New Bar Street houses had been built since 1902 to cater specifically for people who kept a servant. One of the streets, St Andrew's Road, was typically inhabited by clergy, officials at the Town Hall and libraries, and foremen and clerks in good positions. Even relatively short streets often contained a mixture of houses built for artisans, and others maybe twice their size, designed for occupiers who were of the servant-keeping class. Such houses would be differentiated not just by size but also by the degree and nature of their decoration.

In the newer and more distant suburban areas lower middle class standards of housing might predominate, but were rarely universal. In 1881 W. S. Clarke, writing for house seekers in *The Suburban Homes of London,* surveyed the developing parts of the metropolis and noted that only in the most distant areas was building solely for the occupation of the upper middle class taking place. In all those suburbs that ringed London within 15 miles of Charing Cross, the most noticeable feature was the variety of the property available, both already built and in process of development. Whilst most existing property was of a class that rented at over £100 per annum, new property within a mile of a suburban railway station offered accommodation in different proportions and patterns within the rental range of £35 to £120. Previously upper middle class enclaves were under pressure. But by the beginning of the twentieth century, it was the turn of the then established lower middle class suburbs to find themselves under similar pressure. In 1904 *The Times* commented on the already common characteristic of suburban envelopment by artisan property let at between £20 and £25 per annum.[27] Meanwhile those of the lower middle class who could afford it were moving on still further out of town.

This transitory nature of lower middle class settlement was reflected in the variations in the houses themselves. As people progressed up the social scale, rents would rise from those which F. G. D'Aeth in 1910 estimated as coming within the 'artisan' category of 6s 6d to 9s per week, through the 'smaller shopkeeper and clerk category' expending £25 to £35 a year on housing, up to the 'smaller business class' whose average rental was £48.[28] Obviously the precise expenditure, and what was procured for that rental, differed from place to place, but within that range the lower middle class could anticipate some variation on what J. J. Clarke in his classification of types of houses described as the 'parlour-house'.[29] At their best such houses were 'semi-detached', had fair sized gardens, and were built only ten or twelve to the acre. More usually, however, they had only a small garden, enabling from eighteen to twenty-five houses to be built to the acre. The latter type was generally built in rows, being separated from the street by only a few square yards of garden. As variations on the terraced plan, such houses were based on narrow frontages of 16 to 20 feet each. The result was that any extension in the size of such houses had to be accommodated by building back with the common back-extension for kitchen and scullery, or by building upwards into a third storey or more commonly into an attic. Such features were typical of the higher priced houses in this range which were designed to accommodate a servant who lived in. Whatever their size, however, all such houses tended to be planned with rooms behind one another—on the ground floor a sitting room at the front and a dining room at the back, and on the first floor a master bedroom running the width of the house with two or three other bedrooms arranged behind it. The result of this type of layout was that all such houses suffered from the defects of having to have long and dark internal passages, and from the restrictions of narrow sites which on the one hand prevented back access, and on the other limited the circulation of air and the admission of sunlight. Nevertheless, with their reasonably sized rooms and with their separate bathroom and adequate sanitary facilities, these houses, when well built and well cared for, represented a considerable social advance.

This model of lower middle class housing involved gradations in social prestige according to its size and the suburban location of the house. But within this broad pattern there was room for considerable and significant indication of the most minute social distinctions. This was displayed in the decoration and embellishment of the property. A bay window of at least one storey was, as Dyos recognised, *de rigueur* in all grades of suburban housing by the end of the nineteenth century.[30] But beyond this there was infinite scope for the decoration of stone sills and copings; the provision of fretwork ornamental ridge-tiles; the addition to porches and windows of columns with machine-turned capitals; the insertion of coloured or stained bricks and moulded plasterwork; the embellishment of forecourts with coloured tiles, and the adding of distinction with stained glass lights in an arch or in a heavily varnished front door. Inside, the lower middle classes were equally conscious of their social status in their efforts at interior decoration—the imitation marble fireplace, the grained woodwork, the floral wallpapers, the accumulation of bulky, veneered furniture, the careful display of ornaments.[31] Outside the house, the intricacy of the cast iron railings and the variations in the planting of the front garden were equally distinctive of different grades of respectability. Nor did this stop at the house, for, as Dyos has pointed out, the very naming of the streets and the choice of trees had their social overtones, and were 'a subtle acknowledgement of a locality's status in suburban society'.[32] All this was important to the lower middle classes striving so desperately for respectability. It was a condition of life that was understood and accepted. Commenting not unsympathetically on such aspirations, S. F. Bullock wrote of the house of his fictional 'clerk', Robert Thorne:

> Ours was a pleasant enough home, if humble—one of a row of six-roomed cottages in a quiet neighbourhood near Denmark Hill. In front was a privet hedge, behind an oak fence, and a tiny flower bed under the parlour bay window; at the back, within brick walls, was a small garden having a grass plot, two beds with a sub-soil of sardine tins and brickbats, a poplar at the bottom, and a lilac tree near the scullery window. The hall door had its brass knocker and letter-box. The rooms were small but comfortable: downstairs a dining-room, drawing-room, kitchen and scullery, upstairs two bedrooms and a little back room containing a chair, a table, and a shelf of books which it pleased us to call the Study. You will see that despite circumstances, we were finding our feet in the social world, making the best show we could. The brass knocker, the bay window, the dining and drawing rooms, establish the fact; whilst the Study gives evidence that already we had in view the great suburban ideal of being superior to the people next door.[33]

But whatever modifications might be made to his house by the aspiring suburbanite, the fundamental character was set by the ground plan and elevation as provided by the builder, whose concern was to cater for a certain degree of social status as cheaply as possible. As a result, the price of respectability was standardisation and consequent suburban monotony. If the charge of being insanitary could no longer be levelled at the newly expanding lower middle class districts, they certainly came in for much criticism for being dreary and ill-designed:

> Every suburb is being spoiled by the hand of the jerry-builder and the greed of landowners. Instead of swelling hills and grass pastures we see serrated lines of house tops and slated roofs. The vast waste of bricks and mortar grows without any visible manifestation of the architect.[34]

It is true that certain elaborating design features such as the bay window, gable, half timbering, and ingle-nook were to be found, often plagiarised and introduced without any real purpose, but the great majority of these respectable villas were of the ordinary builder's type, and were produced with little variation. Cheapness and speed were the requirements, and these could only be achieved if the same plans and templates, window frames and sashes, the same stone dressings, the same fastenings and ironmongery were used. All this multiplication of identical details and fittings enabled a considerable reduction to be made in the cost of erecting a large number of houses, but it made no allowance for the variations in the taste and requirements of the tenants. As the *Building News* pointed out in 1896, public apathy in this matter meant that suburban estates reflected the builders' views. The ruthless despoliation of nature on the estate meant the cutting down of all trees and subsequently the formation of roads at extremely narrow intervals, bordered by identical redbrick houses with contracted passages and small rooms facing directly on to the thoroughfare.[35]

By 1900 there was increasing awareness that the acquiescence in and virtual encouragement of such suburban development was causing irreparable damage.[36] Green fields were being lost for ever, and the houses being built served neither the best interests of the individual tenants nor of the community at large. Criticism spread beyond the columns of the architectural journals, and both national and local newspapers began to carry various articles and commentaries on the character of contemporary suburban expansion. For example, the *Manchester Guardian* in 1901 ran a series of nine articles on various suburban areas, and the *Manchester City News* followed with a similar feature on the City's residential districts four years later.[37] In Sheffield the despoiling of the West End and the increasing loss of open space were frequent topics for editorials and letter writers to the press at the turn of the century.[38] Intermingled with a certain degree of social alarm over the changing character of suburban population and the debasement of property standards was an increasing realisation that the accustomed pattern of suburban development left much to be desired in environmental terms.

With the rapid outward advance of cheaper lower middle class housing in the later nineteenth century, the old ideal and character of suburban life had been submerged. It seemed that the decline in the quality of the suburban environment was matched by a decline in the quality of suburban life. As *The Times* noted in 1904, the suburbs being formed for the lower middle class and artisans were only tending to reproduce the town in its least interesting or stimulating form:

The hurry and bustle, the lights and excitement of London are gone;

but they are not replaced by the repose of green grass and waving trees, and bright flowers and wide spaces. To land the artisan or the clerk in such surroundings after a hard day's work scarcely repays him for the journey from town; to surround London with acres of such streets is to produce a district of appalling monotony, ugliness and dullness. And every suburban extension makes existing suburbs less desirable. Fifty years ago Brixton and Clapham were on the edge of the country; a walk would take one into lanes and meadows. Now London stretches to Croydon. It is no longer possible to escape from the dull suburbs into unspoiled country. It is the more necessary, if possible, to redeem the suburb from meanness and squalor.[39]

The need for improvement in both the layout and design of suburban housing estates was explicit. In this critical mood, architects and builders were receptive to new ideas on suburban development which sought to transfer to the housing estates of the lower middle class the garden character of the arcadian suburbs of the middle class elite. Not only did the recent rapid expansion of lower middle class housing involve many features that were unsatisfactory to those concerned with both environmental and social reform, but also its inherent deficiencies stimulated criticism and pressure from those seeking houses within this segment of the market. Thus the demand for change arose from within and without. As a result, by the beginning of the twentieth century, the lower middle class was probably the most significant sector in the housing reform movement. This is not to say that it was on them that reformers lavished most attention, for the housing problems of the working classes still predominated in terms of gravity and extent, but rather that the lower middle class included those who were most receptive to change, and who had the means of participating in new housing experiments.

In historical terms it is not surprising that this should have been the situation. The ideals of the lower middle class suburbanites had been set by the standards of the upper middle class, and in consequence they had seen their ideals devalued by the forces of market provision. The estates of the upper middle class had style, variety and distinction in appearance, and in addition possessed an integral life-style. Suburban housing for the lower middle class seemed devoid of all these qualities. Yet that class, compared with the working class, contained those who were sufficiently articulate to demand a better alternative, and those with the financial means to participate in the new standards and patterns of housing design and layout which were sweeping the country in the early years of the twentieth century. Moreover, the lower middle class in the past had played an influential role in this development, and thus in many features it reflected the ideals of that class and was geared to that type of market.

The housing movement which dominated the first two decades of the twentieth century, and in which the lower middle class was so influential, and which in turn had such a profound effect on the design and layout of lower middle class housing, and through that of all levels of working class housing after the First World War, was of course the garden city movement and its various ramifications. Though the initial concept of one man,[40] it was a movement which owed its rapid development to a variety of factors, not least among which was the suburban stimulus of the artisan and lower middle classes. In combination with this, the garden city idea became broadened and in effect applicable to a wide range of suburban estate developments.[41]

The immediate and popular reaction to the garden city idea must be credited largely to its coincidence with a certain eruption of utopianism. This was prompted by various societies, such as the Home Colonisation Society, the Allotments and Small Holdings Association, and the Association for Improving the Condition of the People, and it is quite clear that the rank and file membership of these societies was composed basically of those of artisan and lower middle class status.[42] The earnestness of their concern for the physical and moral deterioration of urban life reflected the growth of social and political involvement amongst these classes in the last decades of the nineteenth century. Typical of this activity was the founding in 1893 of the English Land Colonisation Society which attempted, without particular success, to organise a residential colony in the Home Counties for middle class people anxious to flee from city life.[43]

Such efforts were, however, merely a further reflection of the continuing nineteenth-century search for an alternative to the prevailing conditions and concepts of urban life. Ever since Owen, idealists had propounded the virtues of model towns in virgin territory. But more realistically, since the 1860s and 1870s housing reformers and sanitarians had increasingly seen the alternative to overcrowded urban housing conditions in the encouragement of the directed movement of people from the centre of cities to planned estates beyond the built up area where land values and building costs were lower.[44] The efficacy of such schemes, however, depended on the availability of cheap transport. As long as this was beyond the means of the mass of working men, realistic promoters saw that such schemes could only meet the needs of a lower middle class market. Those below could not afford, and those above did not need assistance. Such schemes that were successful therefore clearly catered for the lower middle class market. Among the first had been those promulgated during the 1850s by the *Freehold Land Times* for the establishment of freehold land society estates adjoining railway stations in the London suburbs, and actually brought to fruition near the Crystal Palace at Sydenham.[45] During the last three decades of the century the most effective schemes for controlled suburban estates, reflecting in some way co-operative ideals of community building, were those of the Artisans, Labourers and General Dwellings Company.[46] As its name implied, its origins lay in the earlier tradition of self-help, but with practical realism it was accepted, after initial problems, that its efforts would be more immediately beneficial if directed to the needs of a higher class. This realisation formed a significant strand in housing reform attitudes throughout this period. When George Cruikshank, the engraver, illustrated a scheme for a model suburban village in 1873, he demonstrated an immensely practical scheme that was clearly designed for the families of respectable white collar workers.[47] When Charles Booth wrote on the value of improved transport for curing the housing ills of London in 1901, he recognised that the immediate beneficiaries would not be the working class but the lower middle class.[48] Solving the housing problem was clearly a matter of stages, and, with the limited capital and impetus available, this would best be applied to those who could take most advantage of it, and whose removal would in turn relieve some of the pressures on the classes below.

Such schemes differed from the generality of lower middle class suburban development in that they capitalised on that group's ability to commute, and combined with it the benefits of community planning. The ideals of such planning had matured in a variety of self-help schemes throughout the Victorian period, all of which had in varying degrees involved the lower middle class. Endeavours such as the freehold land societies, the building societies and indeed the co-operative societies had all attempted to bring to the reform of working class housing those middle class virtues of hard work, thrift and investment. With the application of these bulwarks of self-help, it was argued that housing problems could be solved by the people themselves without outside assistance, and this remained a fundamental feature of the housing reform movement through to the First World War. However, few of such schemes proved to be efficacious for working men, and many that started out with high hopes were eventually taken over by the lower middle class. This was as true of the estates of the Artisans, Labourers and General Dwellings Company in London as it was of the freehold land societies in Lancashire and Yorkshire. A study of the latter estates in Sheffield, for example, reveals that the estates begun in the 1850s rapidly became the preserves of respectable professional people—small masters in the metal trades, clerks, schoolmasters and shopkeepers.[49] A study of the borrowers from provincial building societies at the time of the Royal Commission on Building Societies in 1871,[50] or of the beneficiaries of the housing schemes of the larger co-operative societies at the end of the century, reveals a similar social pattern.[51] Thus once again the lower middle classes took over schemes that had been primarily intended for the working class, but in so doing they made of them practical realities. As a result, valuable experience was gained during the last third of the nineteenth century in the planning and layout of housing estates, and in their social and economic organisation. Although as a means of helping the working class the nineteenth-century housing movement often seems a succession of failures, nevertheless these lower middle class experiments in the creation and organisation of unified housing schemes were significant steps in the development and acceptance of new notions of housing layout and planning by the end of the century.

Equally important in this process was the application of new concepts in housing design and architectural standards. Here again in the last third of the nineteenth century the lower middle class provided the testing ground. The stimulus for a rejuvenation in the physical appearance of housing during this period came from the ideas of Morris and Lethaby, which were translated in architectural terms by Philip Webb and his followers.[52] Initially, of course, their social ideal had been the transformation of the workman's cottage, but the restraints of the profit margin were too great to allow of much architectural idealism except in a few model estate villages and such like. Within the range of the £100 to £150 house there was little scope for innovation, and though developments in upper middle class housing were important architecturally its preconceptions were too far removed from those of ordinary people to be of practical benefit. It was with the housing of the lower middle class in the £200 to £400 range that there was some leeway for experiment and that such endeavours might be of general practical value. Thus it was in occasional schemes in this category that architects of the new school worked out their ideas. What was to become the new suburban style could be traced in its application back to the 1870s at Bedford Park, and the small houses of Voysey and Shaw. Here had been established the town-country scale that was to govern the layout of later garden suburbs.[53] Great attention had been paid to the spatial qualities of layout—the straight street of the bye law—terrace discarded in favour of the picturesque settlement of trees and gardens, with houses built semi-detached, or disposed of in units of five or six. The roads had lost the rigidity of the gridiron, and the houses had provided object lessons in grouping and design. A greater diversity of textures and colours had evidenced a desire for variety in the street picture. From the standards set by this most famous undertaking, which the *Building News* in 1876 rightly recognised as being aimed at the lower end of the middle class market, there developed the first real involvement of architects with cheaper housing.[54] The experience gained at this level in new methods of estate layout and concepts of housing design was to be of crucial importance, together with other coincidental strands of development, in the successful promotion of the garden city movement at the turn of the century.

In the years 1900 to 1914, therefore, the new ideas in housing held a particular appeal for the lower middle class. Not only did the garden city movement owe its character and development in a large part to middle class standards and pressures, but, like earlier housing movements, it had little practical relevance for the working class. Despite the aims and ideals of the initiators of the movement, it could only be made applicable to working class needs in a modified, subsidised form. It was again in the financial range of lower middle class housing that innovation could be attempted. Thus, while that class was predominantly responsible for the very physical expansion of towns against which the garden city movement was a reaction, it also provided the conditions for experimentation with new ideas in housing design and layout, and at the same time modified by its own requirements the garden city movement, and created the garden suburb movement. This allowed those who participated to continue the middle class exodus from town centres, and at the same time to benefit in terms of the quality and planning of their houses; in terms of building costs and rentals, and ultimately in terms of the quality of life.

In the years before the First World War, over sixty estates were undertaken which were categorised as coming within the orbit of the garden city movement, and which were not working class schemes promoted by industrialists or local authorities.[55] The appeal of these estates was definitely to the lower middle classes. This was reflected in the type of houses built; in the range of rentals; in the pattern of life on these estates, and primarily in their financial organisation and promotion. In all these schemes the latter was undertaken by means of tenant co-partnership which was the ultimate refinement of Victorian self-help in housing, and which reflected the middle class ethics and values of that movement, for the co-partnership ideal was to combine corporate control with a personal interest in the profits arising from a right and economical use of the property.[56] The methods adopted by the Tenants Co-partnership Society were: to purchase an estate in the suburb of a growing town and to plan or lay out the same, so as to provide suitable playing sites for the tenants and their children; to insist on the reasonable limitation of the number of houses to the acre, so that each house might have a private garden, and to secure pleasing architectural effects in the grouping and designing of the houses; to erect substantial houses, provided with good sanitary and other arrangements for the convenience of stock-holders desiring to become tenants; to let these at ordinary rents, so as to pay a moderate rate of interest on capital (usually five per cent on shares, and four per cent on loan stock), dividing the surplus profits, after providing for expenses, repairs and sinking fund, among the tenant stock-holders, in proportion to the rents paid by them. Each tenant stock-holder's share of the profits was credited to him in capital instead of being paid in cash, until he held the value of the house tenanted by him, after which all dividends could be withdrawn in cash.[57]

In such societies an individual could obtain practically all the economic advantages which would have arisen from the ownership of his own house. Capital was obtained at a rate of interest below the level at which the individual could usually borrow to build or buy his own house, while the preliminary legal and other expenses were less than would have been the case if incurred individually. Neither did the tenant shareholder run the risk of loss in the event of removal, for his security was in the stock of an association rather than in the deed of a particular site and house. His mobility was not restricted, therefore, by the possession of property.

In promotion, the rudiments of this pattern owed their origin in 1888 to the Tenant Co-operators Limited working within the general framework of the co-operative movement, and definitely aiming at working men with the fundamental principle of the equality of shareholders holding one £1 share.[58] In practice, only 115 houses were built by this company on five London estates and, though the concept survived, by the time it combined with the idea of the garden city, the Co-Partnership in Housing movement, as it was now known, was very clearly appealing to a higher class, with its limitations on voting rights and the insistence on £10 shares.[59] In garden suburbs designed for artisans and the lower middle class, co-partnership societies had financed the building of 11,479 houses by 1913.[60] Although the validity of the movement's principles remained intact, its social evangelism had been curtailed. This was reflected in the cost of the house property built in the co-partnership garden city schemes.

It had been the hope of the promoters of the garden city idea that with the use of cheaper land, and with the introduction of less formal and thus less costly means of layout, it would be possible to build houses for working men that would not only be better designed but would have a certain individuality, and would 'look at least as well as middle class houses'.[61] This meant, in practice, the adaptation of the concepts of the new style in housing to the restrictions of a structure that could be erected for less than £150, and so rent at well below 5s a week exclusive of rates. Even 5s a week rental at 1900 prices would have been beyond the means of a large proportion of the working class. Nevertheless, few of the co-partnership schemes, despite real efforts, were able to build so cheaply. The first houses at Letchworth cost £200 each, and in an effort to secure lower cost houses a Cheap Cottage Exhibition was held in 1905, when competitors were required to build a house for less than £150.[62] Models were produced in wood and timber framing and in a variety of patent materials, but few were satisfactorily resistant to cold and damp, and virtually all were impracticable for living in. Endeavours of a similar nature were attempted on other estates, such as at Sheffield and Newcastle, but nowhere was the hope of breaking the economic impasse to the vision of Victorian housing design realised.[63] Whatever their original ideals, the co-partnership garden suburb schemes before the First World War were of predominantly lower middle class character in fruition.

Thus at Hampstead Garden Suburb, though the initial intention had been to develop a truly mixed community, economic pressures meant that by 1914 the majority of the 1,550 houses built ranged in cost from £300 to £425, and in rentals from 7s 6d to 14s 6d per week, with some more expensive and exclusive properties on the fringe of the scheme.[64] At Gidea Park in Essex, one of the most commercially successful schemes, the building was safely middle class, and the rents ranged from £30 to £100 per annum.[65] In the provinces the pattern was similar. The Manchester Tenants' scheme at Burnage was opened in 1910 with 136 houses completed, at rents varying from 5s to 14s 6d per week excluding rates.[66] At Chorltonville Garden Suburb, on the other side of the same city, the first twenty houses completed in 1909 were designed to attract working class families from the Hulme district of the city.[67] None could be persuaded to come and consequently the estate had to be adapted for an altogether different class of tenants, with the remaining 272 houses letting at rents of £23 per annum and upwards.[68] A survey of the garden city schemes in 1914 shows such figures, with the slight variation in costs between London and the provinces, to be generally applicable. It was estimated that out of 2,955 houses erected by societies connected with the Co-Partnership Tenants Limited by 1913, only 640 rented for below 6s a week, 1,913 rented for between 6s and 12s, while of the remainder 247 let for between 12s and 20s, and 155 for over 20s a week.[69] The societies appealed basically to middle class tenants, as they did to middle class values.

Both these qualities were reflected in the character of the houses built and the environment planned. What in effect the garden city movement achieved was the development of estates on which the lower middle class were able to realise something of their arcadian dreams, and experience, in modified form, the low density and informality of layout which had hitherto been the prerogative of their social superiors. Previously, too, the standard housing of the lower middle class had merely been the product of builders' manuals and their experience. Architects had not concerned themselves with this lower class of property: architectural guides and instruction had been restricted to the houses of the upper middle class.[70] Now, extending the innovations of the new school of housing design, the architects of the garden city movement, primarily Raymond Unwin and Barry Parker, directed attention to the provision of an alternative to the standard terraced unit.[71] In place of the narrow fronted terraced house, with a front and a back room, the lower street-age costs in the garden suburbs enabled the evolution of houses with greater widths. This meant that, in the first place, it was possible to provide more variety in accommodation. Secondly, all the accommodation required was brought under the main roof, and long back projections or detached out-buildings were dispensed with, which effected a reduction of gloom and shade. Thirdly, the increased wall space admitted of more windows, and allowed staircases, landings and larders to be placed on outer walls with direct light and ventilation. Lastly, the proportions of the buildings lent themselves to a treatment more pleasing to the eye. Breadth itself is a valuable aesthetic quality, and when it is associated with the broad casement window of simple framing, and the long lines of a well-pitched roof, then to some degree there is recovered the homely appearance of the English country cottage.[72]

Such houses, placed in large gardens and in a variety of positions along curving tree-lined streets, brought new residential standards within the orbit of the lower middle class. This market having been tested in the pioneer garden suburbs of the early twentieth century, housing of this new type was soon being promoted by speculative builders. On the eve of the First World War in some of the newly expanding middle class areas, in place of the regularity and drabness of the terrace was to be seen the irregularity of elevation of houses which were constructed of lighter brick or covered with rough cast, which had much outside woodwork, whose windows were of the casement type, and whose whole appearance was generally lighter and more cheerful.[73] Such was the appeal of the new style, that its application spread both up and down the social scale, and indeed, what had been pioneered in a speculative way for an artisan and lower middle class market, established the visual norm and universal style in housing after the war.

Furthermore, in these garden suburbs the lower middle class tenants discovered a sense of identity that had hitherto eluded their peers, and set a pattern of community life which was to become the model for twentieth century planners. The exclusive suburbs of the upper middle class had always had a strong sense of identity and had maintained an integral and highly developed social life. This the amorphous areas of lower middle class housing had never possessed, and at the end of the nineteenth century numerous writers bore witness to what Masterman designated as the 'incorrect standards of value' and the 'noticeable absence of vision'.[74] Both Wells and Gissing had drawn attention to the infinite boredom of life in the expanding suburbs of London, while Grossmith and Bullock had highlighted its pettiness and desolation.[75] As against this the organised co-operation of life in the new garden suburbs presented an expression of purpose and concern for the general welfare of the community. As co-partnership estates developed, arrangements were made to foster the expression of such aspirations. With encouragement from the management, tenants organised themselves into committees and arranged flower shows, gardening contests, concerts and winter lectures. As the Secretary of the Liverpool Company explained to the first tenants on the estate:

> Living in a co-partnership suburb did not mean being isolated tenants, but that the whole of the social and recreative life of the estate would be managed by the tenants themselves.[76]

On the larger estates there would be a central hall or institute which provided not only games rooms, lecture room, reading room and library, but also facilities for the organisation of other communal activities. On the smaller estates social activities were organised among the houses.[77] Everywhere the greatest prominence was given to sporting and horticultural activities, as was only to be expected in developments which placed such emphasis on the virtues of fresh air and the outdoor life. By such means, however unsophisticated, the co-partnership estates sought to foster a spirit of neighbourliness which it was felt had been suppressed by the long streets and high yard walls of the terraced dwellings. During the first decade of development, when the ideas were novel, the garden suburbs attracted tenants who were receptive to such ideals, and the spirit of co-operation seems to have flourished.[78]

In such ways the garden suburb movement allowed that class, which for financial reasons could benefit from its development, to overcome some of the problems which had beset the provision of lower middle class housing in the open market during the last three decades of the nineteenth century. An idea originally intended to solve the housing ills of the working class had, like so many earlier reform movements, proved more applicable to the needs of those higher in the social scale. The combination of that highly middle class quality of self-help with the garden city principle had produced a housing programme that was not only financially amenable, but also physically attractive to the lower middle class. Thus from the ranks of those who had been most responsible for the ever increasing pressure on urban land and resources, and who were as a result probably most aware of the limitations of the traditional forms of development, came the vital support for this new solution. The ready acceptance of the garden city idea, at least in its modified form as the garden suburb, owed much to its immediate and practical appeal to the lower middle classes. Their experimentation was to mean the acceptance of the new standards of layout and design in housing as the proper standards for working class housing when subsidised after the First World War.

In the long term, therefore, the irony was that what had been conceived of as an alternative to the pattern and problems of suburban expansion created in the later nineteenth century by the lower middle classes, ultimately served only to exacerbate that very problem. With the increasing expansion of towns between the wars as a result of better transport facilities, the garden suburbs ceased to be able to maintain any separate identity, and planned expansion became increasingly merged into the urban framework. With the development and dilution of the garden city idea, the final product became less well designed, and ultimately increasingly monotonous. The idea of the coherent estate maintaining a balanced development was seemingly forgotten, and the result was urban expansion pressing out aimlessly into the countryside along the main roads. As the interstices were gradually filled in, our towns

180   *The Lower Middle Class in Britain 1870-1914*

became surrounded by the suburbia of semi-detached houses with their own gardens, which assiduously destroyed the balance between town and country that had been at the heart of the garden city concept. At the same time it equally brought the opportunity of a suburban life style, that had been pioneered by the middle class and extended and modified at the behest of the lower middle class between 1870 and 1914, ultimately within the reach of a greater proportion of the working class.

Notes

1. H.B. Rodgers, 'Suburban Growth in Victorian Manchester', *Transactions of Manchester Geographical Society,* 1961-2, pp. 5-9.
2. J.H. Stainton, *The Making of Sheffield, 1865-1914,* Sheffield, 1924, pp. 181-195.
3. J.C. Loudon, *The Suburban Garden and Villa Companion,* London, 1838, *passim*; *The Gardener's Magazine,* vol. XIX, 1843, p. 166; G.F. Chadwick, *The Park and the Town,* London, 1966, pp. 53-65; J. Gloag, *Mr. Loudon's England,* London, 1970, pp. 73-80.
4. M. D. Greville and G.O. Holt, 'Railway Development in Manchester', *Railway Magazine,* 1957, pp. 615-620, 720-726; 'A History of Manchester Railways', *Manchester City News Notes and Queries,* vol. IV, 1882, p. 10.
5. D.A. Reeder, 'A Theatre of Suburbs: Some Patterns of Development in West London, 1801-1911', in *The Study of Urban History,* H.J. Dyos (ed), London, 1968, pp. 254-261, 268-269. A.A. Jackson, *Semi-Detached London,* London, 1973, pp. 21-22.
6. H.J. Dyos, 'Workmen's Fares in South London, 1860-1914', *Journal of Transport History,* vol. I, 1953, pp. 8-19. A.S. Wohl, 'Housing of the Working Classes in London, 1815-1914', in *The History of Working-Class Housing,* S.D.Chapman (ed), Newton Abbot, 1971, pp. 29-34.
7. H.B. Rodgers, op.cit., p. 6.
8. For comparison, see H.J. Dyos, *Victorian Suburb,* Leicester, 1966, pp. 51-53.
9. *Building News,* vol. LI, 1886, p. 373.
10. Ibid., vol. XXII, 1872, p. 52; *Manchester City News,* February 1906.
11. Salford Corporation, Approved Building Plans, 1890-1910, City Architect's Department, Salford Town Hall; *Manchester City News,* 9 December 1905; 3 February 1906; *Manchester Guardian,* 18 October 1901; *Slater's Manchester, Salford and Suburban Directory,* 1906.
12. *Sheffield Independent,* 28 December 1901; Sheffield Medical Officer of Health, *Annual Report,* 1899, p. 11.
13. Township of Nether Hallam Rate Books, 1875-1880. Ordnance Survey, Sheffield, 1850, rev. 1873; W. White, *Directory of Sheffield,* 1876, 1879.
14. *Sheffield Independent,* 28 December 1901.
15. *Sheffield and Rotherham Independent,* 29 April 1865, 4 July 1865, 14 July 1886, 15 September 1866, 4 May 1867, 15 March 1870.
16. Ibid., 15 March 1870; 3 August 1872; 3 January 1874; 19 December 1889. Plan of properties for sale, Heeley, 1872, Sheffield City Library Archives M.D. 3162. W. White, *Directory of Sheffield,* 1872.
17. *Sheffield Independent,* 28 December 1901. A. Gatty, *Sheffield Past and*

Present, Sheffield, 1873, p. 300.
18. W.S. Clarke, *The Suburban Homes of London*, London, 1881, pp. 318, 450, 483-495; G.W. Thornbury, *Old and New London*, vol. VI, London, 1897, p. 539; E.G. Howarth and M. Wilson, *West Ham: A Study in Social and Industrial Problems*, London, 1907, p. 15.
19. A.A.Jackson, op.cit., p. 38.
20. Ibid., pp. 40-41.
21. Sheffield Township Rate Books, 1881, 1891, 1901; Ecclesall Union Rate Books, 1881, 1891, 1901; W. White, *Directory of Sheffield*, 1881, 1891, 1901; *Sheffield Independent*, 11 January 1886, 28 December 1901.
22. W. Birch, Particulars and Conditions of Sale and Plans of . . . properties situate in Machon Bank, to be sold 18 October 1910. E. Holmes, Plan of Freehold and Leasehold Building Estates situate in Sheffield and district for disposal by private treaty, 1892. Pawson and Brailsford, Plans of Properties for sale, 1872, Sheffield City Library Archives M.D. 3162-1-3. Ordnance Survey, Sheffield, 1893.
23. Conveyances of land on the Kenwood Estate from G. Wostenholm to T. Steade, Sheffield City Library Archives, Loan Deposits 610-657. 'The Pleasant Ways of Sharrow', Undated Newspaper Cuttings, Sheffield City Library Local History Collection. M. Walton, *A History of the Parish of Sharrow*, Sheffield, 1968, p. 30.
24. C. Booth, *Life and Labour of the People in London*, vol. I, London, 1889, *passim*.
25. E.G.Howarth and M. Wilson, op.cit., *passim*.
26. Ibid., pp. 47-53.
27. *The Times*, 25 June 1904.
28. F.G. D'Aeth, 'Present Tendencies of Class Differentiation', *Sociological Review*, vol. III, 1910, pp. 270-271.
29. J.J. Clarke, *The Housing Problem. Its History, Growth, Legislation and Procedure*, London, 1920, p. 118.
30. H.J. Dyos, *Victorian Suburb*, Leicester, 1966, p. 178.
31. G. and W. Grossmith, *Diary of a Nobody*, London, 1892, *passim*; H.G. Wells, *Joan and Peter*, London, 1918, *passim*.
32. H.J. Dyos, *Victorian Suburb*, Leicester, 1966, p. 188.
33. S.F. Bullock, *Robert Thorne, the Story of a London Clerk*, London, 1907, p. 249.
34. *Building News*, vol. LXXI, 1896, p. 290.
35. Ibid.
36. *The Architect*, vol. LXI, 1899, Supplement, p. 21; vol. LXIV, 1900, pp. 66-67; *Building News*, vol. LXXVIII, 1900, p. 858; vol. LXXX, 1901, p. 83.
37. *Manchester Guardian*, 20 September 1901 to 14 November 1901; *Manchester City News*, 18 November 1905 to 12 May 1906.
38. *Sheffield Weekly News*, 13 January 1900; *Sheffield Daily Telegraph*, 22 November 1900, 10 February 1906, 3 November 1906; *Sheffield Independent*, 26 December 1896, 27 March 1897, 4 February 1899, 28 December 1901, 28 September 1904, 29 September 1904, 1 October 1904, 4 October 1904, 17 October 1904.
39. *The Times*, 25 June 1904.
40. E. Howard, *Tomorrow: A Peaceful Path to Social Reform*, London, 1898; *Garden Cities of Tomorrow*, London, 1902.
41. E.G. Culpin, *The Garden City Movement Up-to-Date*, London, 1914, *passim*, C.B.Purdom (ed), *Town Theory and Practice*, London, 1921, *passim*. R. Unwin, *Nothing Gained by Overcrowding! How the Garden City Type of Development may Benefit both Owner and Occupier*, London, 1912, *passim*.

42. R. Gill, 'Till We Have Built Jerusalem', University of Sheffield Ph.D. thesis, 1966, p. 226.
43. W.H.G. Armytage, *Heavens Below*, London, 1961, p. 336.
44. *The Architect*, vol. XVI, 1876, p. 162; vol. XXVIII, 1882, p. 10; vol. XXXII, 1884, pp. 191, 199; *Building News*, vol. XIII, 1866, pp. 193, 810; vol. XXIII, 1872, p. 255; vol. XXVII, 1874, p. 482; *Transactions of the National Association for the Promotion of Social Science*, 1864, pp. 585-586; 1866, pp. 620, 732; 1884, p. 464.
45. *Freehold Land Times and Building News*, 1 April 1853, 15 April 1853, 1 June 1853, 1 July 1853, 1 November 1853; *City Press*, 3 October 1857; *The Times*, 2 March 1861.
46. J.N. Tarn, 'Some Pioneer Suburban Housing Estates', *Architectural Review*, vol. CXLIII, 1966, pp. 367-370.
47. G. Cruikshank, *A Suburban Village* (Etching), c.1873, Victoria and Albert Museum, Department of Prints and Drawings, V&A 9528.1.
48. C. Booth, *Improved Means of Locomotion as a Cure for the Housing Difficulties of London*, London, 1901, p. 17.
49. S.M. Gaskell, 'Yorkshire Estate Development and the Freehold Land Societies in the Nineteenth Century', *Yorkshire Archaeological Society Journal*, 1972, p. 161.
50. Royal Commission on Building Societies, *First Report*, 1871, A.A. 5469-92, 6040, 6681-88. *Building Societies and Land Companies Gazette*, 1 January 1873.
51. *Co-operative News*, vol. XXVII, 1896, p. 253; vol. XXIX, 1898, p. 1288; vol. XXXI, 1900, pp. 102, 331, 451, 1475; A. Mansbridge, *Brick Upon Brick: The Co-operative Permanent Building Society, 1884-1934*, London, 1934, p. 39.
52. R.T. Blomfield, *Richard Norman Shaw, R.A., Architect, 1831-1912*, London, 1940, pp. 33-36; N. Pevsner, 'Architecture and William Morris', *R.I.B.A. Journal*, vol. LXIV, 1957, pp. 172-175; N. Pevsner, *Pioneers of Modern Design*, Harmondsworth, rev.ed., 1960, pp. 48-60; A.R.N. Roberts, 'The Life and Work of W.R. Lethaby', *Journal of Royal Society of Arts*, vol. CV, 1957, pp. 355-371; R.N.Shaw, 'The Home and Its Dwelling Rooms', in *The British Home of Today*, W. Shaw Sparrow (ed), London, 1904, pp. cv-cvi; L. Weaver, *The Country Life Book of Cottages*, London, 2nd ed., 1919, *passim*; *The Studio*, vol. IX, 1896, pp. 189-190.
53. W.L. Creese, *The Search for Environment*, New Haven, 1966, pp. 87-107.
54. *Building News*, vol. XXXI, 1876, p. 621.
55. E.G. Culpin, op.cit., facing p. 8.
56. *Co-operative News*, vol. XXXI, 1900, p. 1475; vol. XXXXIV, 1903, p. 360.
57. H. Vivian, 'Garden Cities, Housing and Town Planning', *Quarterly Review*, vol. CCXVI, 1912, p. 51; H. Vivian, *Co-Partnership in Housing in its Health Relationship*, London, 1908, pp. 5-6; E.B., *Co-Partnership in Housing*, London, 1910, *passim*.
58. J.E. Yerbury, *A Short History of the Pioneer Society in Co-operative Housing*, London, 1913, p. 22; E.G. Culpin, op.cit., p. 49.
59. H. Vivian, 'Garden Cities, Housing and Town Planning', *Quarterly Review*, vol. CCXVI, 1912, pp. 512-513.
60. E.G. Culpin, op.cit., facing p. 8.
61. S.D. Adshead, 'The Economies of Estate Development', *Town Planning Review*, vol. III, 1912, pp. 273-275; C.B. Purdom, *The Building of Satellite Towns*, London, new ed., 1949, p. 65; R. Unwin, *Nothing Gained by Overcrowding! How the Garden City Type of Development many benefit both Owner and Occupier*, London, 1913, *passim*.

Housing and the Lower Middle Class 1870-1914 183

62. *The Architect and Contract Reporter*, vol. LXXIV, 1905, supplement p. 23. *British Architect*, vol. LXIV, 1905, p. 15. *Garden City*, n.s. vol. I, 1905, pp. 91-93.
63. *The Architect and Contract Reporter*, vol. LXXVI, 1906, supplement p.23; vol. LXXVII, 1907, supplement p. 23; *The Builder*, vol. XCIII, 1907, p.167; *Town Planning Review*, vol. I, 1910, p. 23.
64. H.O.W. Barnett, 'A Garden Suburb at Hampstead', *Contemporary Review*, vol. LXXXVII, 1905, pp. 231, 234-235; H.O.W. Barnett, *The Story of the Growth of the Hampstead Garden Suburb, 1907-1928*, London, 1928, pp. 14, 19, 26; S.A. Barnett, 'Of Town Planning', in *Practicable Socialism*, London, 1915, p. 226; E.G. Culpin, *op.cit.*, p. 33; Hampstead Tenants Ltd, *Cottages with Gardens for Londoners*, London, 1907, pp. 6-7; Hampstead Garden Suburb Trust, *The Hampstead Garden Suburb. Its Achievement and Significance*, London, 1937, pp. 14-17.
65. *Garden Cities and Town Planning*, n.s. vol. III, 1913, p. 54; *Town Planning Review*, vol. II, 1911, pp. 124, 230; E.G. Culpin, op.cit., p. 30.
66. *The Burnage Journal*, 1930; *Labour Co-Partnership*, vol. XIII, 1907, pp. 12, 129; vol. XIV, 1908, p. 175; vol. XVI, 1910, p. 102; *Manchester City News*, 26 March 1910, 1 September 1910; *Manchester Evening Chronicle*, 25 May 1939, 14 June 1964; *Manchester Guardian*, 26 June 1912; E.G. Culpin, op.cit., p. 53; E.W. Sidebotham, *Burnage*, Manchester, 1925, pp. 19-24.
67. *Manchester City News*, 20 March 1909; *Manchester Guardian*, 26 June 1912; *Chorltonville: Programme of Official Opening, 7th October 1911*, Manchester, 1911, *passim*.
68. *Manchester City News*, 26 May 1927, 29 April 1939; *Manchester County Express*, 10 August 1941.
69. *Town Planning Review*, vol. IV, 1913, p. 65. E.G. Culpin, op.cit., p. 50.
70. For example, see S.H. Brooks, *A Rudimentary Treatise on the Erection of Dwelling Houses*, London, 1860, *passim*; G.W. Poore, *The Dwelling House*, London, 1897, *passim*; C.J. Richardson, *Picturesque Designs for Mansions, Villas, Lodges, etc.*, London, 1870, *passim*.
71. B. Parker, 'Site Planning at New Earswick', *Town Planning Review*, vol. XVII, 1937, pp. 2-9. R. Unwin, *Cottage Plans and Common Sense*, Fabian Tract No. 109, London, 1902, *passim*. L. Weaver, 'Cottages at Earswick', *Country Life*, vol. LVIII, 1925, p. 681.
72. B. Parker and R. Unwin, 'Cottages near a Town', in *The Catalogue of the Northern Art Workers' Guild*, Manchester, 1898; P. Houfton, 'The Raw Material of Town Planning', *Garden City*, vol. IV, 1910, p. 292; *The Building News*, vol. LXXXV, 1903, p. 196; vol. XCVII, 1904, pp. 5-6.
73. A.A. Jackson, op.cit., p. 45.
74. C.F.G. Masterman, *The Condition of England*, London, 3rd ed., 1960, p. 65.
75. S.F. Bullock, *Robert Thorne, the Story of a London Clerk*, London, 1907; G. Gissing, *In the Year of Jubilee*, London, 1893; G. and W. Grossmith, *The Diary of a Nobody*, London, 1892. H.G. Wells, *Ann Veronica*, London, 1909; *First and Last Things*, London, 1908.
76. *Town Planning Review*, vol. II, 1911, p. 128.
77. Ibid., p. 242, J.E. Yerbury, op.cit., p. 56.
78. *Labour Co-Partnership*, August 1894-December 1906; *Co-Partnership*, January 1907-August 1914.

7 THE SMALL SHOPKEEPER IN INDUSTRIAL AND MARKET TOWNS

Thea Vigne and Alun Howkins

Introduction

The term shopkeeper covers a wide area from the barons of the shopocracy, the Gordon Selfridges and John Lewises, down to the itinerant dealer in paraffin and iron-ware who operates from a shed in his back yard. Shopkeepers do not in any sense represent a unified stratum or class but are rather to be seen in the very specific context of the area in which they work and particularly the spread of their trade. Initially we can offer two basic divisions. The first between urban and rural or semi-rural shopkeepers, and the second between those whose trade is firmly linked to the community immediately around their shop, usually general shopkeepers, and those who because of their specialised wares or the size of their business deal with a much wider area. Even these distinctions are only satisfactory up to a point. The specific nature of the community—city slum or rural court—further helps to determine the precise social position and behaviour of individual shopkeepers.

In this essay we seek to confront this problem of diversity head-on. By using oral material from urban and rural areas we try to show both the nature and sources of this diversity mainly through the eyes of the shopkeepers themselves but also through the eyes of the community they serve. It deals with a group of shopkeepers who fall, by and large, at the lower end of the scale (there are no members of the shopocracy included) although it will become clear that in a small pond a relatively small shopkeeper could hold an important place in the community. We will show, if only in outline, how this diversity relates to the particular calling of the individual shopkeeper, but more importantly how it relates to the area and specific community within which he or she operates.

The sources of this piece are almost entirely oral. There are good reasons for this. The standard printed sources, like directories, and even the manuscript sources such as the census returns, while they can provide adequate statistics, are hopelessly inadequate, taken alone, when it comes to any real classification of the social situation of shopkeepers. Indeed they hide the diversity which is the prime characteristic of the group. Even a detailed knowledge of a locality and a fortuitous biography or two cannot provide the kind of information that interviews can in this particularly misty area of class and social division.

The piece is divided into two halves. The first discusses shopkeepers in cities and industrial towns, the second in market towns and villages. Both sections are concerned with class and the social situation of shopkeepers in relation to the community they served although there are differences of approach in the two sections. This is largely a product of the difference between the urban and rural situation.

The Urban Shopkeeper

The oral sources for this section are two groups of interviews taken from the 444 which comprise the survey of family life and work in Great Britain before 1918 undertaken by Paul Thompson and Thea Vigne.[1] They are: (1) Interviews with 13 men and 16 women living in urban areas of England in 1911 who had had one or more parent engaged in keeping a shop for some or all of the period 1880-1914. Three of this group were also themselves owners of shops during that period. (2) Interviews with 71 people (38 men, 33 women) living in Lancashire in 1911. With three exceptions who lived in rural areas they lived in Liverpool, Manchester, Bolton, Farnworth or neighbouring districts. The rural people lived very near Bolton and Farnworth.[2] We have drawn principally on the first, the 'shopkeeper group' of interviews for information about the attitudes towards their place in the social structure of small shopkeepers. The second, 'the Lancashire group' we have used to reconstruct the social role and position of the small shopkeeper in different neighbourhoods of Liverpool, Bolton and Salford as seen by the working and white collar class. We shall discuss the shopkeepers' attitudes first and attempt some explanation of these.

'Class focuses on the divisions which result from the brute facts of economic organization. Status relates to the more subtle distinctions which stem from the values that men set on each others' activities'.[3] Perhaps the obscurity of their position in the economic organisation of society confused small shopkeepers in their attempts to define their social class. For some were owners of property and capital and employed staff while others had assets which were scarcely more and sometimes less than a working man. Booth describes a small shopkeeper whose shop cost 40s consisting of 'a wooden screen betwixt door and fire, two tables, a counter, small and large scales and weights, a good corner cupboard, and some odds and ends'. The rent was 3s 6d a week, stock bought on Fridays usually cost £1 16s 7½d and the shop paid 10s a week beyond its rent, takings averaging about £2 15s. After one year they had saved £25 in the bank.[4] Robert Roberts's father bought their family shop with a £40 loan.[5] In Jarrow, Rodney Atwood's father started an ironmonger's business with three or four dozen corned beef tins which he fetched from a tip and covered with brown paper, filling them with screws and nails. A half-crown grindstone for sharpening scissors completed his stock.[6] But although some small shopkeepers were hazy about class demarcations, they focused with sharp clarity on status. They were very keenly aware of minute degrees of social standing in the communities in which they lived ranking themselves and others confidently in terms of ownership of furnishings, clothing, size of house rented, degree of cleanliness of property and person, sobriety, and, more rarely, education, speech and bearing.

For some of them the most important factor was the size and standing of the shopkeeping business. Edna Oakes,[7] John Minter[8] and Frank Boxall[9] who all came from small shopkeeping families, all remembered the social distinction between themselves and families of big shopkeepers, but were unsure of their social class. Edna Oakes, for example, thought that the important people in Salford had been 'the doctors and the owner of the chemist's shop and the owner of the big grocer's shop and the owner of a big drapery shop . . . We bought from these shops . . . we considered them important because we supposed they were a bit better off than a little shopkeeper and they had big shops and we had to call them "Sir"'. When asked about her family's social position in the period before 1918 she used various descriptions—middle class, better class and lower middle class. Similarly, John Minter who started work in his father's hardware business in Longton, Staffordshire, in 1895, felt that he had belonged to 'the poorer business people, not the big business people, the small shopkeeper and small dealers, like the little grocer, the little butcher, the little general dealer'. He had a more definite view of his social class than Edna Oakes, placing himself in the lower middle class between the employers or upper class and employees or working class. Further south, in Guildford, Surrey, Frank Boxall was sure only of his membership of the small business people and of the distinction between High Street and back street shops in the town.[10]

A similar view, but in this case from the upper rather than the lower echelons of shopkeeping, was expressed by Janet Cheadle[11] whose father was a Bolton wholesale grocer with two warehouses and 30 employees. He was, in addition, a magistrate and a town councillor. Talking of small shopkeepers she said, 'A lot of them had shops in what they used to call their front parlour, you know, of course we being just wholesale those were the people we served a lot you see and they were a very nice lot of people. Very nice. I've always been very fond of that type of person. Had a lot to do with them really in working at the Girls Club too you know, the working girls . . . ' Janet Cheadle and other shopkeepers of the big variety were less concerned with status among shop keepers and more confident of membership of the middle class, but a middle class with two irreconcilable divisions—trade and the professions.

Not all small shopkeepers, however, were uncertain about their family's class position. Some were sure of being middle class and a few remember strong identification with the working class where they lived and worked.[12] Poverty and residence in a neighbourhood entirely working class may partly explain this. It is a phenomenon which requires more investigation.

Some other factors may help throw light on the wide variety of class attitudes held by small shopkeepers and their individual confusion of class identity. First, an outstanding feature of the group was the variety of their work experience before, after and often at the same time as keeping a shop. Shopkeeping was not a job for life. In the shopkeeper group of 29 people, only seven believed that the shopkeeping parent had never had another job, excepting an apprenticeship. Of these seven, four were the only big shopkeepers of the 29. They had servants, family holidays and shop assistants, whereas the other 22 were from families of the small type.[13] The careers of these small people fall mainly into two groups: shopkeeping, often in a family business, followed by a descent into manual or white collar jobs—a predominantly male pattern, and shopkeeping as one episode in a varied career which included both manual and white collar occupations for men and for women, usually manual and domestic. For a few, mainly men, this shopkeeping episode was the most successful and major job of their working lives, for others it was a relatively short-lived enterprise. This second group includes those who hoped that a shop would be a refuge from disaster.[14] In Bolton, for example, corner shops were 'small cramped stores usually kept by disabled miners or widows'.[15] Mrs Levy, a widow, was one of these unfortunates.[16] When her husband died his speculative building and surveying ventures went bankrupt, the comfortable house in Sedgley Park, Manchester, was sold and the three sons at boarding school in Margate were recalled to join their four brothers. Her brothers raised money for her to open a small grocer shop but despite the help of four other relations who lived with the family, it failed. After a second unsuccessful attempt, two of the seven boys were sent to a Jewish orphanage in London and the rest moved with their mother to a 'bug-ridden hovel'. Mrs Levy's shopkeeping episode had followed a moderately leisured life with domestic help and long country holidays, and preceded a time of great hardship in which she was forced to earn her living in a cap works and let lodgings. Another widow who tried shopkeeping was Mrs Grove.[17] Before marriage she had been in domestic service and during the first two years of her widowhood she left her two young children with her mother and went to work for a doctor's family. Finally, her mother rented a shop for her at the end of a row of terrace houses in Leigh, Lancashire, and, like Mrs Levy, she started shopkeeping with the help of four relations. However, unlike Mrs Levy, she was not reduced to factory work but managed after twelve bitterly hard years in the shop, and a brief, disastrous marriage, to start a new life in Bolton with her third husband, a respectable insurance agent with a kindly disposition. As the wife of a white collar worker without vices her social and material position were better than they had ever been. In the shopkeeping game she had been carried up a ladder while Mrs Levy had gone down a snake.

In small shopkeeping families not only had the parents tried their hand at other work at an earlier or later stage, they frequently earned money at additional jobs during the shopkeeping period. A common pattern was a man going out to work while a woman ran a shop, but sometimes both worked in the shop, occasionally or regularly earning money by other means, e.g. letting lodgings, working as a postman, joiner, labourer, collier, bookie's runner. It seems very possible that members of families whose breadwinners had sometimes been self-employed, and at others employed at a number of jobs of widely differing social standing, would be confused about their class affiliation. Of our 29 shopkeeping families four mothers (two of them widowed) ran the shop entirely unaided, eight took an equal or in some cases the greater share in the business, four (all wives of the big shopkeepers)[18] played no part in the shop, their middle class position making this unsuitable. For the remaining 13 the evidence is sometimes a little scanty (e.g. where a mother died before the respondent can remember her) but several seem to have helped their husbands while bringing up children. At least 41 per cent therefore of the shopkeeping families had wives and mothers taking an equal or greater share in shopkeeping than their husbands. As class membership is customarily and officially designated by the occupation of the male parent, the effect on class consciousness of female parents holding jobs of equal or superior status to their husbands' must have been significant.[19]

The Small Shopkeeper in Industrial and Market Towns 189

We have suggested that the great variety of shopkeepers' economic positions, their diverse career patterns and the high proportion of women among their numbers may account for the stronger convictions of status than of class held by some of the shopkeepers. A fourth and final factor should be briefly mentioned. As people's ideas of class and status grow not only from the occupations of their nuclear family but from what they know of their wider kin as well, it seems worth noting that excluding descendants, at least one third of the 'Lancashire group' had a relation who had been a shopkeeper in the period 1880-1914. It is highly probable that the true proportion is considerably higher than one third because information was sought only about the occupations of informants' parents, siblings and brothers-in-law. Information about shopkeeping aunts, uncles, sisters-in-law, cousins and grandparents and parents-in-law occurs therefore, when it does, infrequently and at random. And there is the additional probability that some respondents would have forgotten, or been unaware of, the shopkeeping activities of some of the relations they were not asked about. The fact that many of the white collar and working class friends and relations had had brief careers as shopkeepers must have diluted any sense of cohesive class consciousness of shopkeepers' families. Possibly too, the fact that so many families, had relations who were retailers affected their view of the social class of shopkeepers. This would be difficult to deduce from our evidence, as perceptions about shopkeepers' class arise from memories of contact with neighbourhood shops in childhood and youth. This brings us to a discussion of the shopkeepers' social position as seen by their neighbours, their role in the community they served.

The main factors affecting the Lancashire respondents' placing of shopkeepers were:

1. Their own individual social class and standing in the working class and community.

2. The type of community in which they lived, whether socially diverse or homogeneous. These two variables are of course affected by each other and it is better not to discuss them separately. I shall therefore take three areas in turn, Salford, Bolton and Liverpool and try to assess the relative importance of type of community and individual social class in shaping people's attitudes to their small shopkeepers.

Robert Roberts wrote of Salford: 'Every industrial city, of course, folds within itself a clutter of loosely defined overlapping "villages". Those in the Great Britain of seventy years ago were almost self-contained communities.'[20] It is the self-containment of these communities which powerfully shaped the class perceptions of their members.

Rarely venturing from them, particularly when young, they saw no other social classes. 'We belonged to the working classes and the people round us were working classes and the other side of the world were the people who represented the better off-well off classes'.[21]

Bill Collier[22] grew up in a poor, rough Salford family and Pat O'Mara[23] came from a similar family in a neighbouring district of Manchester. Both suffered hunger and neglect as boys, Bill Turner doing a spell in prison. They were both too far removed from the respectable working class to aspire to nice ways or gentility, and their memory of shopkeepers was of the weight of their economic power. They were ' very, very wealthy' Mr O'Mara said, and had lived on the backs of the poor, overcharging them and, when they ran up a large bill, refusing them credit. They were 'all in with each other' and so you could not start anywhere else. Mr Collier did not consider them wealthy: 'You see —they couldn't make much money or owt like that 'cause there was no money knocking about' but they were nevertheless the most important people in Hankey Park, 'because if mother wanted to borrow a shilling or a couple of shillings, you know, I used to go and say, "Mother wants to know will you lend her two shillings well father gets paid"'. But for these men, power brought with it no trappings of social prestige. Their neighbourhood shops were kept by people who were in no way 'better' or 'posh'.

Mr Doyle,[24] however, who belonged to 'the respectable working men's class but on the poor side', remembered that in the Greengate and Broughton districts of Salford, shopkeepers 'was the only upper class that I knew'. Classed with publicans they were looked up to, and associated mainly with each other though his mother was welcome in their society. Her friends were 'Mrs Finnigan the tobacconist, Mrs Price who had a tripe shop and Mrs Wellesley who had this old-fashioned pub'. Mrs Wellesley filled the important symbolic role which in more heterogeneous neighbourhoods usually fell to one of the gentry or professional classes. 'She was a real lady—she'd help anybody, like, if she could—a down and out'. Another very poor Salford boy, Robert Morgan,[25] and Edna Brooker[26] also recalled the dominance of shopkeepers, their money and their children's superior clothes.

But it was not only poor people who looked up to shopkeepers. Mr Hamley thought that shopkeepers were very important.[27] But it was their glamour, their style rather than their economic hegemony that affected him, as his father, a railway goods checker, was in a white collar occupation and actively engaged in helping those less fortunate than himself, e.g. mill girls to buy clothing. Mr Hamley said 'When I went to school there were certain people, in fact the jewellers where I had been going since I was eight years of age (I'm still friendly with them now). I thought their station in life was higher than mine, which of course it was. They were jewellers, they were in business. They had money; we hadn't. I used to like to be with them—not because I was a snob or other people were outcasts, but when you're young you kind of get dressing nice and you go out for better dress, and I did think I was a bit better than them because I was educating myself a bit more than the ordinary. And we went out in their car on a Wednesday afternoon when it was their half day—they had a car even then before 1918, and we thought we were it'. Another member of the white collar class who shared Mr Hamley's deferential attitude was Enid Newton.[28] Her father was a clerk and her mother had been a pupil teacher. She said that shopkeepers 'you would come in contact with were as the dukes and duchesses' and to work in a mill was 'awful'. The Salford shops provided a little visual glamour in the Newtons' drab world: 'they had all these toffees in the shop and there's the pork and everything in the shops and we used to think it was wonderful to go look in shops because we never saw them lit up'. Shopkeepers in these relatively homogeneous areas were 'ladies and gentlemen' and 'dukes and duchesses' in the minds of their customers, they took on themselves the traditional role of the gentry in the seasonal rituals which survived from rural villages. Mrs Brooker[29] told how in Salford they 'used to do all the shops—they used to always open on a New Year's Day, we used to go round and—our Mag'd hold the bags, they used to always open on a New Year's Day, and you used to go in every shop along Chapel Street and then we'd go to Lower Broughton—we had to be out early morning, they wouldn't give you 'em after dinner—and everybody got orange off every shop.' She received charity from the shopkeepers too—cast off clothing from the greengrocers in Adelphi and the people at the corner pub 'as I say these shopkeepers, me mother used to say "Oh," she said, "she's a lady her you know" . . . probably come or send half a dozen eggs'. Shopkeepers too donated vegetables, oatmeal and scrap meat when Mrs Whitworth,[30] whose husband was in regular work as a corporation horsekeeper, made soup to feed her poor neighbours. Possibly this participation in common charitable effort explains why her daughter did not consider the shopkeepers had power or importance in Salford. Her family were on terms of approximate social equality with them and in 1896 she married a co-op shop manager. The similarity of attitudes of a group of people whose social and economic position were so various, ranging from the desperately poor and rough to the respectable and white collar families, seems to indicate that community structure may have been more important in shaping attitudes than class position. It should be noted however that the Salford group does not contain a family of the skilled working class.

Of the Bolton people in the Lancashire sample, only Miss Foley[31] living in the centre of town, was a child out of sight and contact with the wealth and power of the town. She alone mentioned shopkeepers as important in Bolton. 'The aristocrats we never came in touch with. The real moneyed people were hardly—I don't think we ever—they ever touched our life.' The middle class were 'town councillors, ... members of various committees, Guild of Help, they had a Clog Fund at Queen Street Mission ... they were kind of a benevolent group, you see, many of them shopkeepers of course, who'd got shops in town and were making a fairly comfortable living.'

Mr Benson,[32] Mr Oldfield[33] and Mr Farmer[34] were on the other hand well aware of the elite of the town, lived near Chorley New Road and being male and less poor than Miss Foley explored the town more. Frank Benson knew that Chorley New Road was inhabited by 'mill owners, industrialists with the big houses and stables at the back—these were the aristocrats, the really top class as we knew them in those days ..' Very near Mr Benson's home was situated another group of 'aristocrats' at Astley Bridge. Foremost of these was Col. Hesketh, Mayor of the town and Parliamentary candidate. But Mr Farmer and Mr Oldfield, whose fathers had been an overlooker and gas meter inspector respectively, do not remember shopkeeping as being an important function, although they lived nearer the centre than Mr Benson, further from the rich of the town. These three and Mr Hobson,[35] whose father had been a collier, thought that the people with prestige and power were managers, aldermen, timber merchants and tax collectors. Mr Farmer, who looked up to the clergyman and considered the mill manager a gentleman, was less than warm in his regard for shopkeepers. Some, he considered 'quite friendly and well respected and others—how shall I put it—they were not actually disregarded but they were just tolerated in a business sense.' In nearby Farnworth too, nobody remembered considering shopkeepers of any importance, and in Bolton a fitter's wife employed the wife of a fruit shop owner as her washerwoman.[36]

We have seen that the Salford respondents seemed mostly to see shopkeepers as an elite and the shopkeepers in their turn appeared to play some of the traditional elite roles and reflect some of their charm and glamour. The Boltonians on the other hand seemed to have considered shopkeepers of very little significance. Only Alice Foley's recollections strike an exceptional note and even they lack the sense of deference so marked in the Salford respondents. Probably the size and character of Bolton, its greater penetrability, its smaller slums, were the most important factors, but it must be borne in mind that most of the respondents are men who explored their environments and that they came from respectable families where the father was a skilled man. Their families, though not affluent, are a great deal better off than most of the Salford respondents, and they would have had no reason to fear the shopkeeper or consider him rich.

In Liverpool, the patterns of attitudes are more various. As in Bolton, the majority have no memory of shopkeepers having a significant role and a superior place in the class structure. There are, however, two exceptions to this; both were the children of carters and lived in one-class neighbourhoods of the urban village type. Annie Shaw's street, for example, consisted of families like her own 'just carters and cotton porters'.[37] The shopkeepers were the only people who were any different, 'Mr Moon the grocer and Browns the newsagents and Cartwrights the newsagents. Cartwrights was very, very nice. There were three sons but there was two of 'em in business—the other son didn't carry on with the father's business and that—they were exceptionally nice . . . they were business people really . . . that's what I felt, that they were sort of higher than us sort of thing.' The other carter's family lived in Nursery Street a mile from the docks. Their son was also impressed by the shopkeepers though rather differently from Annie Shaw. There were, he remembered, only two classes: 'those that had what they required or what was necessary in life and our class—my parents' class—having to fight for what they wanted and work hard for it.' Shopkeepers were 'the snobs and toffs' in the community.[38]

Five of the Liverpool people lived very near the Liverpool gentry and professional class with their carriages and servants. The poorest of these was Bob Murphy.[39] Like Bill Collier and Pat O'Mara his family felt the influence of those who gave credit. 'They provided the tick whereby you lived. This is the kind of thing you see . . . I mean even the clothes you wore were on tick—they were on credit, nothing bought for cash.' But this authority over the very poor was not paralleled by any social importance—richer people lived nearby. 'I lived in a neighbourhood where there was—the houses had no bathrooms, no inside toilets—and I could go along the road to the top to where there was houses built with these and sitting rooms. I thought they were a class apart from me. I thought they were a higher class than I was. And further along when I got along the Sheil Road—had the people that had the servants you know. I thought they were another class—higher again. I thought they were in tiers these classes—you see.'

The Waldrons[40] and Stewards[41] lived at Sefton Park, the most fashionable part of Liverpool. Both families were extremely poor and the mothers widowed. Peter Waldron lived in Lark Lane which was a street of 'high class moneyed people. There was lords and judges ... I think the most respected person of the lot was Canon Irwin from Christchurch.' Another gentleman was Mr Hughes who lived in Linnet Lane and ran the Boys' Brigade and the Cadets. He was a bachelor and 'just seemed to want to be amongst the working folk'. Mrs Waldron dealt exclusively with the co-operative stores and Peter knew no shopkeepers. To Lillian Steward too the clergy were the most important people and 'we looked up to the people that was better off than us.' Esther Fookes lived in the next street to Peter Waldron and attended the same church on Sunday and mixed with 'the nice gentlemen'.[42] She thought shopkeepers were important because 'they must have a lot of money to have a shop'. A shipwright's son,[43] living one street away from South Street which backed on to Devonshire Road and Belvedere Road, also observed the social distinctions around him. South Street, he remembered, provided the servants' back entrance for the houses and carriages of Belvedere and Devonshire Roads which bordered Princes Park. He alone of Liverpool people recalled hearing a shopkeeper described as a lady or gentlemen—'people that could adapt themselves to the circumstances', and it is perhaps significant that his aunt kept a shop. Nearby in High Park Street lived the Longtons.[44] Their son Jim had no memory of shopkeepers. His family kept themselves to themselves and avoided the Sefton Park people who 'wouldn't want you' and were 'better off than us'. Yet they were not entirely cut off from the Liverpool patricians, because his idea of 'a real lady' was a 92-year-old vicar's widow who 'was trying to do good to others'.

These Sefton Park people, like the Boltonians, seemed largely unaffected by shopkeepers, and unlike the Bolton group they were socially more diverse including the sons and daughters of skilled men, widows and a labourer, which points again to the overriding influence of the character of the neighbourhood and community. Where the Sefton Park people felt snobbery it was from 'people in offices or shop managers'. 'Anybody worked in an office was a bit above you' and the rent collector was higher class, a 'fellow with a parlour and a piano'.[45]

To conclude, it seems that while small shopkeepers loomed large in the lives of the poorest families, the social respect accorded them and the rank which they were given by most Lancashire respondents of the working and white collar class, were affected more by the type of community than the social class of the respondent's family. In the homogeneous urban villages of Salford and Liverpool they were the ruling class, but where the social structure resembled that of rural villages, they lost their position completely.

The Rural Shopkeeper

The first thing one would wish to stress about shopkeeping in the rural areas was its diversity. The name shopkeeper covers a multitude of differing positions on the social scale. At the lowest point were the casual hawkers, men and women of many occupations and sometimes none, to whom a bit of selling around the villages, be it a box of herrings or some windfall fruit, was just one of many seasonal jobs. At the other end of the scale were the large shopkeepers of the country towns, pillars of respectability and the sociologists' ideal bourgeois. In between lay every conceivable gradation passing through tally men and agents, working in the country districts from town-based department stores, travelling grocers, greengrocers and ironmongers, village shopkeepers and so on up to the established shop selling hunting breeches or fine teas to the gentry.

We wish to concentrate firstly on two rural shopkeepers and their families and communities, one near the bottom of the scale and one near the top. Both lived in country towns which served as markets for the countryside around although even the similarity of situation is only surface deep. The difference between the two comes indeed in the first place from the nature of the country town, unfortunately one of the great unstudied areas of English social history.

The country town of the late nineteenth and early twentieth century was still very much its own social world. It had its own season with the Hunt and Farmers' Ball, its own social hierarchy headed by the big farmers and professional people and its own economic structure based on the servicing of the countryside around it. The agricultural community needed supplying with everything from bricklayers to quality goods, and the country town provided them all in the days when a trip to town meant a trip not to London or even the county town, but to somewhere very much smaller and very much nearer. The young Joseph Ashby's first trip to town was from his village of Tysoe to Banbury 'nine miles of field paths' away. Even so the small country town was a cause of amazement to Joseph. '"Nijni Novgorod", breathed Joseph as the sight burst upon him. (His last school reading book had contained rich descriptions of the world's oddities. There he had read of a giant fair in the Russian city.)'[46] To the inhabitants of Flora Thompson's Lark Rise the city of Oxford 19 miles away was almost unimaginable.

> They often wondered what Oxford was like and asked questions about it. One answer was that it was 'a gert big town' where a man might earn as much as five and twenty shillings a week; but as he would have to pay 'pretty near' half of it on house rent and have nowhere to keep a pig or to grow vegetables, he'd be a fool to go there.[47]

Even Candleford, more like nine miles away, where they once went to visit relations was a different world to the village children.[48]

If the country town was seen by the visiting villager as 'Nijni Novgorod', as a great bustling city then it had another side too—the rural slums. When Flora Thompson visited Candleford for the first time she saw '... at a turning ... a glimpse of a narrow lane of poor houses with ragged washing slung on lines between windows and children sitting on the doorsteps.'[49] This was the other side of the service aspect of the country town: the homes of the unskilled, the domestic servants, the ostlers and the carters, all of whom were as vital in servicing the countryside as the gentleman's outfitters or the high class grocer.

The first shop we wish to examine was situated in North Street, Bicester, in North Oxfordshire, a town of under 3,000 people in the 1900s. North Street, or Top o' the Town as it was known locally, was a long street with brick-and-stone built mid-nineteenth-century cottages on the east side and older cottages on the west. Behind New Buildings, the eastern terrace, was another poorer terrace, Spring Gardens. The shop which was a general store was situated half way up the brick terrace on the eastern side of the street and formed a part of it. It was a family business and was owned in the period which concerns us by a man called Charlie Clifton who had inherited it from his mother. She in turn was a publican and brewer in the town's main street, Sheep Street.[50]

Although North Street was not a rural slum it was a poor area. As an informant said, 'You see we lived in a poor neighbourhood, it was a very poor neighbourhood ... up North Street, you see they were only working people'. As well as the skilled and unskilled working class the street housed in the 1900s among others, Harry Giles, 'a solicitor's clerk and "poor man's lawyer", who for a shilling would write a legally phrased document or will'; a shoemaker; a builder; a pawn shop; Fred Kirtland the Congregationalist postman and Harris's Dairy.[51]

The second shop we wish to look at was also in a country town. This was situated in the main street of Woodstock in West Oxfordshire. If the shop was part of any kind of community it was a commercial one as most of the buildings in the immediate vicinity were shops. The shop was a gentleman's outfitter, and as such a classic service trade for the rural areas around Woodstock. The owner of the shop, Mr Broad, seems to have had lower middle class origins but having served an apprenticeship in Yorkshire, where he was born, he began on his own account in the Woodstock area with a pony and trap taking orders from the countryside. By the 1890s, though, he had established himself in a large shop, Bristol House, in Woodstock's main street.[52] We shall also look briefly at a third shop at the end of this section situated in a large open village, Ingham, in Lincolnshire. In all three cases the oral material comes from surviving relatives: in the case of Charlie Clifton from his daughter Mrs Lovell, in the case of Mr Broad from his daughter, Miss Broad, and in the case of the Hayes family, from a daughter of one of them, Mrs Sharp. If we take the two shops situated in country towns, Charlie Clifton's general store and Mr Broad's gentleman's outfitters, we can see in detail the differences contained within the name shopkeeper in some detail. In an economic sense they represented two different phases of economic development. One was an almost pre-industrial work unit catering for all the needs of a largely homogeneous community whose profit margins were narrow and whose owner's relationship with the community of which he was a member were often difficult. The other was one whose trade was defined not by community but by a class—those who bought high class gentleman's clothing. It was a firm, a secure business in every sense of the word relying on hired labour and in which the family took no part. Indeed it is interesting that Mr Broad's sons both became farmers, a distinct step up the social scale, rather than remaining in the shop which passed to a son-in-law.

Charlie Clifton's shop was described by his daughter as '... grocery, provision you know, and general store ...'. In fact they sold almost literally everything from fresh meat, rabbit, mutton and pork, through to candles and paraffin and in the winter Charlie delivered coal. Although as Mrs Lovell says, 'they didn't have the multiples against them', there were, to my knowledge at least, two similar general stores within easy walking distance (about 200 yards on either side) as well as a butcher's, a wet fish shop, and a greengrocer's even nearer. Thus competition was very tough. One way of stealing the march on competitors was to make the place friendly. In this Charlie seems to have succeeded: the shop seems almost to have been a social club for some customers (Alice

Foley's *A Bolton Childhood* takes a similar view of the slum shop).[53]

> . . . he was very popular he was a jocular man, he'd laugh with them all he'd make a joke out of nothing with them—and that was their entertainment, 'Let's go and see old Charlie'—two or three old women in there—they often come to my mother's—and knock the door and say 'come and control your Charlie'—he'd be telling them such tales, and that was their little bit entertainment.

He also fulfilled a social function as a letter writer:

> He was the type of man then, he'd had the sort of education everybody in the area who couldn't read and write used to come along and say 'Charlie I wants a letter written' and he'd write the letters for them you know . . . or if there was a bit of, you know, a bit of an argument anywhere he could put a letter together for them—they always came to Charlie.

Finally there was the essential function of a small shopkeeper in a poor area to provide credit.

> there was the people who run the little accounts you know, they were glad to . . . they'd have the weekly groceries we'd make the bills out Saturday morning and in they'd come, they'd pay—sometimes they paid the lot all according to what income they had coming in you see . . . they might come in and say to my father—well I can't manage it all today . . .

Charlie Clifton seems to have accepted the vagaries of employment and the serious effects it could have on a family budget. Indeed he seems to have gone even further:

> Mind you, we were fortunate . . . you know my father was though, if there was an old lady or anybody ill and he had a ham or anything he'd just whip her a slice across—a little bit of this—and my mother would . . .

However, the profit margins must always have been very slight and this problem was dealt with in three main ways. Firstly the whole family contributed to the economic unit especially the wife; as Mrs Lovell says, 'wives helped in the shop those days, little businesses you couldn't exist without the wife.' However, it wasn't simply helping in the shop, it was actually providing the shop with some of its stock. Mrs Clifton 'made no end of jams' to be sold in the shop, 'ginger beer 1d a pint . . . people would fetch a pint of beer for supper . . . ', as well as pickled cabbage, pickled walnuts, pickled onions and cakes. The pickles were especially popular on Saturday nights after the Plough closed at eleven and were one of the main reasons for staying open: 'we had to wait 'til they turned out of the Plough 'cause when they come out the Plough they had all sorts of fancies.'

The children also helped. They pricked the walnuts before they were dried and pickled and helped make the lard by cutting up the fat. They also (the girls at least) played an important part in running the house when Mrs Clifton was working in the shop. But they themselves were also expected to help in the business. Mrs Lovell says, 'when I was nine I went into the shop . . . I used to help him in the shop when I could. If anybody came in for—a box of matches say, I could serve that, or two candles, a pennorth of candles, three candles for a penny . . . ' Before they could take money they had to carry customers' baskets home. It is clear that a hardworking wife and family were a valuable economic asset to a small shopkeeper as they had been to the handloom weaver of a hundred years earlier. There is little direct evidence of how this affected the relationship between Mr Clifton and his children, but he does seem to have been remarkably tolerant and unrepressive and his relationship with his children was a very good one and marked by an absence of violence.

Here, in the area of family work, the contrast between Charlie Clifton's shop and Mr Broad's is clear. In the case of the Broads the children did nothing at all in the shop and neither did their mother. They were not even expected to help around the house. What jobs they did were a kind of treat. At Christmas time for instance ' . . . we had to stone the raisins, all those kinds of things little children love to do you know . . . we were allowed to do all that.' Even the mother did very little about the house. According to her daughter she 'didn't do much housework at all' and the only cooking she did was cake making. All this work, performed in the case of the Clifton's shop by family members, was done by wage labour—the girls in the shop and the servants in the house.

Another way profits could be stretched a little was by self sufficiency. Although Charlie Clifton was not a farmer shopkeeper, selling the produce of his own land like the peasant stall holders of French markets, he did, wherever possible, take advantage of the fact that he lived in a country area. We mentioned earlier that he sold fresh meat, this came not from wholesale butchers but from cattle he fattened himself.

> Every week end he bought a pig or a sheep and had it killed and sold the joints see . . . he'd go to market perhaps and buy three he never bought anymore three pigs or three sheep . . .

They were kept in

> a little corner meadow, my father used to have . . . and he'd out his cattle in there you see . . . he never touched bullocks or anything of that . . . and round Bonners garden he had pig sties . . . and as he wanted one he got Blower Wynman to kill it.

He also sold 'the beasts of the field and the birds of the air' and wasn't all that particular where they came from.

> Yes. Oh yes, plenty of Rabbits, Hares, Wild Ducks, all that sort of food, people would come, poachers and otherwise . . . the old poacher was about you know . . . my father bought plenty to sell at fourpence, fourpenny rabbit, that was a treat.

Walnuts for pickling, fruit for jam, vegetable, butter and eggs to sell in the shop all came from small producers in the country round. Another source of produce was the children of the town as, according to another account of the same town, 'Some green grocers of those days used to buy blackberries in bulk . . .'[54]

Not all these goods were paid for in money. The poachers were paid for the rabbits and so were the walnut gatherers, but the farmer who supplied the butter and eggs was paid in goods or credit from the shop. This brings us to the third way a subsistence level shopkeeper could increase his profits: by reciprocal arrangements with other tradesmen and small farmers either to buy together or to give credit in exchange for goods. This network of barter of goods covered most areas of business and family life. Stock for the shop was obtained in this way: 'we used to deal with a farmer at Bainton they used to bring us dairy butter and eggs, we used to sell them. There again they had it out in grocery, see, that's how it was worked.' Those items which could not be obtained in this way, or bought from the country people Charlie bought together with another small shopkeeper.

> ... he and my father bought together, you know, they'd see one another—my father perhaps would say 'I could do with two barrels of vinegar ... it's pickling time' perhaps Mr Scrivener would say. 'Well I could do with two Charlie as well, we shall get a discount on the four see' that's how they went along—they'd do the same with sugar, they'd buy ten sacks of sugar together see. One would have five one would have the other—get the little extra ...

Barter, though, was perhaps more important in supplying the family with clothes since all their food came from the shop anyway whether it got there by barter or purchase in the first place. (Mrs Lovell says they ate most meats but 'not so much beef because we didn't sell beef'.) The cloth for clothes was purchased once a year in Bicester

> My mother only went shopping once a year and that was, she used to go down to Fleming's ... that was one of the biggest drapery stores in Bicester ... and she used to go there once a year and shop and then they had a settling up touch cause we supplied them with grocery.

Once the cloth and other necessities had been got it was taken to a Mrs Wadup in North Street where barter came in again. 'There was a lady who lived about four doors away ... and she was a dress maker ... and she'd take it [material] along ... you see she spent the money, we did a bit of exchange again, and that's how that was ...' However this exchange of goods for services with a social inferior had other ramifications in which shopkeeper could become banker.

> probably he'd want to go perhaps to Banbury Fair ... well if there was a day out like that, they would draw some money see ... they'd say I'll have the money and let the other go on and work it off ... see it was ever such an agreeable agreement ... and it worked very well too.

Despite the fact that the Clifton family were in most senses identical to their neighbours they were less at ease in their community than were the Broads. The most obvious reason for this is that Charlie Clifton lived in the community which provided his livelihood. His customers were, in his daughter's words 'all from North Street' and to mix socially would have meant showing favour since all the community could not be known equally well and to show favour could mean losing custom. Thus when asked if she and her family ever went visiting in the neighbourhood to friends Charlie Clifton's daughter replied 'No . . . my people were a very tight knit little community.'

This affected Charlie and his wife in different ways. His wife, who anyway seems to have been ill at ease in the community and to have been quick tempered, even passionate, but with a strong sense of respectability, stifled part of her nature. Mrs Lovell described her mother's isolation in very moving terms:

> She [her mother] wasn't really a very easy person to approach—she rather well see—let me tell you something of our life, we were trades people we were in a very poor area and you see we had to always be on the same standard as all the other people there, you know what I mean, and she couldn't really be herself, she liked poetry and—but she couldn't be herself because you had to rely on those people for your living so you got to do—when you're in Rome you do the same as Rome does and probably she was—I really seemed to think she was bottled up.

Although Charlie fitted more easily into the community and, as we have seen, had a genuine role in it, indeed seems to have been very popular, he was very conscious of narrow margins and the need not to offend. This precluded him from many community activities. For instance when asked about her father's politics Mrs Lovell said

> he used to have his own version of it and he had to keep his politics very much to his self . . . he had to get his living out of all people . . . you see he dealt with all types and discretion is the better part of valour sometimes isn't it.

Here the contrast with Mr Broad, who feared no community pressure, is very strong. Although he was a Liberal in what was virtually a Tory pocket borough his standing and the specialised nature of his trade, which was class based rather than area based, protected him against any serious discrimination. When his daughter was asked about her father's politics she replied

> I can tell you in one sentence. My father was a Liberal and we were all brought up Liberals. My mother was a Liberal, they voted Liberal, they went to Liberal meetings in the Town Hall.

She was further asked if her father felt himself under any political pressure from his richer customers. Her reply was emphatic: 'No. No . . . Nobody would have dared to question my father . . . My father had one line and it was straight, and he never deviated a scrap.'

The difference between the Broads and the Cliftons is also emphasised by their social relationships. As we have seen Charlie Clifton's family was ill at ease in the community, conscious of the narrow divide between them and their customers. There was no such feeling in the Broad household; theirs was a community bounded not by geography but by class.

> Well in Woodstock—the trades people were always friendly to each other. And the professional people, always held themselves a little aloof- from the trades people. And especially trades people that were uneducated. A lot of people in those days, you see, were not educated at all, they were just homely nice people you know, but —if—if a person was well educated, and a tradesperson of course you had the entrée into what we call the professional people.

It was also a community of religion, both her parents were strong Methodists and on Sunday evenings, for instance, her mother would make coffee and informal religious gatherings were held with her father playing the American organ.

The differences stretched over just as significantly into family life. Here Charlie's family work unit shows itself as a productive unit, rather than the archetypal Victorian family. Again, because of economic pressure the shop was open at all hours and because it was situated in the midst of a community there were customers coming and going at all times. This was made worse by the fact that the living and working areas of the house were scarcely divided—the living room where the family ate all their meals was directly behind the shop, only separated by an ever open door. Thus a meal could never be taken without interruption.

The Broad's house, unlike the Clifton's, was clearly divided into living and working areas. Although they lived next door to the shop there seems to have been no interconnection between the home and the workplace. Although the shop seems to have been open later at night than a modern clothes shop would be the hours were clearly much shorter than those worked by Charlie Clifton. The separation of workplace and home can be seen at meal times. All meals were taken together by the whole family except for dinner which was eaten after the children had gone to bed. There is no indication of any interruption and indeed her father came out of the shop at tea time specifically to be with the children. 'Daddy was generally with us for tea—yes.'

As is to be expected the whole scale of Miss Broad's house and lifestyle was very different from that of the Cliftons. As we have said the shop was next door to but separate from the house. There were at least four bedrooms and a bathroom upstairs and a dining room, living room and kitchen downstairs. All meals, except for Saturday's tea, were taken in the dining room and on Sunday lunch frequently included a visiting Methodist minister. At the Cliftons, Sunday was a day of amiable chaos which Charlie regarded as a true 'day of rest' certainly not to be interrupted by going to church.

The whole question of servants is another significant way of pointing to the differences between the two units. The Broads firstly employed a number of girls in the shop who lived in the town but who stood in a distinctly paternalist relationship with their employers. For instance they came into the Broads' house on Sunday evenings to sing hymns and drink cocoa after chapel. This employment of workers decisively marks the character of Mr Broad's shop as a business as distinct from the family work unit of the Clifton's shop. Secondly, the Broads employed quite a number of domestic servants. Most of the cooking and a good deal of the cleaning was done by Mrs Broad's sister but there were other servants as well. Firstly there was a local girl who came in daily to do the heavy cleaning work and a woman who also came in to do 'the laundry and part of the ironing'. Secondly, the children had a nurse, also a local girl, and thirdly there was a yard boy who looked after the horses, cleaned shoes and did general outside work.

Charlie Clifton stands at one end and Mr Broad at the other of the spectrum of small shopkeepers. Mr Broad was the proprietor of a small business, Charlie Clifton the head of a family work unit. It was possible though in some circumstances to stand half way between the two. This was the case of the Hayes family of Ingham in North Lincolnshire. In the large open parish with no resident landowner the Hayes family built up a small shop Empire.[55]

The Hayes family formed almost a dynasty founded by William Hayes who is shown in the 1856 directory as a farmer and carrier. William had seven sons who lived into adulthood and he set them all up in business. Between them, Mrs Sharp, granddaughter of William Hayes, said, 'it used to be said of the Hayeses that they owned half the village'. They were certainly well represented in the village hierarchy with two farmer/carriers, a grocer and a blacksmith from among the seven sons.

Sam Hayes, who owned the grocer's shop, was a considerable figure. On the 1871 census he is shown in the one shop he had probably been set up in by his father but he soon expanded beyond this. In his first shop he had a bakery: 'they made the bread and sold it to outlying farms and sold it but along with the bread of course they always took grocery orders and everything else.'

Eventually he expanded into two shops, the top shop and the bottom shop and handed these to two of his thirteen children. The top shop was kept by Herbert, the eldest son, who had been apprenticed as a baker. This was mainly a provision shop. The bottom shop was run by George, a younger brother and this was 'principally drapery though it had a grocery section'. A third brother 'divided his time between the two shops'. Sam also bought land and owned a number of houses in the village. Indeed his role in the village was a very important one. Ingham was an open village with no resident gentry and the Hayeses, who had a considerable family presence in the village, as well as a good deal of economic power, played an important social role. This is shown clearly by the dinner Sam Hayes gave every year to those villagers who were members of the shops' club. Mrs Sharp remembers:

In connection with their village grocery and general business they ran a club . . . now, poor people would pay sixpence or a shilling a week to be credited on the club card . . . when club day came round, they came or in fact were fetched . . . to the shops to choose and buy what they wanted . . . and they were entertained to tea and some form of social entertainment . . . and it was all provided by the family and staff.

Here we see a very sharp contrast with Charlie Clifton although even on the surface there was probably not that much difference between the two businesses. In the social situation of Ingham the Hayeses were able to expand socially and economically in a way inconceivable in North Street. Indeed the similarities went much further than just outward appearances for like Charlie Clifton the Hayes kept and killed their own animals, cured their own bacon and made their own lard as well as relying heavily on family labour. All the children, said Mrs Sharp, 'at a certain period in their lives . . . all worked in the business.' Yet the Hayeses were able to expand. The reasons probably lie in the lack of competition in the village but it is interesting to note that in the case of the club dinner for instance the Hayes were prepared to distance themselves from their customers and act almost as squires in a way Charlie Clifton would never have been able to do. Finally, and one is almost loath to raise the ghost of controversy, the Hayeses were Methodists. Again this is a sharp contrast to Charlie Clifton who, if not actively religious, seldom went to church and looked upon Sunday very much as a 'day of rest'.

Conclusion

From the examples we have given, the diversity of the group loosely termed shopkeeper should be abundantly clear. However, a few common factors emerge which serve more as guidelines than firm conclusions. Firstly, a shopkeeper's status and position both in the eyes of the community and his or her own eyes depended crucially on two major factors: first, the position of the shop and secondly, on the type of goods the shop sold. In a socially homogeneous urban area it seems likely the small general shopkeeper was accorded a status above that of his customers because of the great economic power of the small shopkeeper in this kind of area. The less homogeneous an area the clearer the position of the shopkeeper became. In Bolton or Woodstock where there was perception of a clear social hierarchy with 'aristocrats', be they of the mill or the landed estate, the shopkeeper assumed a definite place in that hierarchy, probably quite low down. However, again position is of paramount importance. In a very small town like Woodstock, someone like Mr Broad could move to a position of relative importance, although his business was not that large. A similar case is provided by the Hayeses.

The second major division is that of type of shop, the specialist or general retailer. In urban areas there were poor specialist shopkeepers, for where the clientele was poor the shopkeeper did not grow rich. Certain traders, for example, greengrocers, needed no more capital than general dealing and were, as Booth noted, low in the social order of shopkeepers.[56] Some specialists, however, seem usually to have been higher class, e.g. butchers, chemists, drapers and jewellers. In rural areas where shops were fewer, specialisation nearly always meant a step up the social ladder, for a sparse population could not support a diversity of specialists of varying size and importance.

Within these broad outlines though, broad classifications do not seem realistically possible. A shop could provide a step up the social ladder for the working class. On the other hand it was possible for a shop to remain in the family for generations with little social change. At the bottom end of the scale family labour was absolutely crucial and economic insecurity very great. All kinds of stratagems were resorted to in order to keep customers, ranging from the New Year's gifts of the industrial North West to the annual treat of Lincolnshire. Similarly profit margins were stretched by buying with other shopkeepers and in rural areas by buying from the small producers of the countryside. At the top end the family was rigidly removed from the shop, and although there may have been some economic insecurity the business still provided a firm base of economic prosperity for a local political and social career.

Thus it seems to us that at this level of generality it is unrealistic to speak of shopkeepers as a homogeneous group or stratum. What is vital is to see the shopkeeper in the first place in the context of his community and understand, at least in the first instance, the direct relationship between the specific social and economic situation of the individual shopkeeper and his or her general class position.

Notes

1. The 444 interviews in this collection were carried out for the 'Family Life and Work Experience before 1918' project with financial support from the Social Science Research Council. They constitute a representative quota sample (by sex, occupation, city/town or country, and region) of the British population in 1911. They are located in the Department of Sociology, the University of Essex. We have used pseudonyms in accordance with the guarantee of confidentiality given at the time of the interview, unless respondents have expressed the wish to have their real names used. In the semi-structured, tape recorded interviews all respondents were encouraged to talk about their own class position and that of other people where they lived in the period before the end of the First World War. In order to get as full a picture as possible of the class structure of the neighbourhood and district a number of questions were asked. In particular, the following questions tended to prompt memories of the place of shopkeepers where they were important: 11 j. In the district/village who were considered the most important people? Did you come into contact with them? Why were they considered important? 11 n. What about the shopkeepers: who did they associate with? *Repeat for other local social groups* e.g. clergy, teachers, employers, farmers. 11 t. Do you remember anyone being described as a 'real gentleman' or 'real lady'? Why do you think that was?

    See also, Paul Thompson, 'Note on the interview method in social history', *The Edwardians,* London, 1975, pp. 5-8, and Paul Thompson, *Memory and History SSRC Newsletter* 6, 1969, p. 17 for a discussion of the methodology of oral history and a fuller account of the above mentioned research project.

2. The respondents were classified according to their own occupation in 1911 if they were in full time work or if they were not, by the occupation of their spouse, father or mother, whoever was the main source of financial support. They were Professional 3; managerial or employer 8; clerical or foreman 3; skilled manual 20; semi-skilled 23; unskilled manual 14. Originally, when the research was first projected it was intended to relate the thirteen regional quotas, of which this Lancashire group is one, to the occupational structure within that region. This proved in practice to be

impossible. Each informant had to be classified from the information gained at an original contact meeting. It was quite common for an informant to have moved for a few months in 1911, or for a father to have been promoted to another occupational class, resulting in a change in classification. Given the limitations of our budget, we could not afford to take in very many unusable interviews or to ask that interviewers search indefinitely for persons in obscure combinations of category. We had to keep the quota as straightforward as was compatible with our original aims in order to get the survey completed. In the event the sex: conurbation/urban/rural; occupied/unoccupied and occupational class totals have been strictly fulfilled as *national totals*, but we have been more flexible with the regional totals.

3. David Lockwood, *The Black Coated Worker*, London, p. 208.
4. Charles Booth, *Life and Labour of the People of London*, London, 1896, pp. 69, 70.
5. Robert Roberts, *The Classic Slum: Salford Life in the First Quarter of the Century*, London, 1971, p. 15.
6. Interview 167, p. 50.
7. Interview 45, pp. 31-33.
8. Interview 218, pp. 55, 56.
9. Interview 83, p. 30.
10. For a discussion of the need to see small shopkeepers as 'a separate stratum', distinct from the lower middle class and from the skilled and independent manual workers, see Frank Bechofer and Brian Elliott, *The Petits Bourgeois in the Class Structure: The Case of the Shopkeepers*, presented at the BSA conference, 1973, p. 4.
11. Interview 267, p. 42.
12. For an account of the working class origins and character of some small shopkeepers in Paris 1815-1848 see Adeline Daumard, *Les Bourgeois de Paris au XIXe siècle*, Paris, 1970, pp. 128, 130.
13. See especially interviews 11, 267, 33 and 418 for 'big' shopkeepers.
14. Cf. Bechofer, op.cit., pp. 17, 21-22.
15. Alice Foley, *A Bolton Childhood*, Manchester, 1973, p. 19.
16. Interview 127, pp. 62-64.
17. Interview 87, pp. 1-5.
18. For an account of the role of the big shopkeeper's wife see W.F. Fish, *The Career of Andrew Carter, A Romance of the Drapery Trade*, London, 1930, p. 225, 'The business had grown far beyond any help that Annie could give, but *her* contribution to its success was in "keeping the home fires burning" with cheerfulness, love, and sympathy, which was more valuable to him than the services of many a highly paid buyer in his vast establishment'.
19. For an account of the family life and work of two women shopkeepers see the autobiographies of A.L. Rowse, *A Cornish Childhood*, London, 1942, and of Louis Heren, *Growing Up Poor in London*, London, 1973.
20. Roberts, op.cit., p. 16.
21. Interview 108, p. 21.
22. Interview 90, pp. 43, 68.
23. Interview 102; appendix pp. 5, 6.
24. Interview 55, pp. 17, 26-27, 32.
25. Interview 89, p. 4.
26. Interview 52, p. 36.
27. Interview 47, pp. 43-44.
28. Interview 135, pp. 3-4.

29. Interview 138, pp. 34, 39.
30. Interview 61, pp. 1, 14.
31. Interview 72, cf. Alice Foley, op.cit., p. 70.
32. Interview 54, p. 28a.
33. Interview 106, pp. 31-32.
34. Interview 67, pp. 29, 30 and 35.
35. Interview 104, p. 27.
36. Interview 137, pp. 4, 5.
37. Interview 51, pp. 27, 28.
38. Interview 86, pp. 17 and 18.
39. Interview 120, pp. 19 and 20.
40. Interview 43, pp. 32, 36.
41. Interview 117, pp. 22, 24.
42. Interview 116, pp. 27-29.
43. Interview 32, pp. 27, 32.
44. Interview 118, pp. 20, 23-24.
45. Interview 99.
46. Mabel K. Ashby, *Joseph Ashby of Tysoe*, Cambridge, 1961, p. 27.
47. Flora Thompson, *Lark Rise to Candleford*, Oxford, 1954, p. 20.
48. Ibid., pp. 331-2.
49. Ibid., p. 347.
50. Interview, Alun Howkins/Mrs Lovell, Bicester. In author's possession. For ease of reference all material on the Clifton family comes from this interview and will not be footnoted again.
51. Sid Hedges ('S.G.'), *Bicester wuz a little town,* Bicester, 1968, pp. 109-129.
52. Interview 450, 'Family Life and Work Experience before 1918', Thompson and Vigne. Again all the material comes from this interview and will not be referred to again. See especially pp. 2, 3, 7, 12, 23, 29, 30, 34, 45.
53. Foley, op.cit., p. 19.
54. Hedges, op.cit., p. 120.
55. Interview Eve Hostettler/Mrs Sharp, Keddington, Lincs. In Ms Hostettler's possession. I am grateful to Eve Hostettler for allowing me to use this material.
56. Charles Booth, op.cit., p. 227.

INDEX

Allen, A.P. 21, 47
Answers 34
apprenticeships 126
artisans 12
Artisans Labourers and General Dwellings Company 172
Association of Teachers in Technical Institutions 26

Bairoch, Paul 20
bank clerks 63, 113, 114-16
Belgium 16-17, 27, 45
Besant, Sir Walter 96
Birmingham 33, 51
Bolton 50, 186-7, 192-3
Booth, Charles 12, 14, 33, 50, 63, 64, 65, 172, 185
bourgeoisie 13-14
bowling clubs 140
Boys' Brigade 138-9, 141, 145, 156-7n
building societies 173
Bullock, S.F. 178

Calvinism 141
capitalist economy 46-7
Cardiff 123
Caudwell, Christopher 27, 46
charity 71-2
charivari 91-2
children 72, 89
Christian World, The 112n
Church of Scotland, Established 136
churches 28, 61-88, 203; and business 142; and culture 141-51; attendance 66-7, 79, 84-8, 137; denominations 66-7, 136-41; in Edinburgh 134-58; membership of 136-41, 146, 155-7n; missionary work 145; suburban congregations 137
civil servants 12, 25
Clarion Clubs 78
Clarke, W.S. 166
class 185, 186-8
clergy 12
clerks 12, 14, 17-21, 62, 113-33;

associations 122-4, 131n; careers 35-6, 114-19; distressed 119-27; earnings 34, 131-4n; embezzlement by 124-5; employment bureau for 121-3; female 55n, 104-5, 127; German 104, 127-9; jingoism and 91, 97-108; labour market for 103-7, 126-9, 131-4n; railway 36; sickness 124; standards expected of 72, 102; status of 97-108; unions 47, 63, 107, 132n; work done by 114-15
Clifford, John 76
Club and Institute Journal 40, 52
collectivism 96
commerce 20-21, 113, 114
commercial travellers 21, 22-3, 26, 47, 59n, 62, 76-7, 79n
Commercial Travellers' Christian Association 76-7
commuting 33, 160, 172
concentration, business 16, 118
conservation 39-48
co-operation 16, 17
Cornford, James 40
Crew, David 23
Crewe 50
Cruikshank, George 172
cultural innovation 143-51

D'Aeth, F.G. 34, 36, 166
Daily Chronicle 31
Daily Mail 34, 95-6
Daily News 64
Davis, Natalie 91
department stores 16
Derby 50
drink 75
Dyos, H.J. 167

earnings 34-5
Edinburgh 33, 40, 134-58; housing 50
education 38; adult 28
emigration 122
employers 24-5, 104-5

211

Index

Engels, Friedrich 64
English Land Colonisation Society 171
expenditure 35

family, the 71-2, 198-9
Fish, W.J. 77
France 14, 20-21, 23, 24, 31-2, 38-9, 41-2, 53
Free Church 136, 144
free trade 46-7
Freehold Land Times 172

Garden cities 159, 171-80
Germany 11, 13, 16, 17, 20, 23, 24, 28, 29, 41-6
Gerschenkron, A. 21
Gibbs, T.E. 49
Giddens, A. 46-7
Gissing, George 13, 31, 178
Gordon, G. 50
Grocer 17
Grossmith, G. and W. 29-30, 178
Guildford 73, 186

Hamilton, Lord George 40
Hannah, L. 15-16
Harrigan, Patrick 38-9
Harrison, J.S. 62, 78
Haw, George 64
Henning, H. 29
Hobsbawm, Eric 110n
Hobson, John 89
housing 32-4, 93, 159-83; co-partnership 175-7; design and layout 166-74; expansion of, beyond town boundaries 162; in Edinburgh 138-9; segregation by class 49 *see also* suburbs
housing estates 173
housing reform movement 170
Howard, Keble 27
Howarth, E.G. 165
Hull 117
Hyde, Francis 117

ideology 27, 39, 43-8, 143-51
Imperial Patriotic League 96
Imperialism 90, 96, 107
insecurity *see* security
insurance 113, 114

Jackson, Gordon 117
jingoism 89-102
jobs: obtaining 38; searching for 125-26, 131n

Kellett, John 34
Kocka, Jurgen 13

labour aristocrats 13
labour market 22-3; for clerks 103-7
labour movement 48
Labour Party 76
Lancashire 185-95
Layard, G.S. 44
Le Bon, Gustave 89
lecture programmes 149
Leeds 123
leisure 71, 73, 148-50, 178-9
Lethaby, W.R. 173
Levi, Leone 12
Liberal Party 76
Liberalism 90
Liverpool 33, 40, 87, 101; churches 66-7, 78, 79, 87-8n; clerks 116, 117, 123-4; shopkeepers 193-5
local government officers 19
London 14, 40, 123; churches 65, 66, 79, 86-7n; housing 33, 50, 51, 160, 163-4, 165-6, 175-7
lower middle class: defined 12-15

McEwan, Robert 149

magazines 148
managers 12
Manchester 33, 122, 123-4; housing in 159, 160, 162
Manchester Guardian 169
manufacturing industry 20
Masterman, C.F.G. 27, 29, 30, 39, 40-41, 64-5
Mayer, Arno 41
mechanics' institutions 51
Methodism 143, 145
middle class, the: differentials within 93, 99
Middle Classes Union 44
Mills, C. Wright 52
Mittelstand 11, 13, 16, 28, 41-6
mobility 35-9, 58n, 63, 80n, 119; aspirations 21-2, 37; downward 105-6
morality 75, 92-3, 102
Morris, William 173
multiple shops 16, 197
music hall 148
mutual improvement association 139, 143

National Association of Local Government Officers 26
National Union of Clerks 47, 63, 107
National Union of Teachers 32
neighbours 70, 71
Newcastle 123, 176
Nonconformists 74-6
obligations 67-8
On the Road 47
Orchard, B.G. 18, 101, 105, 116-17
Oxfordshire 195-206

Parker, Barry 177
parochialism 68
Pelling, Henry 40
People's Friend 148
petty bourgeoisie *see* shopkeepers *and* small businessmen
political commitments 74
Presbyterian Church 136, 144
Preston 50-51

railways 33, 160
Rees, J. Aubrey 17
religion *see* churches
rents 166, 176
respectability 30, 61-2, 92-5, 97, 106-7; and religion 67, 73
retail price maintenance 17
retailers *see* shopkeepers
Robertson, J.M. 89
rowdyism 94-5
Royal Exchange Assurance 114, 115
ruling class 135-6

salary *see* earnings
Salford 186, 189-92
school teachers 12, 19, 25-6, 31-2, 151
Scottish Clerks Association 123
security: of employment 22-4, 34-5, 40, 68-9, 100; of status 99-100
Seddon, F.H. 80n
self-ascription 12-13
Selfridges 34
selling, careers in 119
semi-skilled workers 48
servants 63, 137, 204
Shaw, George Bernard 24, 107
Sheffield 123; housing in 160, 163, 164-5, 169, 173, 176
shop assistants 12, 72, 77, 105-6
shopkeepers 12, 14, 15-17, 100-101, 106, 184-209; additional jobs 188; bartering 199-201; rural 195-207; status 185-9, 206-7; urban 185-95

skilled workers 13, 48
small businessmen 12, 15-17, 35, 134-5
social relationships 13, 2-3; isolation 27-8; with neighbours 70
socialism 78, 96, 107
Spectator 31
standards, maintenance of 71-2
status 61-3, 185-9; 206-7; and jingoism 89-112; aspirations 30; consciousness 29-31, 49, 186; insecurities 92; maintaining 37-8
Stephens, Fitzjames 30
Sturmthal, A. 25, 26
suburbs 32-3, 63n, 101, 159-83, *passim*

technological change 118
Tenants Co-partnership Society 175-7
terraced houses 161, 162
Thompson, Flora 196
Thompson, Paul 70, 74, 81n, 185-209
Tit-Bits 34
trade *see* commerce
trade unions 24-7, 40, 48, 107 *see also specific unions*
transport 33, 160, 171-2, 179

unemployment 92, 119-27, 130n
United Kingdom Commercial Travellers' Association 26
Unwin, Raymond 177
utopianism 171

values 46-7, 91-2, 149, 150-51
Vigne, Thea 70, 74, 81n, 185-209
villadom 93, 95, 101
voluntary associations 121-3

wages *see* earnings
Webb, Philip 173
Weber, Eugen 42
Wells H.G. 38, 100-101, 106, 178
white collar workers 12, 17-27, 134, 187; female 18, 20; numbers of 19
Wilson, Charles 16
Wilson, M. 165
Winkler, H.A. 45
Wolverhampton 51
women 18, 20, 22, 147; clerks 55n, 104-5, 127
working class, the 48-52, 106, 140-41; and religion 66; clubs 52

YMCA 30, 77, 121-3, 141

Zeldin, Theodore 53

For Product Safety Concerns and Information please contact our EU
representative GPSR@taylorandfrancis.com
Taylor & Francis Verlag GmbH, Kaufingerstraße 24, 80331 München, Germany

www.ingramcontent.com/pod-product-compliance
Lightning Source LLC
Chambersburg PA
CBHW052115300426
44116CB00010B/1665